Frontispiece: Le Triomphe de la République : les despotes cruels dont nous bravons la rage, eux mêmes, sur leur tête ont provoqué l'orage. De la montagne enfin ils son précipités ces monstres furieux par le crime enfantés; et les traits foudroyans qu'ils lançoient sur leur proie, sont pour nous, aujourd'hui le plus beau feu de joie: [estampe] / Boissieux pinxit; P.M. Alix sculpsit. (Paris: chez Bance, entre 1792 et 1794). Bibliothèque nationale de France.

Reimagining Society in Eighteenth-Century French Literature

The French revolutionary shift from monarchical to popular sovereignty came clothed in a new political language, a significant part of which was a strange coupling of happiness and rights. In Old Regime ideology, Frenchmen were considered subjects who had no need of understanding why what was prescribed to them would be in the interest of their happiness. The 1789 Declaration of the Rights of Man and of the Citizen equipped the French with a list of inalienable rights, and if society would respect those rights, the happiness of all would materialize.

This volume explores the authors of fictional literature who contributed alongside pamphleteers, politicians, and philosophers to the establishment of this new political arena, filled with sometimes vague yet insisting notions of happiness and rights. The shift from monarchical to popular sovereignty and the corollary transition from subjects to citizens culminated in the summer of 1789, but it was preceded by an immense piece of imaginative work. Because of their medium, authors of fictional literature were well placed to help imagine society anew. New political bodies and conceptions of sovereignty, alternative codes of civil conduct, and forms of interpersonal interaction flourished in the rich generic landscape of late eighteenth-century French literature. These works of literature, the forgotten as well as the canonized ones, continuously intervened in that burgeoning social imaginary within which the struggle to define the happiness of all took place.

Jonas Ross Kjærgård, PhD, is Assistant Professor of Comparative Literature at Aarhus University and recipient of the Elite Research travel grant. He acquired his PhD at Aarhus University, Denmark, with a dissertation on French revolutionary rights and literature. He has published articles and book chapters on literature and the French revolution, and edited the volume *Discursive Framings of Human Rights: Negotiating Agency and Victimhood* (with Karen-Margrethe Simonsen), published by Birkbeck Law Press. He has begun a new research project on the literary history of the Haitian revolution.

Routledge Studies in Eighteenth-Century Literature

11 **Women and Gift Exchange in Eighteenth-Century Fiction**
   Richardson, Burney, Austen
   Linda Zionkowski

12 **New Perspectives on Delarivier Manley and Eighteenth-Century Literature**
   Power, Sex, and Text
   Edited by Aleksondra Hultquist and Elizabeth J. Mathews

13 **Daniel Defoe and the Representation of Personal Identity**
   Christopher Borsing

14 **The Future of Feminist Eighteenth-Century Scholarship**
   Beyond Recovery
   Edited by Robin Runia

15 **Wordsworth Before Coleridge**
   The Growth of the Poet's Philosophical Mind, 1785–1797
   Mark Bruhn

16 **Political Economy, Literature & the Formation of Knowledge, 1720–1850**
   Richard Adelman and Catherine Packham

17 **Errors and Reconciliations**
   Marriage in the Plays and Novels of Henry Fielding
   Anaclara Castro-Santana

18 **Reimagining Society in Eighteenth-Century French Literature**
   Happiness and Human Rights
   Jonas Ross Kjærgård

For a full list of titles published in the series, please visit www.routledge.com.

Reimagining Society in Eighteenth-Century French Literature

Happiness and Human Rights

Jonas Ross Kjærgård

NEW YORK AND LONDON

First published 2018
by Routledge
711 Third Avenue, New York, NY 10017

and by Routledge
2 Park Square, Milton Park, Abingdon, Oxon OX14 4RN

Routledge is an imprint of the Taylor & Francis Group, an informa business

© 2018 Taylor & Francis

The right of Jonas Ross Kjærgård to be identified as author of this work has been asserted by him in accordance with sections 77 and 78 of the Copyright, Designs and Patents Act 1988.

All rights reserved. No part of this book may be reprinted or reproduced or utilised in any form or by any electronic, mechanical, or other means, now known or hereafter invented, including photocopying and recording, or in any information storage or retrieval system, without permission in writing from the publishers.

Trademark notice: Product or corporate names may be trademarks or registered trademarks, and are used only for identification and explanation without intent to infringe.

Library of Congress Cataloging-in-Publication Data
Names: Kjaergêard, Jonas Ross author.
Title: Reimagining society in 18th century French literature: happiness and human rights / by Jonas Ross Kjaergêard.
Description: New York: Routledge, 2018. | Series: Routledge studies in eighteenth-century literature; 18 | Includes bibliographical references and index.
Identifiers: LCCN 2018009639 | Subjects: LCSH: French fiction—18th century—History and criticism. | Happiness in literature. | Human rights in literature. | Literature and society—France—History—18th century.
Classification: LCC PQ637.H37 K53 2018 |
DDC 840.9/3584404—dc23
LC record available at https://lccn.loc.gov/2018009639

ISBN: 978-1-138-61174-0 (hbk)
ISBN: 978-0-429-46526-0 (ebk)

Typeset in Sabon
by codeMantra

Dedicated to all the people who bring happiness
Particularly to my wonderful wife, Signe, and our beautiful
kids Frieda, Sofus, and Laura

Contents

List of Figures   xi
Preface   xiii

Introduction   1
Happiness and the Politics of Words   6
*The Political Anthropology of Happiness
  and Rights*   10
Literature   19

1   **The Unfinished Declaration**   22
Debating the Declaration   25
Nature and Society   29
Rights and Duties   32
Enmity and Passive Citizenship   38
Literature   49

2   **What Was Literature?**   53
The Author-Politician and the Code of History   55
*Louis-Sébastien Mercier and the Reawakening of
  Patriotic Virtue*   59
*Choderlos de Laclos's Reinterpretation of
  Dulce et Utile*   66
Marie-Joseph Chénier and the Author-Legislator   72
Literature   89

3   **Louis-Sébastien Mercier and the Dream of a
Happy Future**   93
Temporality in Mercier's Utopian Thought   96
The Form of Government in L'an 2440   102
Taxation and the Duty of Patriotism   108
Literature   125

x Contents

4 The Search for Order in Choderlos de Laclos's *Liaisons dangereuses* 129
   The Politics of Social Forms 131
   The Rhythm of Social Forms 136
   The Hierarchies of Social Forms 144
   Literature 160

5 The Regeneration of the State in Marie-Joseph Chénier's *Fénelon ou les religieuses de Cambrai* 164
   Convent Life and Paternal Inflexibility 167
   The Problem of Humanness 173
   Political Agency: From Unhappiness to Happiness 178
   The Tableau Vivant: *The Politics of the Happy Ending 185*
   Literature 197

   Conclusion 201
   Literature 206

   Index 209

List of Figures

Frontispiece: *Le Triomphe de la République : les despotes cruels dont nous bravons la rage, eux mêmes, sur leur tête ont provoqué l'orage. De la montagne enfin ils son précipités ces monstres furieux par le crime enfantés; et les traits foudroyans qu'ils lançoient sur leur proie, sont pour nous, aujourd'hui le plus beau feu de joie*: [estampe] / Boissieux pinxit; P.M. Alix sculpsit. (Paris: chez Bance, entre 1792 et 1794). Bibliothèque nationale de France   i

I.1   *Bonheur* and *Liberté*. Numbers are compiled using the ARTFL FRANTEXT database   7

1.1   *Déclaration des droits de l'homme et du citoyen*: [estampe]. (Paris: chez Jaufret, 1789]. Bibliothèque nationale de France   23

1.2   *La Tyrannie revolutionnaire écrasée par les amis de la Constitution de l'an III*: [estampe]/Queverdo del.; Massol sculp. (Paris, chez l'auteur, 1795–1796). Bibliothèque nationale de France   34

2.1   *M … r l'ane comme il n ' y en a point: peu m'importent les chefs d'oeuvres de tous les arts, pourvu que j'écrase, que je m 'élève, et que le chardon ne me manque pas. Ô gens de goût reconnaissez la bête!*: inspiré par Crémier: [estampe]/[non identifié]. (Paris: [s.n.], 1798). Bibliothèque nationale de France   61

3.1   *Projet de l'impot patriotique donné par Mad. e de Gouges, dans le mois de sept.re 1788: tout citoyen se verrait dans le même miroir ce portrait touchant caracteriseroit à la fois l'ame, le coeur et l'esprit français*: [estampe] / Desrais inv.; Frussotte sculp. (Paris: [s.n.], 1788). Bibliothèque nationale de France   113

3.2   *Patience… ça ira : y n' faut qu' sentendre*: [estampe] / [non identifié]. (Paris: [n.p.], 1789). Bibliothèque nationale de France. The angel at the bottom left is inscribing the name of Necker at the bust   117

4.1	*L'Amour et la Raison*: [estampe] / Fr. Bartolozzy delineav.; Elisab. G. Herhan sculpsit. (Paris: Chez Joubert, 1794). Bibliothèque nationale de France	136
5.1	*L'Erreur et la folie nous avoit jetté dans des cloîtres, mais la raison nous rend au monde*: [estampe] / [non identifié]. (Paris: [s.n.], 1790). Bibliothèque nationale de France	172
5.2	*Le Grand abus*: [estampe] / [Villeneuve]. (Paris: chez Villeneuve, 1790). Bibliothèque nationale de France	183
5.3	*La Bonne justice*: [estampe] / [Villeneuve]. (Paris: chez Villeneuve, 1790). Bibliothèque nationale de France	184

Preface

This is a book about French eighteenth-century literature and politics, but it actually began as a worried bewilderment about present-day global politics. To my mind, the war in Iraq and the horrible scenes from Abu Graib were unlawful attacks on justice and human rights. Yet some proposed that the war was actually a humanitarian intervention designed to protect the rights of subjected Iraqis. To my mind, the Danish, and eventually global, Cartoon Crisis seemed designed to offend a Muslim minority in Denmark. Yet some insisted that it was nothing less than a defense of the freedom of expression. The war in Iraq and the Cartoon Crisis were complex tragedies on very different scales, but to me, the public discussions that surrounded these events were emblematic of a strange phenomenon. People who held completely different views on these conflicts would oftentimes draw upon the human rights vocabulary when trying to legitimize their opinions. Was the human rights discourse really so flexible that it could encompass opposite views on one and the same conflict?

I wanted to understand this flexibility of the human rights discourse. Apparently, opposite actions and opinions could be defended in the name of freedom of speech or protection of the individual. That in itself was strange, but why would agents and groups, with very different political agendas, try to position themselves and their actions as a defense of human rights in the first place? To me, it seemed that the human rights discourse had a legitimacy, which liberals and conservatives alike wanted to draw upon, but in order to do that, they had to twist the meaning of equal rights according to their different political goals. What I initially wanted to understand was this highly authoritative yet flexible discourse of rights. Scholars of international law would approach such a problem in *their* way, but to me, it seemed productive to bring these questions to my field of knowledge: eighteenth-century literature and politics.

The period of the late Enlightenment and the French revolution is not the only point of origin of human rights. Scholars have located all kinds of origins in earlier historical periods and other geographical regions. I appreciate the ambition of those studies, but my interest was not the philosophical origins of rights but the practical negotiations of the meaning of rights. The French revolution and its development of a new political culture was a privileged site for this kind of investigation. What really attracted my attention as a literary scholar, however, was the multitude of writers who tried to develop what they considered a new kind of politically engaged literature. The emotional appeal of literature, these authors argued, could be used for political purposes. This might sound like propaganda, and for some, I believe it was, but other writers were directed by a genuine wish to reinvent literature and use it to build the moral foundation of a new France. These authors did not necessarily agree on the direction of the new France, but they all referred to common happiness, *droits de l'homme*, and the natural order. What I found in the literature of this period, in other words, were attempts to imagine a new France that respected the rights of individuals and secured the happiness of all.

Somewhere along the way, the strangeness of French eighteenth-century literature and politics assumed a life of its own for me. I got interested in the peculiar conflicts of the historical agents and particularly in their political and literary attempts to balance collective joy with individual rights. My initial impetus, however, were present-day global concerns, and even though I have deliberately chosen to focus solely on eighteenth-century France in the pages that follow, I'd like to think that the historical analysis resonates with and casts its own light on frighteningly present conflicts and the contemporary search for collective happiness.

* * *

While working on this book I have benefitted enormously from the advice and suggestions of a multitude of friends and colleagues from near and far. What makes Kasernen a great place to work is primarily all the wonderful people there. I especially want to thank my colleagues from the Department of Comparative Literature. Thank you for welcoming and accepting me, despite my unimaginative lunch boxes and ambivalent attitude toward shoes. You know who you are.

During my time as a PhD student, I had the much appreciated opportunity to discuss some of the topics treated in this book with inspiring academics, among which were Dan Edelstein; Keith Michael Baker; Antoine Lilti; Joseph Slaughter; Costas Douzinas; Michael Kwass; Paul Cheney; and, most importantly, Madeleine Dobie and Susan Maslan. Susan and Madeleine served on my PhD committee, and their critical and encouraging comments on that occasion – and others – were particularly useful in the long process of rewriting my dissertation and turning it into this book. Thank you. Thanks also to the people at Routledge and the anonymous reviewers who offered valuable suggestions.

My warmest thanks and my greatest academic debts, however, I owe to four people. Thank you to my three dissertation supervisors, Karen-Margrethe Simonsen, Anne Fastrup, and Mikkel Thorup. Your knowledge, your academic commitment, and your readiness to discuss whatever strange eighteenth-century text I found on whatever bizarre topic was amazing. Thank you for the hours and hours you have spent talking and listening to me. It made all the difference. An enormous thank you also to my friend and academic partner in crime Jakob Ladegaard. It has been a thrill to discuss literature, politics, and history with you in the past years, and I hope we can continue the discussion for years to come.

Introduction

On 23 June, 1789, the French king Louis XVI addressed the members of the National Assembly and declared the recent founding of their assembly as well as the ensuing deliberations "illegal and unconstitutional."[1] He wanted the Old Regime distinction between the three orders – the clerics, the nobles, and the commoners – to be entirely conserved. In legitimizing these counterrevolutionary orders, the king pointed to the fact that the Estates General had been open for two months, but so far, it had proven completely unable to deliver the solutions that were expected of it. As a consequence of their failings and of the great turmoil their uncommissioned political actions had occasioned, the king now attempted to invoke the sum of his royal authority and bring an end to the revolutionary efforts. He said,

> Gentlemen, I thought I had done everything in my power for the good of my people when I made the resolution to summon you; when I had surmounted all the difficulties surrounding your convocation; when I had, so to speak, gone beyond the vows of the nation in manifesting in advance what I would do for its happiness. [...]
>
> I owe it to the good of my kingdom and I owe it to myself to put an end to these disastrous divisions. It is with this resolution, gentlemen, that I assemble you around me once more; it is as the father of all my subjects, it is as the defender of the laws of my kingdom that I come to retrace the true spirit [of the nation], and repress the attacks that may have been made.[2]

In his speech, Louis XVI relied on the authority of traditional royalist ideology.[3] The king is the responsible father of all the nation's children, and the benefits of this stable paternal power structure are unity, order, and general happiness. Happiness is here the result of a trade-off; the king rules, the subjects obey, and mutual happiness flourishes. In the words of Étienne Balibar, under absolutism, "the subject is he who has no need of *knowing*, much less *understanding*, why what is prescribed to him is in the interest of his own happiness."[4] The subject simply follows the orders of the benevolent sovereign. When the king next addressed the National

Assembly eighteen days later, he had had to accept that the distinction between the three orders was not reinstated, but defending his recent policies, he still relied on the same version of happiness and absolute rule. On 11 July, the king had summoned the military and placed troupes around Paris to avoid, as he wrote, general "disorder and scandalous scenes."[5] In his estimation, this was the only way to "maintain order" and "public security."[6] Again, Louis XVI invoked his royal authority as the only guarantee not only of the people's security but also of its happiness:

> Only ill-intentioned people would mislead my people regarding the true motives of the precautionary measures I take; I have constantly tried to do everything that could lead to its happiness, and I have always had reason to be sure of the love and fidelity of my people.[7]

In this monarchical world of now bygone days, the paternal king acts, and the people responds happily with love and fidelity.

The king's absolutist arguments were ill received by the majority of the deputies and by the Parisian population. In the days succeeding the presentation of the king's wishes, Parisian crowds stormed prisons and liberated inmates, they burned down forty of the fifty-four tollgates surrounding Paris, and they searched the Monastère Saint-Lazare for weapons. These riots culminated with what has become the symbol of the revolution: the storming of the Bastille on 14 July.[8] Within the high political arena of the National Assembly, deputies received the king's letter first with suspicious murmurs and then with verbal attacks and fierce criticism.[9] Their skepticism is unsurprising given the fact that in establishing the National Assembly, the deputies had deliberately challenged the royalist assumptions inherent in both of the king's addresses. Thus, in his response to the king's 23 June speech, the influential pamphleteer Abbé Sieyès addressed the role of the deputies: "Are we only mandates, officers of the King? Then we must obey and withdraw. But, are we the envoys of the people – let us then fulfill our mission, freely, courageously."[10] In opposition to the king's speech, this proposal to stand firm as a National Assembly and to insist on being something other than the king's children was "covered in applause."[11] In holding their ground on this issue, the deputies redefined their political role; instead of being the king's subjects, they now thought of themselves as the people's representatives. Hereby, they also contested the royalist meaning of happiness. On 26 August, the deputies finished the deliberations of the single most important document of the French revolution: the *Declaration of the Rights of Man and of the Citizen*. The preface of this document proposed a wholly different interpretation of happiness and of the roads leading to this goal:

> The representatives of the French people, constituted as a National Assembly, and considering that ignorance, neglect or contempt of

the rights of man are the sole causes of public misfortunes [malheurs publics] and governmental corruption, have resolved to set forth in a solemn declaration the natural, inalienable and sacred rights of man: so that by being constantly present to all members of the social body this declaration may always remind them of their rights and duties; so that by being liable at every moment to comparison with the aim of any and all political institutions the acts of the legislative and executive powers may be the more fully respected; and so that by being founded henceforward on simple and incontestable principles the demands of the citizens may always tend toward maintaining the constitution and the general welfare [bonheur de tous].[12]

The *raison d'être* of politics is here presented as the maintenance of the constitution and as the establishment of the happiness of all. The Declaration of Rights is meant to secure these two ambitions by functioning as a constant checklist. Are the actions of the members of society in alignment with their rights and duties? Do the legislative and executive powers act in accordance with the overall goal of the political institutions? Should the grievances of citizens be accepted or denied? The proclaimed ambition of the Declaration of Rights is to render these difficult questions easily answerable. In comparison with the royalist ideology of Louis XVI, the role of every single member of society has here changed. In principle, no one is any longer a subject obeying the orders of the king. Instead, everyone is a citizen equipped with a list of inalienable rights that may be used to judge political representatives and their actions. The political role of the citizenry has changed from obedience to participation, and this alteration, such is the hope of the revolutionaries, shall initiate a process leading from unhappiness to happiness, from "*malheur public*" to "*bonheur de tous.*" The deputies' coupling of general happiness and individual rights is a cornerstone in the French revolutionary shift from monarchical to popular sovereignty. This coupling and its troublesome political and literary history are the subject of this book.

* * *

My general thesis is that fictional literature not only intervened in but also helped establish that social imaginary within which the deputies debated the Declaration of Rights and its established linkage of happiness and rights. The shift from monarchical to popular sovereignty and the corollary transition from subjects to citizens culminated in the summer of 1789, but it was preceded by an immense piece of *imaginative* work. After hundreds of years of absolutist rule, after an 175-year wait since the last assembly of the general estates, it took considerable courage and intellectual creativity to think society anew, to reimagine what general happiness could be. Because of their imaginative medium, authors of fictional literature were well placed to help lift this task. Fictional literature partook in the struggle to reimagine France by proposing alternative political scenarios, other ways of organizing civil society, and different kinds of interpersonal relations. In opposition to the parliamentary rhetoric of politicians and the abstract rationality of pamphleteers, authors of fiction aimed to write in an emotionally moving and personally resonating way. Literature had the ability to concretize abstract questions of liberty, equality, and happiness, and to question them using the examples of ordinary men and women, friends and foes. The combination of literature's emotional appeal, individual focus, and imaginary commitment allowed it to co-establish that new social imaginary within which the struggles to define the happiness of all took place. This hypothesis rests on two historical premises.

First, the 1789 Declaration of Rights and its combination of rights and happiness was a poignant, yet highly ambiguous political document. Its mere seventeen articles suggest confidence and fixity but in fact contain multiple contradictions, the most striking of which is Article Ten. Article Ten initially stresses absolute freedom of opinion, even in religious matters, only to add the significant disclaimer "provided that their manifestation does not trouble public order as established by law."[13] In other words, you have absolute freedom of opinion unless the manifestation of your opinion troubles public order. This ambiguity increases when we take into consideration the thirty official and the hundreds of unofficial declaration proposals that predate the final document;[14] when we analyze the wildly heated National Assembly debates of July and August 1789 that, according to a commentator, reveal "bitter argument, inevitable linguistic compromises, and dramatic theoretical tensions;"[15] and when we consider the fact that the deputies themselves, at the end of their August deliberations, agreed that the Declaration of Rights "is not finished."[16] In addition, the 1789 Declaration was twice supplanted by other rights declarations in the revolutionary decade: first by the Jacobins in 1793 and later by the Directory in 1795. During the strenuous summer debates preceding the adoption of the 1789 Declaration of Rights, the Third Estate deputy Jean-Baptiste Crenière put the blatant tension between the alleged invariable yet in fact ever-changing rights into words:

> Our rights are invariable, always constant, always the same, and yet they increase or decrease according to the opinions of the authors of the declarations of rights. The Committee of Five has presented us with a draft of nineteen articles; a member showed us one of twenty; another of thirty; finally they counted sometimes up to seventy-six.[17]

We should pause and consider the significance of the political ambiguity and instability of this foundational document. Too often, it is thought to contain an "unqualified moral universalism" or any other such unwavering principle.[18] The flux and the contradictions of the Declaration of Rights challenge us to write histories of an open document, a compromise text written in a moment of great social unrest and of major intellectual disagreement. Individuals and interest groups strove to influence the wording of the 1789 Declaration, and this document, in all its fascinating contradictions and uncertainties, bears witness to these political struggles. I read the document and the multiple oral and written discussions surrounding it not as any one fixed set of political ideas breaking forth but as a momentary end-result in an ongoing negotiation of the relationship between individual and society, rights and duties, universality and particularity. This, the document's open-endedness, was an important reason why it was debated not only in the National Assembly but also in pamphlets, political clubs, salons, songs, and literature. I want to study its significance within this outlined space of uncertainty. I want to understand the implications of the deputies' own claim that the Declaration of Rights "was unfinished," and I argue that authors of fiction used their means of expression to prepare and influence this open, public debate about a happy future for France.

My thesis hinges on one more historical premise. The social function of literature and the role of the author changed in the last third of the eighteenth century. Because the political field of discourse was made up of opposing definitions of keywords and hence encompassed immense uncertainty and disagreement regarding the goals of a new society, authors felt impelled to propose imaginative solutions and interrogative interventions. The ambition to recreate France, to define happiness and rights through literature, was further fueled by marginal authors' common experience of not being taken seriously by the literary *monde*. I suggest that this double feeling of being drawn toward politics and of standing outside the literary elite awakened a wish to redefine the role of the author. No longer should the morals and aesthetic norms of tradition rule. Instead, authors should attempt to use literature and theater politically. They should make and contest claims about happiness and rights in the hope of creating what author-politician Marie-Joseph Chénier termed "new men for the new laws."[19] Pursuing this ambition, they carved out a new *literary field*, which is here understood as an intellectual space giving direction to discussions of "what it means to be a writer."[20]

The sociological background of the attempts to develop a new literature is the late Old Regime divide between the high Enlightenment and the low-life of literature. As emphasized by Robert Darnton, central *philosophes*, such as Voltaire, Rousseau, Diderot, Condillac, d'Alembert, and Mably, all died between 1778 and 1785, something which left a void to be filled by younger writers. This generational shift had consequences for what had been the heroic Enlightenment movement. "[I]t lost its fire," writes Darnton, "and became a mere tranquil diffusion of light, a comfortable ascent toward progress."[21] The social background of this tamed Enlightenment lay in the financial realities of life as an author. Successful writers earned a living not primarily by selling their books but by being appointed to lucrative positions, such as royal censor, newspaper editor, or member of the French Academy, or by receiving a pension. A book-market structured in this way produced a homogeneous *monde* that defined and strengthened itself by carefully selecting like-minded persons whenever subsidies were distributed: "While the literary rabble held out its hands to the government, the government gave its handouts to writers situated safely within *le monde*."[22]

Confronted with this impenetrable elite, Grub Street authors reacted by developing a libelous literature whose target was the exclusive *monde* and its alliance with the monarchical state apparatus. Slander, sexual sensationalism, and verbal rage directed at public figures had the benefit of being easy to sell, which made it possible to ease the accumulated frustrations while making a living. And the moral outrage of the *libelles* was more than a rhetorical pose:

> It expressed a feeling of total contempt for a totally corrupt elite. So if the *libelles* lacked a coherent ideology, they communicated a revolutionary point of view: they showed that social rot was consuming French society, eating its way downward from the top.[23]

I agree that the lack of recognition and financial success prompted Grub Street authors to write furious slander, but other writers reacted differently in a sociologically similar situation. Rather than attacking the elite, these authors decided to go elsewhere, to develop what they considered a new literature, with specific aesthetic and political goals. The literary field of the period was characterized by a divide between an elitist *monde* and a literary rabble, but my set of authors saw the development of a politically intervening and emotionally moving literature as a way out of that deadlock. The push away from the literary elite and the pull toward the open political culture are the two premises that explain the political ambition and involvement of the period's literature as it is here represented by Louis-Sébastien Mercier (1740–1814), Choderlos de Laclos (1741–1803), and Marie-Joseph Chénier (1764–1811).

Before closing this introduction, I want to further open up the historical problems of happiness and rights. After all, making individual rights meet general happiness was a political ambition, but the road toward that goal contained multiple pitfalls.

Happiness and the Politics of Words

This study benefits from combining elements of intellectual history with literary analysis. Following the lead of the Cambridge School and the

German *Begriffsgeschichte*, I think of politics as a struggle to define contested concepts according to specific ideological agendas. Concepts like democracy, rights, and happiness are interpreted differently by various agents and interest groups, and Quentin Skinner, Reinhart Kosseleck, Walter Bryce Gallie, and others have shown that such struggles to define key-concepts have real-life social implications.[24] I am aware of the "social" criticisms directed at this kind of intellectual history, but I see great potential in combining a discursive understanding of politics with literary analysis.[25] Literature, like philosophy, makes and contests claims but does so by presenting individual characters that experience lifelike situations. Abstract principles are concretized as men and women, servants and kings, struggle to find happiness in imaginative scenarios. Particularly, the concept of happiness – which is personal and political, rational and emotional – has been scrutinized by authors of fiction, and their accumulated knowledge needs to be confronted with the political discussions of the day.[26] Literary analysis improves our understanding of the period's vocabulary, of its understanding of rights and happiness, and it helps make fathomable the popular engagement with eighteenth-century politics.

According to Jacobin leader Louis Antoine Léon de Saint-Just, "happiness is a new idea in Europe."[27] Historian Darrin McMahon is right to insist that Saint-Just's "claim was overstated" because, as McMahon's *longue durée* study – stretching from the Greek *eudaimonia* over the Latin *felicitas* to Enlightenment *bonheur* and Samuel Beckett's *Happy Days* (1961) – shows, happiness was no new idea in 1794.[28] Yet Saint-Just's claim should not be rejected too easily. Figure I.1 illustrates the shifting frequency with which "*bonheur*" and "*liberté*" were used in a vast corpus of French texts over a period of 350 years. The columns

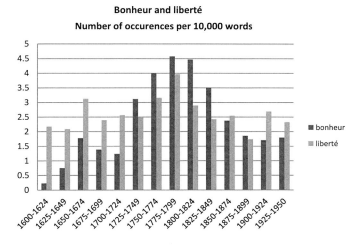

Figure I.1 Bonheur and *Liberté*. Numbers are compiled using the ARTFL FRANTEXT database.

show that the frequency rate of the word happiness increased drastically in the prerevolutionary years. In comparison with the fluctuations of another key revolutionary term, *liberté*, those of *bonheur* demonstrate a considerably steeper rise in the late eighteenth century. This suggests that happiness, without being a new idea (which of course it was not), assumed some poignancy in these years; a poignancy, which it is a historical challenge to understand and explain. Why this interest in happiness? What did it mean?

In the *Encyclopedia* of Diderot and d'Alambert, theologian Jean Pestré contributed with the article "Happiness." Here, he initially defines happiness in nonpolitical terms in its opposition to pleasure. Whereas pleasure is a short and passing feeling, happiness is "a state or situation which we would like to see continue forever unchanged."[29] But a happiness that is not animated by pleasure from time to time is not so much true happiness as "a state of tranquility, a very sorry kind of happiness indeed!"[30] Thus, in order to achieve happiness, it is not enough to linger in a situation of tranquility. Tranquility needs to be interrupted every so often by "pleasant feelings, [...] gentle shocks, filled with delightful variety [mouvemens délicieux]" and by "pure pleasure [une volupté pure]," as Pestré writes in his strongly sexualized vocabulary.[31] The closest anyone comes to true happiness, then, is "a state of tranquility *that is enlivened from time to time by moments of pleasure.*"[32] Happiness, in other words, is tranquility mixed up with the occasional brawl.

Pestré's definition is strikingly apolitical in comparison with the royal edicts and declarations discussed earlier. His definition is a presentation of an individual's ideal state of being which actually combines elements from two conflicting understandings of happiness. Enlightenment happiness, claims McMahon, stood in opposition to classical Greek *Eudaimonia*. The ideal of the latter was to "minimize pain," while Enlightenment *philosophes* strove to "maximize pleasure."[33] McMahon illustrates the search for pleasure with a wonderful anecdote about the materialist philosopher and lover of all kinds of pleasure Julien Offray de la Mettrie (1709–1751), who – according to legend – "collapsed in his plate, the victim of too much pâté and a life far too sweet."[34] In La Mettrie's *Anti-Seneca or the Sovereign Good*, sometimes referred to simply as *Discourse on Happiness*, the author himself does much to build up to McMahon's later anecdotal portrait as he practically equates pleasure with happiness: "If the impression created by this feeling [that pleases us] is short, it constitutes pleasure; if longer, sensuality and if permanent, happiness. It is always the same feeling; only its duration and intensity differ."[35]

With his sexualized vocabulary and emphasis upon agreeable feelings, Pestré's definition of happiness does include La Mettrie's characteristic emphasis on pleasure. But in opposition to La Mettrie, Pestré insists that with the brevity of pleasure follows a qualitative difference from happiness. Pleasure is not equal to happiness but can result in happiness if it alternates with a tranquil feeling devoid of pain. McMahon, in my opinion, underestimates the complexity of Enlightenment happiness and especially the importance of a less hedonistic version of eighteenth-century happiness.[36] Fénelon, Rousseau, and later Robespierre are prominent examples of the tendency to equate happiness with a moderate and virtuous life. "What a shame," says Mentor, the divine instructor from Fénelon's didactic novel *Telemachus, son of Ulysses* (1699),

> that men of the highest rank should place their greatness in the dainties of a luxurious table, by which they enervate their minds, and quickly ruin the health and vigor of their bodies! They ought to account it their happiness to be moderate.[37]

Moderation is not a luxurious, pleasure-seeking life-form, but for many, including Mercier and Chénier, happiness is best found in material and culinary simplicity.

Neither hedonism nor moderation is a political term. How, then, did happiness become politicized? Returning to Pestré's article, his understanding of the concept does suggest one possible answer. When he presents happiness as a common goal of mankind, he also transports the concept from an individual to a collective sphere:

> All men are one in their desire for happiness. Nature has made happiness a law of our being, and all that is not happiness is alien to our disposition. It alone has unmistakable power over our hearts, it attracts us all through an instant inclination, a powerful charm, and an irresistible attraction. Happiness is the charm and perfection of Nature and she has indelibly engraved it on our hearts.[38]

In *The Promise of Happiness*, Sara Ahmed begins by noticing that happiness is "consistently described as the object of human desire."[39] The Pestré quotation is an example of what Ahmed finds again and again in the history of philosophy, in commercial society, and in various cultural products. Happiness is a force field, a charming power that man is pulled toward independent of his conscious will. It is what everyone wishes for, and Ahmed asks the critical questions: "Do we consent to happiness? And what are we consenting to, if or when we consent to happiness?"[40] The historical context in which Ahmed works is radically different from the French revolutionary one, but her general question is relevant: If happiness is held up as an ideal for everyone, if it is repeatedly promoted by politicians and authors of fiction, what kind of goal is it people are invited to pursue? The tranquil life interrupted every so often with "*mouvemens délicieux*" might seem enticing, but what do such ostentatious descriptions amount to when they are politicized? And is this actually what politicians have in mind for the citizenry when they present *"le bonheur de tous"* as the goal of society?

Happiness is a vague but luring idea. That duality makes it an effective catchphrase for anyone wishing to create society anew. It can inspire and motivate, but it can also be manipulated. The authors studied here are prime investigators of the aesthetic and political twists and turns of happiness and rights. They contest existing definitions of these concepts and propose alternative ones. Depending on how authors (*and* politicians) understand the link between happiness and rights, the citizens of the new France were considered either pleasure-seeking adventurers or virtuous ascetics, politically competent agents or subjected victims. Using the philosophical vocabulary of Étienne Balibar, we may here speak of the "anthropological dilemmas of citizenship" or of competing brands of "political anthropology."[41]

The Political Anthropology of Happiness and Rights

By political anthropology, I refer to the problem of the individual's role and place in a political community. With any idea of the constitution of the commons follows a set of ideals, rules, or assumptions about individual behavior. The well-being of the state necessitates codes of conduct, and the respect for the rights of citizens presents limitations on the state. The postulate of the Declaration of Rights is that individual rights and collective happiness go hand in hand, but that is far from given. The concept of political anthropology draws attention to the often implicit idea of the human inherent in a specific political movement or ideology. Phrased closer to the vocabulary of Michel Foucault, there is a constant process of subjectivization in human culture, meaning that the individual is produced and finds his or her subjectivity in society.[42] I follow Balibar in using political anthropology as a designation of the interrelationship of the individual and society. Being true to Foucault, Balibar knows well that the individuals both *"precede"* and *"follow"* society in the sense that their subjectivity is produced by society, while society is equally produced by its members.[43]

This anthropological problem is pertinent to the 1789 Declaration of Rights because of its much debated dual subject: the *Declaration of the Rights of Man and of the Citizen*. Who or what is this strange creature, the man/citizen? One approach to the man/citizen-schism, favored by Karl Marx and Samuel Moyn, is to suggest that the French revolutionaries operated with a universal concept of man and a national conception of the citizen. French citizens, in other words, had rights that man as such did not have because they, being citizens, belonged to the French community. For Marx, this means that the emancipation promised by the Declaration of Rights is only partial, limited as it is by the rules set by membership of the nation-state.[44] For Moyn, the 1789 Declaration's tie to the nation-state means that the rights contained in it have nothing to do with universal human rights. Truly universal human rights only gain ground in the 1970s and are supranational and depend on global institutions and NGO commitment.[45]

Balibar is critical of such national readings of the man/citizen-schism: "Reread the *Declaration* and you will see that there is in reality no gap between the rights of man and the rights of the citizen, no difference in content: they are exactly the same."[46] Man and citizen are used interchangeably in the Declaration of Rights, and that is pivotal for Balibar:

> [T]he signification of the equation Man=Citizen is not so much the definition of a political right as the affirmation of a universal right to politics. Formally, at least – but this is the very type of a form that can become a material weapon – the *Declaration* opens an indefinite sphere for the politicization of rights claims, each of which reiterates in its own way the demand for citizenship or for an institutional, public inscription of freedom and equality.[47]

By equating man and citizen, what the Declaration of Rights ultimately declares is a universal right to politics, but this immediately raises the question of what universalism is. In his work, Balibar distinguishes between "extensive" and "intensive" universalism.[48] Extensive universalism relies on an idea of a delimited space without internal borders, a place guided by a set of universally applicable positive laws. The typical example is the nation-state inside which a set of laws apply to all. Intensive universalism, on the other hand, rejects all kinds of arbitrary rule and insists upon the validity of a principle, no matter what positive law may or may not dictate within a given space. When Balibar emphasizes a universal right to politics, it should be taken in the sense of intensive universalism. The Declaration of Rights marks that moment in history when everyone, independent of their class, color, nationality, or gender, acquired the right to partake in politics and the language to lay claim to that right. As Balibar is well aware, this universal right to politics does not mean that everyone from 26 August, 1789 onward has had the possibility to participate equally in politics. Nor does it mean that the Declaration of Rights contains no internal contradictions. What it does mean, however, is that after the adoption of the 1789 Declaration, its opponents themselves were obliged to criticize it "in its own language, based on its own implications."[49] The Declaration of Rights invokes a new paradigm, sets up a new arena of political disagreement.

Literary historian Susan Maslan has set out to write a literary genealogy of this universal man/citizen-linkage, noting that "in the early modern political imagination to be a citizen meant to cease to be human."[50] What she has shown in a number of articles is how literature and especially theater, from the early modern period to the late Enlightenment, have negotiated and problematized the sharp separation of man and the citizen in a way that has prepared the revolutionary equation of man and citizen, and thereby paved the way for what she calls "the feeling citizen."[51] Mediating between man and citizen, the individual and his or her communitarian duties, is one task assumed by late eighteenth-century literature (and I shall have more to say about it in the analytical chapters), but Balibar presents another kind of anthropological dilemma which is important here.

The Declaration of Rights equates man and citizen, and in doing that, it also equates equality and liberty. Equaliberty is Balibar's portmanteau concept for the "historical discovery" that the extensions of equality and liberty are "necessarily identical"; the "(de facto) historical conditions of freedom are exactly the same as the (de facto) historical conditions of equality."[52] What interests me is not the proposed (and somewhat speculative) identity of liberty and equality but rather the anthropological contradictions that equaliberty, according to Balibar, produces when institutions or societies attempt to realize it. Equaliberty, and its inherent universal right to politics, needs a system of mediation to be operational, and Balibar points to two such systems of mediation in Enlightenment philosophy. These are competing ones entailing two different political anthropologies:

> I have emphasized the fact that, historically, there was not a single system of mediation but two partly competing systems: the first based on the hypothesis that man as a citizen in power is a *subject* in the Rousseauian sense, that is, an individual who frees himself from all external or transcendent subjection and thus chooses to freely obey a law he makes himself, as a member of a sovereign community of equal citizens. The second is based on the hypothesis that man as citizen in power is an *agent*, 'proprietor of his own person' in Locke's sense, which means that he and his fellows have an equal right, and equivalent capacity, to engage in 'commerce' in the general sense of this term (*Verkehr*, 'intercourse') on the basis of his absolute disposal over his own person and the unlimited responsibility that follows from it.[53]

Balibar presents two different political anthropologies when he distinguishes between subjects and agents. Rousseau's idea of the general will implies that man is subjected to a law that he himself helps create. Freedom is not to live without regulating laws but to exist in a community where one is subjected only to legislation one has oneself cocreated.[54] Locke's theory of property and commerce is founded on the assumption that "every Man has a *Property* in his own *Person*."[55] The agent owns himself, and when land is worked upon, the labor of the self-owned body mixes with things found in nature. The result of the meeting of labor and natural goods is added value, and everyone can lay a legitimate claim to the value produced by his or her labor. Equaliberty, according to Balibar, needs one of these two competing systems of mediation – Rousseauian community or Lockian property – to be realized.

If Balibar's distinction between the subject and the agent, between Rousseau and Locke, seems more philosophically stringent than historically pertinent, Charly Coleman has recently made a similar yet more historically grounded argument that can help unpack the difficulties inherent in combining general happiness with individual rights. Coleman too distinguishes between different anthropologies or what he calls "opposing cultures of personhood."[56] "On one side," Coleman writes, "orthodox Catholic theologians, mainstream philosophers, and apologists for venal officeholding and luxury consumption defended a multifaceted *culture of self-ownership*, according to which men and women were thought to possess and stand accountable for themselves and their actions."[57] This is the Lockian sense of personhood in which existence is thought of as property of the self. This self-ownership is then the basis of the accumulation of goods, including privileges, consumer products, and spiritual gifts. In opposition to the culture of self-ownership stands a *culture of dispossession* "that valorized the human person's loss of ownership over itself and external objects."[58] Subscribers to this idea – and they included Christian mystics, materialist philosophers, and political thinkers – criticized the idea that the self owned its person. Instead, they "sought to reduce men and women to mere objects of totalizing forces outside the self – at first identified with the God of mystical devotion, and ultimately situated in Enlightenment conceptions of nature and the revolutionary body politic."[59] Personhood, and Coleman develops this idea in dialogue with precisely Rousseau and his concept of the general will, only exists in so far as one is member of a larger body – be that God, nature, or the revolutionary state.

I use these opposing ideas of what Coleman calls cultures of personhood and what Balibar calls political anthropology as analytical concepts throughout this book. In combination, they provide the tools to unlock the 1789 Declaration linkage of individual rights and general happiness. When happiness is politicized, it is also collectivized, as in "*bonheur de tous*" or "*bonheur commun*," and that collectivity makes it potentially difficult to reconcile with individual rights. Equipping the citizen with a list of inalienable rights is very different from encouraging him or her to regulate all individual behavior according to the shifting needs of a happy communality. The Declaration of Rights claims that individual rights lead to general happiness, but that was not always the case. Literature is well equipped to investigate the potential clashes of happiness and rights. It does this on a personal level, thus bringing the conflicting cultures of personhood to life. These fictional personal conflicts should never be relegated to mere curious epiphenomena of late

14 *Introduction*

Enlightenment entertainment. They are also deep reflections on personhood and anthropology at a time when these categories change their meaning in tandem with the political revolution. Society produces the subjectivity of its members in a process in which its members can just as well be said to alter the collectivity they belong to. These negotiations are what the period's literature engages with. And as this book will explain, it very often does so by imagining how individual rights can be tied to the happiness of all.

* * *

I begin by closely analyzing the 1789 *Declaration of Rights and the Declaration Debate*. I seek to take seriously the idea of the deputies themselves that the Declaration of Rights was unfinished. Instead of considering the document as a stable set of unambiguous opinions, I think of the Declaration of Rights as a compromise text that consists of preliminary conclusions to lasting questions. I emphasize three dilemmas that caused the deputies much concern and debate before and after the adoption of the Declaration of Rights: nature versus society, rights versus duties, and dual forms of political exclusion. This chapter is methodologically aligned with the Cambridge School kind of intellectual political history, and its ambition is to lay bare the dilemmas of happiness and rights. I here wish to not only present the Declaration Debate but also prepare the later examination of the ways in which literature responded to, intervened in, and affected the revolutionary coupling of happiness and human rights.

Chapter 2 offers a general presentation of the three author-politicians whose works are analyzed in this book: Louis-Sébastien Mercier, Choderlos de Laclos, and Marie-Joseph Chénier. The ambition of the chapter is to explain how and why these authors believed that literature could have political effects. I take my methodological cue here from literary sociologists such as Alain Viala, Christian Jouhaud, and Robert Darnton, and argue that my set of authors, in their differences and similarities, helped carve out a historically specific *literary field*. In poetics, prefaces, letters, and articles, they continuously reflected on what it meant to be an author at this exact time, and I argue that their historically specific understandings of literature and the author role made them well suited to help lift the political task of reimagining France.

Chapters 3, 4, and 5 are analytical chapters that analyze, respectively, Mercier's *L'an 2440, rêve s'il en fût jamais* (1771), Laclos's *Les Liaisons dangereuses* (1782), and Chénier's *Fénelon ou les religieuses de Cambrai* (1793). My choice of these three works is motivated first by important similarities between the three authors: All three believed in the social effects of literature. All three worked as both professional writers and professional politicians, and they shared an interest in the tension between individual and society. Equally important, however, was a set of differences between them. Together, they provide a timeline spanning roughly from the Maupeou coup in 1771 to the rise and fall of Robespierre in the Year II of the Republic. The philosophical utopianism of Mercier contrasts completely with the ironic style of Laclos's libertine epistolary novel, and both novels, each in their way, differ from Chénier's sentimental theatrical piece. Hence, they offer a diverse selection of late eighteenth-century French literature, which is useful in critically reexamining Lynn Hunt's influential understanding of literature and French revolutionary human rights.[60] It is in fact one of the ambitions of this study to go beyond Hunt's focus on the sentimental, epistolary novel and thus offer a broader investigation of the multiple ways in which literature of different kinds and genres contributed to the task of imagining society anew. The three works considered here are thus chosen because their authors shared a wish to use literature politically *and* because of the different ways in which Mercier, Laclos, and Chénier set out to do that.

Chapter 3 presents a reading of Mercier's utopian – or *uchronian* – depiction of a perfect future society. *L'an 2440* is arguably the novel that most directly assumed the task of imagining a happy future society, and it turned out to be a massive hit on the clandestine literary market from the time of its publication until the time of the revolution. My analysis focuses on three things. I start by examining the peculiar temporality of Mercier's novel, a temporality I juxtapose with the equally famous futuristic vision of the philosopher Marquis de Condorcet and describe as a prophetic voice. I then investigate Mercier's proposed form of government in dialogue with the political philosophy of Jean-Jacques Rousseau and Montesquieu. The analysis finally scrutinizes the future form of taxation and highlights similarities between ideas put forth by Mercier, Olympe de Gouges, and the abbé Sieyès. My recurring argument is that the politics of Mercier's novel resides in its attempt to create a communitarian bond with its readers. *L'an 2440* not only presents a singular and even contradictory vision of happiness but also urges its reader to become a part of this happy society and the values it celebrates.

Choderlos de Laclos's masterpiece *Les liaisons dangereuses* is the focus of Chapter 4. Much scholarship in the field of eighteenth-century literature and human rights has focused on sentimental literature and its ability to awaken empathy in its readers. Laclos wrote an entirely different kind of literature that nonetheless contains sustained reflections upon happiness and rights. The novel atypically presents rights not as the citizen's legitimate claims vis-à-vis the state but as relational expectations, as the entitlement an individual has to expect a specific kind of behavior from another in a shared space of social conventions. In dialogue with historians such as Suzanne Desan and Carol Blum, I argue that interpersonal relationships, not least between men and women, were intricately intertwined with politics in this period. This means that

16 Introduction

Laclos's juxtaposition of competing and mutually threatening forms of sociality functioned as a brutal attack on late Old Regime elite society. While Mercier aimed to create a vision of future happiness by contrasting it with a depiction of eighteenth-century unhappiness, Laclos offers no transparent solutions, but he uses his artistic power to expose the interpersonal corruption of his day. Instead of building up, his contribution to the collective task of imagining society anew lay in his attempt to clear the ground by destroying the old.

In Chapter 5, I turn to revolutionary theater and Marie-Joseph Chénier's *Fénelon or the Nuns of Cambrai*, the most performed of his plays. He was personally involved in revolutionary politics, and he consciously tried to use theater to promote the revolutionary cause. His choice, however, to present the historical figure of François Fénelon on stage proved controversial when he was attacked by Jacobin journalists. I argue that Chénier tried to regenerate the nation and use Fénelon as an inspiring example of Enlightenment virtue. In his regeneration proposal, Chénier's play focuses particularly on the importance of destigmatizing the natural child who had long been excluded from society but was at the end of the century seen as a potential societal resource. Chénier's *drame*, and the subgenre of convent narratives it belongs to, however, also tended to sharply condemn their political adversaries and relegate them to a category of nonhuman enemies. This becomes especially clear in the final *tableau vivant* of the play, and it raises important questions about the universality of sentimental communities and, by extension, about the universality of French revolutionary human rights. When interpreted within the context of the Declaration Debate and the period's shifting ideas of authorship and literature, the three works reveal the diverse and sometimes contradictory way in which literature, for better or worse, helped set France on the course of future happiness.

Notes

1 23 June 1789, Le Roi in *Archives parlementaires de 1787 à 1860* (Paris: Librairie administrative de P. Dupont, 1862–), 8:143.
2 23 June 1789, Le Roi in *AP* 8:143.
3 On royalist ideology in its relation to the French revolution, see Michael Walzer, *Regicide and Revolution* (London and New York: Cambridge University Press, 1974), 8–35.
4 Étienne Balibar, "Citizen Subject" in E. Cadava, P. Connor, and J.-L. Nancy (eds.), *Who Comes After the Subject?* (New York: Routledge, 1991), 40.
5 11 July 1789, Louis XVI (read by Clermont-Tonnerre), *AP* 8:219.
6 11 July 1789, Louis XVI (read by Clermont-Tonnerre), *AP* 8:219.
7 11 July 1789, Louis XVI (read by Clermont-Tonnerre), *AP* 8:219.
8 These riots are described in detail in Hans-Jürgen Lüsebrink and Rolf Reichardt, *The Bastille: A History of a Symbol of Despotism and Freedom*. Trans. N. Schürer (Durham, NC and London: Duke University Press, 1997), 38–79 and, with a special emphasis on the burning of the tollgates, in

Michael Kwass, *Contraband: Louis Mandrin and the Making of a Global Underground* (Cambridge and London: Harvard University Press, 2014), 325–336.
9 *AP* 8:219–220.
10 23 June 1789, Abbé Sieyès in *AP* 8:146.
11 *AP* 8:147.
12 *Déclaration des droits de l'homme et du citoyen* in Antoine de Baecque, Wolfgang Schmale, and Michel Vovelle (eds.), *L'an 1 des droits de l'homme* (Paris: Presses du CNRS, 1988), 198. English translation taken from Lynn Hunt, *Inventing Human Rights: A History* (New York and London: W. W. Norton & Company, 2008), 220.
13 Hunt, *Inventing Human Rights*, 222.
14 The total count of declaration drafts is slightly uncertain. Marcel Gauchet reaches twenty-eight or twenty-nine drafts, while Baecque finds thirty (Marcel Gauchet, *La révolution des droits de l'homme* (Paris: Gallimard, 1989), 61; Baecque et al., *L'an 1*, 219). Some of the extra-parliamentary drafts, such as the one by Marquis de Condorcet, were highly important, and counting these, Gauchet, following S.-J. Samwer, mentions a total of 110 contributions (Gauchet, *La révolution*, 62n1).
15 Keith Michael Baker, "The Idea of a Declaration of Rights" in Dale Van Kley (ed.), *The French Idea of Freedom: The Old Regime and the Declaration of Rights of 1789* (Stanford, CA: Stanford University Press, 1994), 157.
16 27 August 1789, M. Bouche in *AP* VIII, 492/*L'an 1*, 196.
17 M. Crenière, 18 August 1789, in Baecque et al., *L'an 1*, 131.
18 Jonathan Israel, *Democratic Enlightenment: Philosophy, Revolution, and Human Rights 1750–1790* (Oxford: Oxford University Press, 2011), 937.
19 Marie-Joseph Chénier, "Discours préliminaire (1793)" in Gauthier Ambrus and François Jacob (ed.), *Théâtre* (Paris: Flammarion, 2002), 253.
20 Quoted from Christian Jouhaud, "Power and Literature: The Terms of the Exchange 1624–42" in Richard Burt (ed.), *Administration of Aesthetics: Censorship, Political Criticism, and the Public Sphere* (Minneapolis: University of Minnesota Press, 1994), 34. The concept of *field* is taken from the sociology of Pierre Bourdieu and is discussed, e.g., in Pierre Bourdieu, "Champ intellectuel et projet créateur" in *Les temps modernes* (November 1966): 865–906.
21 Robert Darnton, *The Literary Underground of the Old Regime* (Cambridge and London: Harvard University Press, 1982), 15.
22 Darnton, *The Literary Underground*, 10.
23 Darnton, *The Literary Underground*, 35.
24 Classic presentations of this branch of intellectual history are W. B. Gallie, "Essentially Contested Concepts" in *Proceedings of the Aristotelian Society*, Vol. 56 (1955–1956): 167–198; Reinhart Kosseleck, "Social History and Conceptual History" in Reinhart Kosseleck (ed.), *The Practice of Conceptual History: Timing History, Spacing Concepts* (Stanford, CA: Stanford University Press, 2002), 20–38; Quentin Skinner, "Meaning and Understanding in the History of Ideas" in Quentin Skinner (ed.), *Visions of Politics: Regarding Method*, Vol. 1 (Cambridge: Cambridge University Press, 2002), 57–90. For a study of the French revolution within this tradition, see Keith Michael Baker, *Inventing the French Revolution: Essays on French Political Culture in the Eighteenth Century* (Cambridge: Cambridge University Press, 1990).
25 See, e.g., Ellen Meiksins Wood, "The Social History of Political Theory" in Ellen Meiksins Wood (ed.), *Citizens to Lords: A Social History of Western*

18 Introduction

    Political Thought from Antiquity to the Middle Ages (London and New York: Verso, 2008), 1–28, and William H. Sewell Jr., "Refiguring the 'Social' in Social Science: An Interpretivist Manifesto" in William H. Sewell Jr., *Logics of History: Social Theory and Social Transformation* (Chicago, IL: University of Chicago Press, 2005), 318–373.
26 The most thorough study of eighteenth-century happiness is still Robert Mauzi, *L'idée de bonheur au XVIIIe siècle*. Troisième édition (Paris: Armand Colin, 1967).
27 Louis Antoine Léon de Saint-Just, *Rapport sur le mode d'execution du decret contre les ennemis de la republique, présenté au nom du Comité de salut public à la Convention nationale à la séance du 13 ventôse an II* in Saint-Just, *Œuvres complètes* (Paris: Éditions Gérard Lebovici, 1984), 715.
28 Darrin M. McMahon, *The Pursuit of Happiness: A History from the Greeks to the Present* (London: Penguin Books, 2007), 262.
29 Jean Pestré, "Happiness." *The Encyclopedia of Diderot & d'Alembert Collaborative Translation Project*. Trans. N. S. Hoyt and T. Cassirer. Ann Arbor: Michigan Publishing, University of Michigan Library, 2003. http://hdl.handle.net/2027/spo.did2222.0000.153 (accessed 21 December 2017). Originally published as "Bonheur," Encyclopédie ou Dictionnaire raisonné des sciences, des arts et des métiers, 2:322–323 (Paris, 1752).
30 Pestré, "Happiness." *The Encyclopedia of Diderot & d'Alembert*.
31 Pestré, "Happiness." *The Encyclopedia of Diderot & d'Alembert*.
32 Pestré, "Happiness." *The Encyclopedia of Diderot & d'Alembert*.
33 McMahon, *The Pursuit of Happiness*, 209–210.
34 McMahon, *The Pursuit of Happiness*, 222.
35 Julien Offray de La Mettrie, "Anti-Seneca or the Sovereign Good" in *Machine Man and Other Writings*. Trans. and ed. Ann Thomson (Cambridge: Cambridge University Press, 1996), 120.
36 Mauzi distinguishes between four aspects of happiness, the first of which is a *"bilan d'états de conscience"*; the second focuses on "la forme d'une totalité," the third is a Rousseauian *"conscience d'exister,"* and the fourth depends on *"l'existence en mouvement."* Mauzi, *L'idée de bonheur*, 113–114.
37 François de Fénelon, *Telemachus, son of Ulysses* (Cambridge: Cambridge University Press, 1994), 162.
38 Pestré, "Happiness." *The Encyclopedia of Diderot & d'Alembert*.
39 Sara Ahmed, *The Promise of Happiness* (Durham, NC and London: Duke University Press, 2010), 1.
40 Ahmed, *The Promise of Happiness*, 1.
41 Étienne Balibar, *Equaliberty: Political Essays*. Trans. James Ingram (Durham, NC and London: Duke University Press, 2014), 119; 79.
42 For a systematic exposition of this problem, see Michel Foucault, "Le sujet et le pouvoir" in *Dits et écrits II. 1976–1988* (Paris: Gallimard, 2001), 1041–1062.
43 Balibar, *Equaliberty*, 107–108.
44 Karl Marx, "Zur Judenfrage" in Karl Marx and Friedrich Engels (eds.), *Werke* band 1 (Berlin: Dietz Verlag, 1976), 347–377.
45 Samuel Moyn, *The Last Utopia: Human Rights in History* (Cambridge and London: The Belknap Press of Harvard University Press, 2012), 25–26. Moyn repeats this argument in his afterword to Kate E. Tunstall (ed.), *Self-Evident Truths? Human Rights and the Enlightenment* (New York and London: Bloomsbury Academic, 2012), writing,

    [W]hile it is incontestable that the French declaration of the Rights of Man and Citizen of 1789 was about rights, it was just as much directed in the first instance towards founding a state, on the ruins of absolute monarchy. In fact, from their seventeenth-century origins, the assertion of natural rights had typically been bound up with state-formation, and modern history until recently only amplified the connection.

(256–257)

46 Balibar, *Equaliberty*, 44.
47 Balibar, *Equaliberty*, 50.
48 Balibar, *Equaliberty*, 106.
49 Balibar, *Equaliberty*, 120.
50 Susan Maslan, "The Anti-Human: Man and Citizen before the Declaration of the Rights of Man and of the Citizen" in *The South Atlantic Quarterly*, Vol. 103, No. 2/3 (2004): 372.
51 Susan Maslan, "The Dream of the Feeling Citizen: Law and Emotion in Corneille and Montesquieu" in *SubStance*, Vol. 35, No. 1 (2006): 69–84.
52 Balibar, *Equaliberty*, 48.
53 Balibar, *Equaliberty*, 120.
54 In *Of the Social Contract* (1762), Rousseau defines moral freedom in the civil state as "obedience to the law one has prescribed to oneself." Jean-Jacques Rousseau, *Of the Social Contract* in Jean-Jacques Rousseau, *The Social Contract and Other Later Political Writings*. Ed. V. Gourevitch (Cambridge: Cambridge University Press, 2012), 54.
55 John Locke, *Two Treatises of Government*. Ed. P. Laslett (Cambridge: Cambridge University Press, 2009), 287.
56 Charly Coleman, *The Virtues of Abandon: An Anti-Individualist History of the French Enlightenment* (Stanford, CA: Stanford University Press, 2014), 3.
57 Coleman, *The Virtues of Abandon*, 3.
58 Coleman, *The Virtues of Abandon*, 4.
59 Coleman, *The Virtues of Abandon*, 4.
60 Hunt, *Inventing Human Rights*, Chapter 1.

Literature

Ahmed, Sara: *The Promise of Happiness*. Durham, NC and London: Duke University Press, 2010.

Archives parlementaires de 1787 à 1860. Paris: Librairie administrative de P. Dupont, 1862–.

Baecque, Antoine de, Wolfgang Schmale, and Michel Vovelle (eds.): *L'an 1 des droits de l'homme*. Paris: Presses du CNRS, 1988.

Baker, Keith Michael: *Inventing the French Revolution: Essays on French Political Culture in the Eighteenth Century*. Cambridge: Cambridge University Press, 1990, 154–199.

Baker, Keith Michael: "The Idea of a Declaration of Rights" in D. V. Kley (ed.), *The French Idea of Freedom: The Old Regime and the Declaration of Rights of 1789*. Stanford, CA: Stanford University Press, 1994.

Balibar, Étienne: "Citizen Subject" in E. Cadava, P. Connor, and J.-L. Nancy (eds.), *Who Comes After the Subject?* New York: Routledge, 1991.

Balibar, Étienne: *Equaliberty: Political Essays*. Trans. J. Ingram. Durham, NC and London: Duke University Press, 2014.

Bourdieu, Pierre: "Champ intellectual et projet créateur." *Les temps modernes*, No. 246 (November) 1966: 865–906.

Chénier, Marie-Joseph: *Théâtre*. Eds. G. Ambrus and F. Jacob. Paris: Flammarion, 2002.

Coleman, Charly: *The Virtues of Abandon: An Anti-Individualist History of the French Enlightenment*. Stanford, CA: Stanford University Press, 2014.

Darnton, Robert: *The Literary Underground of the Old Regime*. Cambridge and London: Harvard University Press, 1982.

Diderot, Denis and Jean le Rond d'Alembert (eds.): *Encyclopédie, ou dictionnaire raisonné des sciences, des arts et des métiers, par une société de gens de lettres*. University of Chicago: ARTFL Encyclopédie Project (Spring 2013 Edition).

Diderot, Denis and Jean le Rond d'Alembert (eds.): *The Encyclopedia of Diderot & d'Alembert Collaborative Translation Project*. Ann Arbor: Michigan Publishing, University of Michigan Library, 2017. Web. http://hdl.handle.net/2027/spo.did2222.0003.409.

Fénelon, François de: *Telemachus, Son of Ulysses*. Trans. P. Riley. Cambridge: Cambridge University Press, 1994.

Foucault, Michel: "Le sujet et le pouvoir" in Michel Foucault (ed.), *Dits et écrits II. 1976–1988*, 1041–1062. Paris: Gallimard, 2001.

Gallie, Walter B. "Essentially Contested Concepts." *Proceedings of the Aristotelian Society*, Vol. 56 (1955–1956): 167–198.

Gauchet, Marcel: *La révolution des droits de l'homme*. Paris: Gallimard, 1989.

Hunt, Lynn: *Inventing Human Rights: A History*. New York and London: W. W. Norton & Company, 2008.

Israel, Jonathan: *Democratic Enlightenment: Philosophy, Revolution, and Human Rights 1750–1790*. Oxford: Oxford University Press, 2011.

Jouhaud, Christian: "Power and Literature: The Terms of the Exchange 1624–42" in R. Burt (ed.), *Administration of Aesthetics: Censorship, Political Criticism, and the Public Sphere*, 34–82. Minneapolis: University of Minnesota Press, 1994.

Kosseleck, Reinhart: *The Practice of Conceptual History: Timing History, Spacing Concepts*. Trans. T. S. Presner et al. Stanford, CA: Stanford University Press, 2002.

Kwass, Michael: *Contraband: Louis Mandrin and the Making of a Global Underground*. Cambridge and London: Harvard University Press, 2014.

La Mettrie, Julien Offray de: *Machine Man and Other Writings*. Ed. and trans. A. Thomson. Cambridge: Cambridge University Press, 1996.

Locke, John: *Two Treatises of Government*. Ed. Peter Laslett. Cambridge: Cambridge University Press, 2009.

Lüsebrink, Hans-Jürgen and Rolf Reichardt: *The Bastille: A History of a Symbol of Despotism and Freedom*. Trans. Norbert Schürer. Durham, NC and London: Duke University Press, 1997.

Marx, Karl: "Zur Judenfrage" in Karl Marx and Friedrich Engels (eds.), *Werke*. Vol. 1, 347–377. Berlin: Dietz Verlag, 1976.

Maslan, Susan: "The Anti-Human: Man and Citizen before the Declaration of the Rights of Man and of the Citizen." *The South Atlantic Quarterly*, Vol. 103, No. 2/3 (2004), 357–374.

Maslan, Susan: "The Dream of the Feeling Citizen: Law and Emotion in Corneille and Montesquieu." *SubStance*, Vol. 35, No. 1 (2006), 69–84.

Mauzi, Robert: *L'idée de bonheur au XVIIIe siècle*. 3rd edition. Paris: Armand Colin, 1967.
McMahon, Darrin M.: *The Pursuit of Happiness: A History from the Greeks to the Present*. London: Penguin Books, 2007.
Moyn, Samuel: *The Last Utopia: Human Rights in History*. Cambridge and London: The Belknap Press of Harvard University Press, 2012, 249–263.
Moyn, Samuel: "Afterword" in Kate E. Tunstall (ed.), *Self-Evident Truths? Human Rights and the Enlightenment*. New York and London: Bloomsbury Academic, 2012.
Rousseau, Jean-Jacques: *Œuvres completes*. Vol. 3. Paris: Gallimard, 2011.
Saint-Just, Louis Antoine Léon de: *Rapport sur le mode d'execution du decret contre les ennemis de la republique, présenté au nom du Comité de salut public à la Convention nationale à la séance du 13 ventôse an II* in Saint-Just: *Œuvres completes*. Paris: Éditions Gérard Lebovici, 1984.
Sewell Jr., William H.: *Logics of History: Social Theory and Social Transformation*. Chicago, IL: University of Chicago Press, 2005.
Skinner, Quentin: *Visions of Politics: Regarding Method*. Cambridge: Cambridge University Press, 2002.
Walzer, Michael: *Regicide and Revolution*. London and New York: Cambridge University Press, 1974.
Wood, Ellen Meiksins: *Citizens to Lords: A Social History of Western Political thought from Antiquity to the Middle Ages*. London and New York: Verso, 2008.

1 The Unfinished Declaration

"Do I contradict myself? / Very well, then I contradict myself, / (I am large, I contain multitudes.)"[1] Greatness, Walt Whitman famously writes in these lines from *Leaves of Grass*, lies not in unwavering certainty. True greatness, on the contrary, is the ability to contain multitudes, to bridge contradictions.

Scholars agree that the 1789 Declaration of the Rights of Man and of the Citizen is a great historical document, but in their approach to it, not all agree with Whitman's poetic definition of greatness. Instead, scholars often remark on the Declaration's solidity and firm principles. Thus, the "universalism" of the Declaration of Rights is a "major stride forward" that would sadly be "superseded by a nationalist reaction" during the reign of Napoleon Bonaparte.[2] The human rights of 1789 were a "clearly formulated package of basic human rights" that amounted to an "unqualified moral universalism."[3] And if the universal equality was not always actually enjoyed by eighteenth-century men and women, this lamentable fact was not because of inherent contradictions in the document but because it was "prescriptive" and not "descriptive."[4] There is, writes Christine Fauré, a myth of the fixed and stable 1789 rights of man, and despite ambitious genealogies, we sometimes get the impression that the actual Declaration of Rights appeared "pre-armed from the brain of God."[5]

In opposition to scholars emphasizing the unambiguity of the document stands a body of work that underscores the contradictions of the Declaration of Rights. This work – more in line with a Whitmanian understanding of greatness – tends to close-read the Declaration Debate in which the multiple ideological tensions and paradoxes discernible in the Declaration stand out and unmistakably so. Historians, claims Antoine de Baecque, have been overly influenced by a dominant "history of political ideas," which has led them to neglect the forms of the parliamentary debate in order to "privilege the enunciated 'values' and 'principles' in the declaration of rights."[6] These historians of ideas have forgotten that which Marcel Gauchet emphasizes, namely that "before being a text, the Declaration is an act."[7] Much practical negotiation preceded and influenced the document. Had historians of ideas remembered that prehistory, perhaps they would have seen that the Declaration of Rights is an "immensely complex document [...] drawn up with enormous difficulty and great urgency, at the cost of bitter argument, inevitable linguistic compromises, and dramatic theoretical tensions, by an assembly profoundly divided over the nature and purpose of the text."[8] (Figure 1.1).

In this chapter, I revisit the Declaration Debate. My analysis adds to the second body of work and emphasizes the document's Whitmanian greatness. I consider the debate the intellectual machine room of the

Figure 1.1 Déclaration des droits de l'homme et du citoyen: [estampe]. (Paris: chez Jaufret, 1789]. Bibliothèque nationale de France.

early revolution. Here, we find crystallized the problems inherent in the revolutionary break with absolutism, inherent in the revolutionary movement itself, and we get first glimpses of the issues that would haunt the 1790s: active/passive citizenship, the limits of political membership, and the philosophical anthropological premises for considering citizens free and equal. Rather than an unwavering declaration of self-evident truths, I seek to understand what the deputies meant when they, at the very conclusion of their deliberations, called the Declaration of Rights "unfinished."[9]

There is, however, a danger inherent in emphasizing the incompleteness and openness of the Declaration of Rights. Do its openness and inconsistencies not make it an empty document? How do we avoid reducing the Declaration to empty talk while insisting upon its compromise character? I believe the Declaration of Rights in fact follows two different historical trajectories in the revolutionary decade. The first trajectory is one in which the fundamental problems presented by the 1789 Declaration keep looming large over later political developments. In 1793, when the Jacobins renegotiated the Declaration of Rights, they were, in the words of Gauchet, "inside the same sphere of possibilities and questions" as the 1789 deputies.[10] As soon as the Directory in 1795 opened its declaration debate, "the antagonisms and dilemmas of the first day reappeared."[11] Following this line of thought, there may be great political differences between 1789, 1793, and 1795, but revolutionaries kept returning to the dilemmas of the 1789 Declaration Debate.

There is another trajectory, however, in which the Declaration of Rights assumed "a virtually sacred status" almost immediately after its adoption.[12] Lynn Hunt has argued that the idea of equal rights came to seem self-evident around 1789 in part because of Enlightenment campaigns against torture and because of the slowly acquired ability to feel empathy and compassion across social, geographical, and gender lines.[13] The self-evidence of rights, in other words, has a history and one going back to the Enlightenment. But this self-evidence or this sacredness of rights and of the Declaration also has an important *post*-1789 history. In the revolutionary decade, there was, Valentine Zuber writes, "a cult of the rights of man;" a cult that was built up through the confident wording of the Declaration, through revolutionary iconography, through widely circulated catechisms for school use, and through civil ceremonies.[14] A significant amount of labor went into producing the image of the Declaration of Rights as sacred and into promoting the idea that it was a stable, self-evident foundation upon which the revolution and the new France rested.

In what follows, I shall pursue the first of these trajectories as I unfold the ideological ambiguities of the Declaration of Rights. I emphasize the importance of the second trajectory, however, because I believe part of the imaginative and intellectual appeal of happiness and rights lay in their simultaneous openness and authority. That duality – contradiction and sacredness – reached a climax in the revolutionary decade, but it was prefigured in the years before as the language of happiness and rights gained momentum in political and aesthetic discourse. In fact, the complementarity of contradiction and sacredness, of ambiguity and self-evidence, was a crucial reason for the pull toward politics felt by the period's authors of fiction. I shall begin the analysis with an overview of the political atmosphere and institutional framework within which the Declaration Debate took place.

Debating the Declaration

When the deputies were still debating whether or not they needed a declaration of rights, one of the document's most fervent supporters, the Third Estate member Rabaut de Saint-Etienne, addressed the Assembly. He drew a parallel between the American Founding Fathers and the French revolutionaries, saying that, despite their many differences, one similarity to the North Americans was the wish to "regenerate ourselves [nous régénérer]." This was essentially what the Declaration should be about, he said: "The first thing it reminds us of is less to declare our rights than to constitute ourselves."[15] The task of the deputies was not solely to agree upon a list of rights but also, and simultaneously, to constitute the Assembly – and even the new France – as a political subject. There was an "apprenticeship of politics" involved in this act of self-constitution which was both philosophical and practical.[16] What did it mean to write a constitution, to constitute France? And how would the approximately 1,200 deputies organize their work, where would they sit, and who would talk when and for how long? All these practical uncertainties of constituting a new political subject were confronted during the Declaration Debate and influenced the final wording of the Declaration of Rights.

The French Revolution, and this is a rare instance in which most historians agree, "was the immediate result of the insolvency of the Bourbon state at the end of the 1780s."[17] Involvement in the Seven Years' War (1756–1763) and the American Revolutionary War (1775–1783) had prompted the French state to take out massive public loans, essentially because the inefficient Old Regime fiscal system was unable to generate sufficient revenue.[18] Seeking to steer clear of the threatening state bankruptcy, Louis XVI, after a disastrous meeting with the Assembly of the Notables, decided to convene the Estates General. The Estates General was an assembly consisting of representatives from all three estates – the clerics, the nobles, and the commoners – and it was last assembled in 1614. Formally, however, it was the only political body with the authority to impose new taxes, and after the failed attempt to persuade the nobles to voluntarily accept new taxes, its assembly seemed the only way out. But it was a politically hazardous move to convene the Estates General because it signaled an element of popular sovereignty.

Enlightenment *philosophes* had long aimed to develop the intellectual foundation for a move from absolutist monarchical sovereignty to popular sovereignty, and assembling the Estates General could accelerate and make real this shift.

Louis XVI summoned the Estates General in January 1789, and four months later, representatives from all the regions of France arrived in Paris. As this happened, the initially economic question of avoiding state bankruptcy gave way to a set of distinctly political problems. Should the members of the Estates General vote by head or by estate? Should the Third Estate – the commoners – have more members since they represented roughly 99% of the French population? Should the king be allowed to veto any decision the Estates General might reach? The impossibility of reaching satisfactory compromises on these questions prompted the Third Estate members to officially declare themselves the National Assembly in June 1789, a decision that was confirmed on 20 June with the Tennis Court Oath. The establishment of the National Assembly marks the beginnings of the French revolution and of the "political apprenticeship" of the deputies.[19] Most of the deputies were lawyers, and despite their obvious interest in politics, they lacked knowledge of its practicalities. The downside to this unfamiliarity with politics, and the learning process it necessitated, was a slow legislative procedure in the early years of the revolution, but the democratic benefit was a debate in which the ways of politics were continuously discussed.

The first problem on the agenda of the National Assembly was a declaration of rights. Prior to the assembly of the Estates General, all the provinces of France had equipped their representatives with lists of grievances, collectively named the *Cahiers de doléances*. These grievance lists' "well-nigh *unanimous*" demand for fiscal reform together with their repeated calls for a constitution and a list of individual rights were considered high priority tasks by the deputies.[20] On behalf of the *Comité de distribution du travail sur la Constitution*, Third Estate deputy Jean-Joseph Mounier presented the task of writing a declaration of rights to the Assembly on 9 July 1789, saying,

> Since the goal of all societies is the general happiness [le bonheur general], a government that distances itself from this goal or is opposed to it is essentially vicious. For a constitution to be good, it must be founded on the rights of men and it must evidently protect them; to prepare a constitution it is hence necessary to know the rights that the natural justice accords to all individuals.[21]

The linkage of collective happiness (*bonheur générale*) and individual rights (*les droits à tous les individus*) was present from the very beginnings of the Declaration Debate. But what caused much immediate discussion was the relationship between the Declaration of Rights and the Constitution.

As presented by Mounier, the rights of man should *found* the constitution and ensure its high quality. There is an exponential logic to the idea he proposes: The Declaration should briefly express the foundation of the Constitution, which, in turn, should lay the ground for all further legislation. This explains why the Declaration Debate is all about the politics of semantics. Any miniscule change in the wording of the Declaration of Rights was seen to affect the future Constitution, which would, in turn, influence the positive laws to be written for the new France. The deputies would come to discuss whether the Declaration should succeed or, as Mounier here argued, precede the Declaration, and the reason this was worth arguing about was the exponential logic of Mounier's presentation. Had the Declaration of Rights succeeded the Constitution, it would have become an appendix to and not a foundation of it.

The National Assembly Declaration Debate took place between 9 July and 27 August, and can be heuristically subdivided into four phases.[22] The first phase ran from 9 to 31 July and was characterized by the preparation and discussion of the thirty official declaration proposals, some of which were written by individuals, others of which were written by groups. Three of the proposals stand out. Marquis de Lafayette, the veteran of the American Revolutionary War and personal friend of George Washington and Thomas Jefferson, presented a version written with the wish to "say what everyone knows, what everyone feels."[23] He favored a brief, easily understandable declaration in line with the sentiments engraved by nature "into the hearts of all men."[24] Abbé Sieyes, who had published the widespread pamphlet *What Is the Third Estate?* in January 1789, took a different approach in his philosophically advanced proposal presented on 20–21 July. Sieyès wanted to present a rational foundation for the Declaration of Rights, an attempt that gave his proposal the reputation of being brilliant but too complex or, to use a word that would later stick to Sieyès, too *metaphysical*.[25] The third proposal that should be highlighted is the collective proposal of the Sixth Bureau. All through July, the Assembly was subdivided into thirty bureaus that would all discuss the Declaration of Rights. The proposal of the Sixth Bureau received no initial attention but would become important later, arguably because of its anonymous or "lacklustre" character.[26]

The second phase of the deliberations ran from 1 to 4 August and was initiated by Louis-Jean-Henry Darnaudat, who had had more than enough of the endless bureau discussions. He suggested that the Assembly should put an immediate stop to the Declaration Debate and dedicate all its time to the Constitution.[27] His proposal was rejected, but it set the tone for the conflictual and philosophically charged discussions of the next days. July and early August, the days of *la Grand Peur*, were characterized by an increasing fear of rural unrest and of an Aristocratic counterrevolutionary conspiracy. In combination with this general fear, Darnaudat's blunt proposal had paved the way for other Declaration critics who now argued that the rights of man could lead to anarchy and chaos, that they were more fit for animals living in a state of nature than for civilized human beings, and that the list of rights should at the very least be supplemented by a list of the duties of all citizens. This phase ended with the deputies rejecting the idea of an additional list of duties (an idea that would resurface later in the decade) in the morning session of 4 August. The almost mythological night session of this date, in which the deputies brought an end to the system of privileges, put the Declaration Debate on hold until 12 August.[28]

When the deputies turned their attention to the Declaration of Rights again, they entered the third phase of the deliberations. By now, they had decided that they wanted a Declaration of Rights – with no list of duties – to precede the Constitution, but they still had multiple declaration proposals to choose from. They wanted to reduce this number to one and then proceed to negotiate each article at a time. On 13 August, the Assembly set down a committee, *le Comité de cinq*, and commissioned it to boil down the amount of proposals. The head of the committee was the great rhetorician of the revolution, the comte de Mirabeau, but after days of hard work, he and his group had to acknowledge that it was "a difficult task."[29] The second estate member, Marquis de Bonnay, agreed as he strongly criticized Mirabeau's proposal the day after its presentation, saying, "This comity has just offered you its work but it's far from perfect. It does not meet our expectations. I will even say that it is not what we asked for."[30] Mirabeau had, writes Rials, committed a "faux-pas."[31] His oratorical skills had failed him, and his colleagues – including his own brother – had gotten the impression that he was trying to "seduce with his eloquence,"[32] that he was guiding "the Assembly towards opposite ends."[33] In the tumult arising from the failure of Mirabeau's proposal, Abbé Grégoire succeeded in planting the idea that God's name ought to be in the Declaration of Rights, something that could have been controversial but was not at this time.[34] Somewhat surprisingly, however, the deputies after a vote on 19 August decided to return to the proposal of the Sixth Bureau and use that as the point of departure for their final negotiation of the Declaration's articles. Receiving 605 votes, 360 more than that of Sieyès, which came in second, the unremarkable proposal won a great victory and its anonymity seems to have been precisely what the deputies needed at this point.[35]

In the final phase of the debate, the deputies debated and rewrote every article from the Sixth Bureau proposal one at a time in order to land at the final wording of the document. The Sixth Bureau proposal contained twenty-four articles, seven more than the final Declaration of Rights.[36] But not only were the number of articles reduced, the wording of all articles underwent significant change in all but two cases.[37] The result of this strenuous editing process was that elements from many of the rejected proposals reentered the debate and fundamentally altered the document. It was also the fourth phase of the debate that really gave the Declaration its compromise character because deputies had to give and take. These were discussions of linguistic nuances, choosing one word over another, that were thought to cause major long-term political differences because of the exponential logic of the debate. This phase ended when the deputies decided to move on to the Constitution and hence not deliberate on the planned eighteenth article about "the social supports."[38] They did promise each other to later resume the tiring work on the unfinished declaration, which, in a sense they did in 1793 and 1795, but that was long after King Louis XVI had reluctantly accepted the Declaration's seventeen articles.

Multiple principled dilemmas arose in the course of the debate, many of which remained unsolved. In what follows, I focus on three of them; three problems that were also given in depth attention by the period's authors of fiction.

Nature and Society

In the second phase of the Declaration Debate, moderates and conservatives launched what Stéphane Rials calls the first "counterattack" against the Declaration of Rights.[39] In immediate succession of the outspoken colonialist Pierre-Victor Malouet, Third Estate deputy and monarchist Antoine-François Delandine mounted the rostrum.[40] Malouet and Delandine both relied on a juxtaposition of natural man and social man in their proposals to abandon the whole idea of a declaration of rights. Delandine said,

> Instead of returning to the origins of the social order, let us improve the situation we're placed in. Let us abandon natural man and spend our time on civilized man. Instead of looking for what we have been, or for what we are, let us determine what we ought to be.[41]

The distinction between natural and civilized man, Delandine explained, is one between abstract philosophy and realist politics. Why bother with discussions about natural rights and the nature state? People are in the streets asking for immediate legislative action and the deputies should honor their call by skipping the Declaration of Rights and begin writing the constitution instead. The resulting nature/society discussion had profound historical, philosophical, and political resonances.

Historically, the nature/society debate was informed by the American revolutionary example. Declaring their independence, the Founding Fathers had pointed to the "Laws of Nature" and famously written,[42] "We hold these truths to be self-evident, that all men are created equal, that they are endowed by their Creator with certain unalienable Rights, that among these are Life, Liberty and the pursuit of Happiness."[43]

30 *The Unfinished Declaration*

America was an ideal for some, including the American revolutionary war veteran, Mathieu de Montmorency, who urged his colleagues to follow and even surpass the American example: "They have offered a great example to the new hemisphere; let us offer one to the universe. Let us set an example worthy of being admired."[44] His ambition was to give to the world what the Americans had given to their hemisphere, to offer, in the words of Gauchet, a "universalist surpassing of the glorious precedent."[45]

The protagonists of the first "counter attack" were less enthusiastic. In his long intervention, Malouet picked up on the American parallel and developed its nature/society linkage:

> I know that the Americans [...] have taken man in the bosom of nature and have presented him to the universe in his primitive sovereignty. But the newly formed American society is wholly made up of proprietors already accustomed to equality, strangers to luxury and poverty alike, barely aware of the burden of taxation. The prejudice that are dominant with us have found no fecundity in the soil they cultivate. Such men were no doubt prepared to receive freedom in all of its energy because their tastes, their mores, and their position drew them towards democracy.[46]

The indigenous population is clearly not a part of Malouet's narrative of the Americas. To him, the United States is made up of proprietors who are ready and able to manage the responsibility that comes with natural freedom and equality. France, on the other hand, is made up of "an immense multitude of men without property who, before anything else, expect their subsistence from a guaranteed job, from an exacting police force, and from a continuous protection."[47] Malouet's argument, as Susan Maslan emphasizes, is "clearly associated" with the philosophical vocabulary of Jean-Jacques Rousseau and especially with the Genevan's *Second Discourse*.[48] Let me recuperate the implications of Rousseau's nature/society distinction before returning to the Declaration Debate.

Rousseau's idea of the natural state is multifaceted but in the *Second Discourse* he juxtaposes it with a description of the civil state while underscoring that his writings on nature should not "be taken for historical truths" but only as "hypothetical and conditional reasonings."[49] His text sometimes seems like an eighteenth-century anthropological book but, strangely, his descriptions of life in the natural state are purely hypothetical, which does seem to undermine his criticism of the luxurious and superficial modern lifestyle. After all, if the ideal from which society has strayed is nothing but a hypothesis, the alleged unnaturalness of society marks only a difference from a strange fiction and straying from a strange fiction would appear less catastrophic than having strayed from the ways of nature herself. And yet Rousseau writes, it is no light undertaking to disentangle what is original from what is artificial in man's present Nature, and to know accurately a state which no longer exists, which perhaps never did exist, which probably never will exist, and about which it is nevertheless necessary to have exact Notions in order accurately to judge of our present state.[50]

In his reading of the *Second Discourse*, Paul de Man takes this paradoxical insistence upon the importance of a purely fictive state of nature as his point of departure. What, de Man asks, is the connection between a deliberately fictional or metaphorical language on the one hand and a treatise on very real political topics such as property rights and civil society on the other? To answer this question he returns to a passage from Rousseau's *First Discourse* where "a primitive man" meets other men for the first time in his life.[51] Struck with fear, the primitive man gives the strangers the name *giants*. Only after having met these strangers numerous times does the primitive man begin to see the resemblances between himself and the others. This is when the word *man* is invoked for the first time. The strangers, who initially seemed different, scary, and large, now appear to be the equal of the primitive man and the word *man* comes to designate the equality or the sameness of what at this point comes to be regarded as a group. Paul de Man writes,

> [T]he invention of the word man makes it possible for 'men' to exist by establishing the equality within inequality, the sameness within difference of civil society, in which the suspended, potential truth of the original fear is domesticated by the illusion of identity. The concept interprets the metaphor of numerical sameness as if it were a statement of literal fact.[52]

The importance of the word *man* is not anthropological; it does not capture the "true essence" of man. Rather, *man* posits a state of equality where there used to be inequality and thereby washes away the insecurity and fear prompted by the initial word *giant*. The state of nature has the same effect in Rousseau, de Man claims. It's a deliberately fictive concept that can be used to expose the unnaturalness of society. Knowing full well that it's a fiction, the concept of the state of nature can nonetheless be used to articulate the depravity of the social state. In her reading of the Declaration Debate, Susan Maslan picks up on de Man's reading of Rousseau and claims that in the National Assembly "[t]he fiction of nature made possible a fictive equality, a willed, artificial political equality capable of overcoming naturalized, social inequality."[53] The organization of the social state, what political philosopher Jacques Rancière calls its "distribution of the sensible," is not a naturally given, it's not a historical necessity.[54] Society can be restructured, its distribution of the sensible can be "reconfigured," but it needs to be challenged by an alternative vision. The possibility of social change has to be made fathomable and this is the task Rousseau assumes when he invokes the deliberately unreal state of nature and uses it as the foundation for his categorical condemnation of the depravity of life in the social state.

Malouet's fear was the introduction of such alternative visions of society. His strategy was to ridicule the idea of a state of nature and natural rights and thereby prompt others to focus on what was immediately at hand. What the nation needed was not abstract principles of equality and liberty, but stability and order. "Why then begin by transporting man to the top of a mountain and show him his limitless empire when he will necessarily have to descend from it and find limits everywhere?"[55] Delandine similarly argued that it was preposterous, and potentially dangerous, to promise people universal, natural rights in the Declaration of Rights, when everything they would meet in society would reveal inequality and limitations.[56] Following Maslan and de Man's reading of Rousseau, what these Declaration critics criticize is not only the philosophical tradition of natural rights nor the American example but the very idea that the deputies could *politically* choose to reorganize society; that they could choose to bring an end to the existing social inequalities. These historical, philosophical, and political implications functioned as subtext to the parliamentary discussion of nature and society.

The first counterattack on the rights of man failed as the deputies continued their deliberations. But a second, less overt attack proved more successful. On 4 August, before the famous night session, the Abbé Grégoire suggested that a declaration should not only show the citizen "the circle that he can move around in but also the barrier, which he cannot transgress,"[57] and Baron Joseph-Henri Jessé stated that "liberty is a generous liquor that needs a solid vase to contain it."[58] These containment metaphors signaled an ambition to limit the rights of man, to ensure that they would not result in anarchy and chaos. According to his 1792 memoirs, Jean-Joseph Mounier, whose views became increasingly moderate during the debate, at one point realized that a declaration of rights was inevitable, and from then on his negotiating strategy was to avoid the frightening American example by "inserting only the principles that did not seem dangerous to me."[59] The dilemma of balancing rights with duties arose from this wish to limit the universal expansion of rights.

Rights and Duties

The explicit discussion of rights and duties took place in the second phase of the Declaration Debate and forms what Rials calls the "second counter-attack."[60] The duties of man were mentioned by the cleric

François-Marie-Christophe Grandin on 1 August and again, primarily by clerics, on 4 August.[61] In the words of M. de Lubersac,

> The flattering expression of *rights* must be managed adroitly; it must be accompanied by that of *duties*, which will serve it as a corrective. It would be fitting if, at the head of this work, there were some nobly expressed religious ideas.[62]

His explicitly religious wish to "manage" the rights of man would be realized in the 1795 Declaration of the Rights and Duties of Man and the Citizen. But in the 1789 Declaration of Rights, duties only appeared in the preface, which stated that the Declaration would remind citizens of "their rights and their duties." The demands to include a list of duties in the document or to insert duties in the title were rejected. What interests me is the ambiguous way in which this was done. Thus, M. de Clermont-Lodève made the successful proposal to exclude duties from the Declaration of Rights because, as he said, duties were implicitly there in the notion of citizenship:

> In the body of the declaration, it would perhaps be possible to detail a couple of those duties but I think the title should only announce *a declaration of the rights of the citizen*, and not *the duties*. The word citizen announces a correlation with the other citizens and with this correlation comes the duties.[63]

In his *Encyclopédie* article "Devoir," Louis de Jaucourt distinguished between three kinds of duty. The first was the duty to God, the second concerned man's relation to himself, and the third his obligations toward his co-citizens.[64] When the abbé Grégoire insisted that rights and duties "march along parallel lines,"[65] and when he fought – successfully – to include the name of God in the Declaration, he was clearly committed to the religious kind of duty. But the politically most significant one, and the one invoked by Clermont-Lodève, was the third kind, man's duty toward other men. In other words, Clermont-Lodève raised the question of what man was obliged to offer to the commons in order to secure general happiness, to secure the happiness of all. Speaking in philosophical anthropological terms the stakes of the discussion were whether man existed primarily as a lone individual, a self-possessive person who pursued his own happiness or as a member of a community whose collective happiness dwarfed any [...] the self-abandonment of the individual (Figure 1.2).

The revolutionaries had inherited the challenge of encouraging citizens to contribute economically to the state from the Old Regime. State bankruptcy was a very likely scenario and the *cahiers des doléances*

34 *The Unfinished Declaration*

Figure 1.2 La Tyrannie revolutionnaire écrasée par les amis de la Constitution de l'an III: [estampe]/Queverdo del.; Massol sculp. (Paris, chez l'auteur, 1795–1796). Bibliothèque nationale de France.

had unmistakably expressed the popular wish for major fiscal reform. The deputies were well aware of this situation and Article Thirteen on the necessity of paying taxes was a response to it.[66] While there was an explicit discussion of the citizen's religious duties, Clermont-Lodève was right to notice another implicit idea of duty inherent in the revolutionary idea of citizenship. Citizenship came with a set of requirements, of duties, and only he (for it was always a he) who fulfilled these requirements obtained full political membership. The deputies would confront this problem of citizenship in the fourth phase of the Declaration Debate as they deliberated on Article Six, one of the most difficult articles to pass and one that provoked "disorder" and "sinister blows [sinistres flambeaux]."[67] What became Article Six in the final version was originally three separate articles in the Sixth Bureau proposal:

> Art. 11. The first duty of every citizen being to serve the society according to his capacity and his talents, he has the right to be called to any public employment.
> Art. 12. The law being the expression of the general will, every citizen must have cooperated immediately in the formation of the law.
> Art. 13. The law must be the same for everyone; and no political authority is obliging for the citizen unless it commands in the name of the law.[68]

These three articles cover different ground: the right of every capable citizen to hold any public office, the right of every citizen to cooperate immediately in the formation of the law, and equality before the law. The quoted article eleven reiterates the claim made by the abbé Grégoire that rights and duties march along parallel lines, and even though the word duty would be removed in the editing process its presence here showcases the degree to which Clermont-Lodève was right to notice the implicit duties inherent in the idea of citizenship. The problem raised by this article, the right to hold public office, caused much debate but what further complicated the discussion, and what would cause major political struggle later on, was the Rousseuaian concept of the general will and that concept's inherent incompatibility with political representation.

In *Of the Social Contract* (1762), Rousseau distinguished between the will of all (*la volonté de tous*) and the general will (*la volonté générale*), writing,

> the latter looks only to the common interest, the former looks to private interest, and is nothing but a sum of particular wills; but if, from these same wills, one takes away the pluses and the minuses which cancel each other out, what is left as the sum of the differences is the general will.[69]

The general will is that which is common to the members of the polity once their different wants and wishes are wiped away. That definition has consequences with regard to the political organization of society and more specifically to the legitimacy of representation: "Since the law is nothing but the declaration of the general will, it is clear that the People cannot be represented in its Legislative power."[70] The general will cannot, and Rousseau insists upon this, be represented because no individual has the ability to determine what is common to everyone. This illegitimacy of political representation is the basis of the Sixth Bureau proposal's Article Twelve.

In their wish to simplify the Declaration of Rights as much as possible, the deputies reduced the three articles to one. The most successful of the combination proposals was that of First Estate member Talleyrand-Périgord. But with his numeric reduction came political alterations that frustrated the deputies.

> The law being the expression of the general will, all the citizens must take part, in person or by their representatives, in its formation; it must be the same for everyone whether it protects or penalizes. All citizens being equal in its eyes are admissible to all the public positions and employments, according to their capacity. [Tous les citoyens étant égaux à ses yeux, sont susceptibles de toutes les places, de tous les emplois publics, selon leur capacité].[71]

This proposal contains the elements from all three Sixth Bureau articles, and it closely resembles the wording of the final version. Gone is the explicit mention of duties and inserted is the idea of representation. The deputies remained indebted to Rousseau's notion of the general will but pragmatically, they considered it necessary to underscore the legitimacy of political representation. In his writings, the Abbé Sieyès did much to argue not just for the practical benefits of political representation but also for its principled legitimacy.[72] Major political struggles would ensue from the early revolutionary understanding of political representation but during the Article Six debate what caused problems was the wording of the last sentence of Talleyrand-Périgord's proposal and hence the question of holding public office. One unknown deputy suggested adding "without distinction [sans distinction]" at the very end of the article, and another proposed adding "without distinction by birth."[73] The reason for these proposed additions was the ambiguity of the word "capacity," which could suggest the prevalent Old Regime idea that some had a natural, birth-given capacity to perform specific tasks, such as a natural aristocratic ability to rule. Fittingly, the assembly was filled with "outcries against the aristocracy" at this moment.[74]

Second Estate member Lally-Tollendal eased the tension of the debate when he suggested a different kind of addition to the final sentence. Instead of "without distinction by birth," he proposed "with no other distinction than that of their talents and of their virtues."[75] This addition made it into the final version. What Lally-Tollendal did may seem a small adjustment, a mere "amendment," as Edelstein writes, but he actually reversed the logic of the clause.[76] Instead of making the negative statement that the nobles – for they were the antagonists at this point in the debate – could make no legitimate claim to any office, Lally-Tollendal positively stated the requirements for holding an office: talents and virtues. This formulation won the approval of the deputies because, I believe, it resonated powerfully with the early revolutionary ideology expressed most influentially by the Abbé Sieyès in his *What Is the Third Estate?* Herein, Sieyès had listed "the activities that support society" and used that list in an uncompromising attack upon the privileges of the nobility.[77] He divided the necessary work into four categories:

1. work on the land.
2. the handiwork [that] adds further amounts of additional value to these primary goods.
3. the merchants and dealers.
4. the liberal and scientific professions.[78]

Much can be said about these four categories and their relation to the political economic thinkers of the century. I tend to agree with William Sewell who sees the whole "foundation of Sieyès's argument" in these few lines.[79] Sieyès's attack on the nobility was based on this positive statement of the needs of society. Because the nobility performed none of the "useful work," Sieyès insisted that their class of men was "a heavy burden to impose upon a nation!"[80] Elsewhere, he termed the privileged nobles a "nation within the nation" and "a pernicious excrescence […], pressing on the springs of the public machine."[81] In saying that talents and virtues were the necessary prerequisites for holding public office, Lally-Tollendal made an argument structurally identical to that of Sieyès. The point was not simply to reject the outmoded feudal principle that positions should follow birth. The ambition, rather, was to present the new and different prerequisites for full social and political participation. Lally-Tollendal's proposal made it into the final version of Article Six:

> The law is the expression of the general will. All citizens have the right to take part, in person or by their representatives, in its formation. It must be the same for everyone whether it protects or penalizes. All citizens being equal in its eyes are equally admissible to all public dignities, offices and employments, according to their ability, and with no other distinction than that of their virtues and talents.[82]

By accentuating virtues and talents the deputies presented the requirements for holding an office, requirements that were in principle independent of birth. Simultaneously, they presented the values upon which the new regime rested. The emphasis upon virtues and talents was not only a massive blow to the Old Regime privileges of the nobility. It also marked the beginnings of the establishment of another kind of social hierarchy; one based not on birth but on the ability of citizens to be of common utility (Article One), or to demonstrate talents and virtues (Article Six). This was a different way of legitimizing social hierarchies, and one that put enormous pressure on the definition of terms such as "common utility," "talent," "ability," and "virtue" since these became gatekeepers for full political membership. These words designated the duty of citizens toward their fellow Frenchmen. The deputies understood well the potential of linguistic finesse and used it to develop rhetorical weapons against Old Regime privilege. Simultaneously, however, they were involved in creating the positive ideological basis for new kinds of social distinctions, which, in turn, resulted in the political exclusion of the "useless" in the top *and* at the bottom of society. As later chapters will show, authors of fiction continuously intervened in such discussions of the implied duties of citizenship and often treated it as a moral question of *mœurs* or social conventions. In what follows, however, I continue the analysis of social inclusion and exclusion by shifting the focus from rights and duties to enmity and passive citizenship.

Enmity and Passive Citizenship

As explained in the introduction to this book, philosopher Étienne Balibar and historian Charly Coleman make similar distinctions between two competing kinds of Enlightenment political anthropology. On the one hand there is the *subject* who acquires his sense of self when subjected to the laws of a greater community; a community that can take different forms but which in Rousseau's philosophy is identified with the general will. On the other hand there is the self-possessive, Lockian *individual* who claims ownership of his or her self and uses this self-possession as the basis for entering social and commercial relations with others. Balibar continues his argument by suggesting that not only do these competing varieties of political anthropology mark different ways of constituting society, different ways of practicing equaliberty. They also result in dissimilar forms of political exclusion, different ways of drawing the line between humanity and inhumanity:

> Clearly, it does not at all amount to the same thing to think this line of demarcation between the human and the inhuman in moral terms, by referring to 'alienated' (*entäusserte*) subjects, or in pragmatic or utilitarian terms, by referring to 'dependent' or 'impeached' agents, those unable to act in an autonomous manner.[83]

Theoretically, Balibar advances these forms of political exclusion in a sustained reflection upon Enlightenment philosophy but analytically, he develops them primarily in readings of modern globalization era conflicts (the "Headscarf Affair" and *Banlieues* uprisings). With some modification, however, they can help conceptualize the two major forms of political exclusion visible in the Declaration Debate and its aftermath, namely the idea of passive citizenship and the figure of the *hostis humani generis*. The passive citizen resembles Balibar's "impeached agent," that is the incapacitated opposite of Locke's autonomous individual, while the enemy of the human race could be interpreted as the outside, alienated threat to the (Rousseauian) subjects who make up the general will. For reasons that will become clear, I prefer to distinguish between *internal* and *external* political exclusion. Whereas the former is a line drawn inside the political community between full and partial members, the latter is a line drawn between inside members and outside nonmembers.

The theory of active and passive citizenship is the intellectual and practical culmination of the French revolutionary *internal political exclusion*. It forms a response to what some regarded as the need to limit the expansion of political membership. One way of excluding select citizens from full political participation was to present certain abilities and kinds of work (Lally Tollendal's virtues and talents and Sieyès's useful work) as the requirements for holding public office. But with the theory of active and passive citizenship, the internal political exclusion became a question of voting rights. The distinction appeared in one of Condorcet's declaration proposals[84] but it was Sieyès who presented it most forcefully in his declaration proposal:

> All the inhabitants of a country ought to enjoy within it the *passive* rights of a citizen; all have a right to the protection of their person, of their property, of their liberty, etc.; but all do not have a right to take an active part in the formation of public powers: not all are *active* citizens. Women, at least in the present situation, children, foreigners, and those who contribute nothing to the support of the public establishment, ought not to exercise an active influence on the public weal [la chose publique]. All may enjoy the advantages of society; but those alone who contribute to the public establishment can be likened to the true shareholders [actionnaires] of the great social enterprise. They alone are the true active citizens, the true members of the association.[85]

Whereas the citizens' *passive* rights to protection, property, and freedom are equally enjoyed by every member of the state, the *active* right to co-determine the contours of the political body is reserved for those contributing to the social enterprise.[86] As such, the line drawn here between passive inhabitants and the "true shareholders" of society is internal to the political community. And while Sieyès's description of the passive citizens resembles Balibar's "impeached agents," there are also important differences. Balibar's theory is property based but for Sieyès the determining factor for political participation is not property but useful work and social contributions. It here again becomes visible that Sieyès's theory is designed as an attack on the landholding aristocracy. Equally visible is the moral and moralizing potentials of Sieyès's utilitarian distinction: *At least for the time being*, women are unfit for politics, only those who contribute are *real* shareholders and *veritable* members of the association. While passive citizens are certainly "impeached agents," the premises for political exclusion differ from Balibar's explanation because it is both utilitarian and moral and because it is premised on useful labor instead of property.

The active/passive distinction was eventually omitted from the Declaration of Rights but in late 1789 the deputies agreed to include it in what became the 1791 Constitution. According to the calculations made by the members of *The New Constitutional Committee*, the proposed distinction would mean that of a total French population of 26 million, only 4.4 million would have political rights and be active citizens.[87] The distinction served two main functions in the Constitution with regard to the national election process. In contrast to a system of direct election, where citizens would cast their votes on whomever they wanted as their representative, the 1791 Constitution was based on an indirect system of election. It held that active citizens should assemble in Primary Assemblies in the various cities and cantons of France, every other March, to appoint electors. Two weeks after the electors were appointed, they would meet in Electoral Assemblies, and only at this point would representatives for the National Legislative Assembly be elected. In addition, only active citizens could be elected as deputies of the Assembly. In other words, active citizens should appoint electors who would afterward elect the deputies from among those active citizens who were running for office. In order to qualify as active citizen, one would have to fulfill the following seven requirements:

> to be born or to become a Frenchman;
> to be fully twenty-five years of age;
> to be domiciled in the city or in the canton for the time fixed by the law;
> To pay in some place of the kingdom a direct tax at the least equal to the value of three days of labor, and to present the receipt therefor;
> Not to be in a state of domestic service, that is to say, not to be a servant for wages;
> To be registered upon the roll of the national guards in the municipality of his domicile;
> To have taken the civic oath.[88]

Besides the need to meet these criteria – and besides being a man, which was implicit – anyone who was accused of a crime, and those who, after having gone bankrupt, were unable to prove that they had been acquitted by their creditors, were also "excluded from the exercise of the rights of the active citizen."[89] But the technicalities of the voting system contained further possibilities for internal political exclusion; possibilities directly linked with the principle of representation introduced with Talleyrand-Périgord's changes to what became Article Six of the 1789 Declaration of Rights. Thus, the requirements for qualifying as an elector were listed in the Constitution's first chapter, Section II, Article 7. Depending on the place of residence, an elector had to be the proprietor or usufructuary of a property assessed at a worth equal to the local value of 150 or 200 days' labor, depending on region. The assembly deputies were in reality the representatives of representatives, and monetary and proprietary requirements functioned to limit the field of representatives in both election phases. When it was necessary to not only be an active citizen, but also to dispose of quite valuable property to qualify as elector, clearly some members of the community were excluded from full political participation. The technicalities of the election processes demonstrate that the inclusion of the possibility of political representation in Article Six of the Declaration of Rights was not a mere practicality. It also created a further basis for establishing a distinction between those with and without the right to political participation.

Maximilien Robespierre was among the most fervent critics of this kind of political exclusion. He demonstrated an acute awareness of the far-reaching implications of the active/passive division in his speech "On the Silver Mark," which was published during the debates on the 1791 Constitution.[90] The silver mark in the title of his speech was motivated by a draft proposal circulated by *The New Constitutional Committee* on 29 September 1789, a committee that counted Abbé Sieyès among its members. Besides from the distinction between active and passive citizens, this draft suggested that in order to be eligible to the National Assembly, not only should one be an active citizen, one should also pay "a direct contribution equivalent to the value of a silver mark."[91] Robespierre argued that such an idea was in opposition to the 1789 Declaration of Rights, a document that in his opinion too contained "the eternal foundations" of the Constitution.[92] Following a Rousseauian understanding of freedom, he insisted that liberty was to abide by rules one had prescribed to oneself.[93] But if political sovereignty, the right to legislate, was limited to the few, the result would be an aristocracy that practically enslaved the disenfranchised subjects. "And what an aristocracy!" Robespierre continued, "The most unbearable of all, that of the rich."[94]

In continuation of his critique of internal political exclusion, Robespierre would go on to emphasize the equal right to political participation in his own 1793 declaration proposal: "All citizens have an equal right to contribute to the appointment of the people's representatives, and to the formation of the law."[95] With this criticism of a line drawn between full and partial members of the social body, however, comes a proposition to distinguish sharply between members and nonmembers of the community. Robespierre, in other words, sharply criticizes the internal political exclusion of the active/passive distinction but he also steps forth as a strong proponent of *external political exclusion*.

Robespierre relaunched the 1789 discussion about the relationship between natural and positive law in his declaration proposal. Malouet, Delandine, and Lally-Tollendal had all urged the National Assembly to quickly pass from natural law to positive law because they feared the potentially anarchical consequences of the former. Robespierre, on the other hand, sought to equate positive and natural law: "Any law that violates the imprescriptible rights of man is essentially unjust and tyrannical: it is not a law."[96] Natural law and the Declaration of Rights were not dangerous or liable to misinterpretation. They were "the principles of justice" and "how could we possibly apply them falsely?"[97] In his interpretation of French revolutionary natural republicanism, Dan Edelstein argues that the Jacobins developed an image of a Golden Age which was closely associated with their understanding of natural law. The infallibility of nature – how could its rules be applied falsely? – came at the price of alleged outside enemies; enemies that continuously threatened the equilibrium of the natural community within. These extraordinary enemies were strongly condemned in Robespierre's declaration proposal:

> XXXVII. Those who make war on a people to arrest the progress of liberty and annihilate the rights of man should be punished by all, not as ordinary enemies but as murderers and rebellious brigands.
> XXXVIII. Kings, aristocrats, tyrants, whatever they be, are slaves in revolt against the sovereign power of the earth, which is the human race, and against the legislator of the universe, which is nature.[98]

These extraordinary enemies – assassins, tyrants, aristocrats etc. – received special attention in the terror laws of the French revolution. Particularly pertinent was the *hors-la-loi* legislative category which took "shape around the figure of the king" but soon came to include a wider variety of vaguely defined counterrevolutionaries.[99] This enemy figure transcended acceptable human behavior and waged war upon the very principles of humanity. Legislatively, the importance of the figure culminated with the Terror and in the context of the Vendée insurgents but culturally and historically, it had both longer and broader implications.[100] In his *Encyclopédie* article "Natural rights," Denis Diderot commented on the unholy creature that was unwilling to seek out truth by way of reason. This creature, he wrote, "renounces his human condition and must be treated by the rest of his species as a wild beast." This is an "unnatural being [être denaturé]," Diderot suggests, and it is best to "stifle him without an answer [l'étouffer sans lui répondre]."[101] In the 1792 *Marsaillaise*, the French national anthem, this figure reappears when French soldiers are initially encouraged to spare their victims. No mercy, however, should be shown to "[a]ll these tigers who, mercilessly, Rip their mother's breast!"[102]

External political exclusion happens when adversaries are regarded not as simple opponents but as threats to humanity. Diderot, Robespierre, and others draw an absolute line between humans and nonhumans with the wish to exclude the latter category from the political body. Internal political exclusion distinguishes between full and partial members of the community. In the process of drawing this internal line, Abbé Sieyès and other revolutionaries simultaneously encouraged a specific behavior, which they found particularly useful for the new France. Authors of fiction from this period commented on and made use of both these types of political exclusion. The sentimental narrative mode operates, almost per definition, with sharp dichotomies of good and evil and it tends to both build upon the image of the extraordinary enemy and produce emotionally appealing descriptions of virtuous and useful citizens.

* * *

With its mere seventeen articles, the Declaration of the Rights of Man and of the Citizen seems deceptively simple. Should the new France choose to respect the rights of man, surely the result would be common happiness. But upon closer inspection the deputies are fundamentally divided on a number of key questions and their divisions would go on and haunt the entire revolutionary decade. The precise relationship between the laws of nature and the laws of society remains disputed. Whether duties march along a line parallel with that of rights, if they are simply irrelevant, or if they are implicitly present in the notion of citizenship itself likewise remains unclear. As does, finally, the relationship between internal and external political exclusion. But how should the significance of such an open document be assessed? One answer to that question can be found in Gail Bossenga's book, *The Politics of Privilege*. Her point is that, rather than bringing an end to social inequality, the French revolution altered the premises of social conflict.

> The Revolution created new possibilities and patterns for mobilization and social conflict. As a result of the Revolution, membership in the national state, or citizenship, became the source of all civic

rights. Although in theory the rights of citizens were inalienable and universal, in fact they were inequitably distributed. Thus, after the Revolution, conflict was to revolve significantly around the acquisition and definition of the full rights of citizenship by disenfranchised groups. [...] Thus the Revolution laid the foundations for future battles waged by disadvantaged groups, whether defined by class, gender, belief or race.[103]

Bossenga argues that the French revolution, in spite of its liberal and egalitarian ideology, was fundamentally unsuccessful in inaugurating a free and equal society. However, it was successful in abolishing the Old Regime *kinds* of inequality, which were based on privileges and feudal principles. Rather than postulating absolute uniformity between revolutionary ideology and practice, and rather than suggesting a revolution without consequences, Bossenga claims that the revolution facilitated new types of political struggle. The struggle against Old Regime privileges was replaced by one centered on the definition and acquisition of citizenship or membership in the nation state. True to her revisionist interpretation of the revolution, Bossenga argues that these new political conflicts cannot be reduced to class struggle; some were class based, but others were structured around gender, race, or religion.

In what follows I focus on fictional literature and its contributions to the development and examination of this new political imaginary. Literature and theatre were used sometimes as interrogative media, sometimes as argumentative or propagandist media. Fiction was well-suited to reflect upon and develop the tensions inherent in coupling happiness with rights. Its imaginary character was used to present new scenarios and its reliance on individuals made it less abstract than the contemporary pamphlets and treatises. But before beginning the detailed analyses of specific literary works of art and their interventions in the rights/happiness-linkage, I will raise a question of literary sociology: How did the authors of this period understand their own work? In other words, what was literature?

Notes

1 Walt Whitman, *Leaves of Grass and Other Writings* (New York: W. W. Norton & Company, Inc., 2002), 77.
2 Micheline R. Ishay, *The History of Human Rights: From Ancient Times to the Globalization Era* (Berkeley: University of California Press, 2004), 4.
3 Jonathan Israel, *Democratic Enlightenment*, 12; 937.
4 Costas Douzinas, *Human Rights and Empire: The Political Philosophy of Cosmopolitanism* (London: Routledge-Cavendish, 2007), 10.
5 Christine Fauré, "Les déclarations des droits de l'homme" in Christine Fauré (ed.), *Les déclarations des droits de l'homme de 1789* (Paris: Éditions Payot, 1988), 17.

The Unfinished Declaration 45

6 Antoine de Baecque, "'Le choc des opinions': Le débat des droits de l'homme, juillet-août 1789" in Antoine de Baecque, Wolfgang Schmale, and Michel Vovelle (eds.), *L'an 1 des droits de l'homme* (Paris: Presses du CNRS, 1988), 7.
7 Gauchet, *La Révolution des droits de l'homme*, 107.
8 Keith Michael Baker, "The Idea of a Declaration of Rights" in Dale Van Kley (ed.), *The French Idea of Freedom: The Old Regime and the Declaration of Rights of 1789* (Stanford: Stanford University Press, 1994), 157.
9 27 August 1789, M. Bouche in *AP* VIII, 492/Baecque et al., *L'an 1*, 196. I refer to both the *Archives Parlementaires* and to the convenient documentation of the debate in *L'an 1*. The latter includes the relevant discussion from the *Archives Parlementaires* in addition to materials from other sources.
10 Gauchet, *La Révolution des droits de l'homme*, 207.
11 Gauchet, *La Révolution des droits de l'homme*, 257.
12 Baker, "The Idea of a Declaration of Rights" in Van Kley (ed.), *The French Idea of Freedom*, 190.
13 Hunt, *Inventing Human Rights*, esp. Chapters one and two.
14 Valentine Zuber, *Le culte des droits de l'homme* (Paris: Gallimard, 2014), esp. 122–151 & 224–244.
15 18 August 1789, Rabaut de Saint-Etienne in *AP* VIII, 452/ Baecque et al., *L'an 1*, 138. For a differently turned interpretation of this passage, see Gauchet, 51. M. Créniere makes a similar claim on 1 August 1789 as he says, "a rightly understood declaration of rights is nothing but the people's act of constitution." (*AP* VIII, 319/ Baecque et al., *L'an 1*, 98).
16 Baecque, "'Le choc des opinions'" in Baecque et al., *L'an 1*, 8.
17 Thomas Kaiser & Dale Van Kley, "Introduction" in Thomas Kaiser & Dale Van Kley (eds.), *From Deficit to Deluge: The Origins of the French Revolution* (Stanford: Stanford University Press, 2011), 1.
18 On the financial origins of the French Revolution, see Michael Sonenscher, *Before the Deluge: Public Debt, Inequality, and the Intellectual Origins of the French Revolution.* (Princeton and Oxford: Princeton University Press, 2007); Michael Kwass, *Privilege and the Politics of Taxation in Eighteenth-Century France: Liberté, Égalité, Fiscalité.* (Cambridge: Cambridge University Press, 2000) and Gail Bossenga, "Financial Origins of the French Revolution" in Thomas E. Kaiser and Dale K. Van Kley (eds.), *From Deficit to Deluge: The Origins of the French Revolution* (Stanford: Stanford University Press, 2011), 37–67.
19 Timothy Tackett, *Becoming a Revolutionary: The Deputies of the French National Assembly and the Emergence of a Revolutionary Culture (1789–1790)* (Princeton: Princeton University Press, 1996), 77–117 and Baecque, "'Le choc des opinions'" in Baecque et al., *L'an 1*, 8.
20 Beatrice F. Hyslop, *French Nationalism in 1789 according to the General Cahiers* (New York: Columbia University Press, 1934), 84.
21 9 July 1789, M. Mounier in *AP* VIII, 216/ Baecque et al., *L'an 1*, 62.
22 My division resembles that of Antoine de Baecque, cf. Baecque et al., *L'an 1*, 7–37. For alternative subdivisions, see Stéphane Rials, *La declaration des droits de l'homme et du citoyen* (Paris: Hachette, 1988), 115–321 and Zuber, *Le culte des droits de l'homme*, 19–20.
23 11 July 1789, Marquis de Lafayette in *AP* VIII, 221/ Baecque et al., *L'an 1*, 65.
24 11 July 1789, Marquis de Lafayette in *AP* VIII, 221/ Baecque et al., *L'an 1*, 65.
25 When the representative of the *Constitutional committee*, M. Champion de Cicé, archevêque de Bordeaux, presented the work of the committee on 27 July to the National Assembly, he presented Sieyès's draft as brilliant but

also as problematical because it supposed "much more than it is permitted to expect from the universality of those who must read and understand it. And everyone must read and understand it." In other words, the contents were good, but because of its rational philosophic character, it failed to be universally understandable, which it had to be.

26 Edelstein, "A response to Jonathan Israel" in K. E. Tunstall (ed.), *Self-Evident Truths? Human Rights and the Enlightenment.* (New York and London: Bloomsbury Academic, 2012), 130.
27 1 August 1789, M. Darnaudat in *AP* VIII, 315/Baecque et al., *L'an 1*, 94.
28 On the 4 August session, see Tackett, *Becoming a Revolutionary*, 169–175.
29 17 August 1789, M. le comte de Mirabeau in *AP* VIII, 438/Baecque et al., *L'an 1*, 127.
30 18 August 1789, M. le marquis de Bonnay in *AP* VIII, 452/Baecque et al., *L'an 1*, 134.
31 Rials, *La déclaration des droits*, 203.
32 18 August 1789, M. le vicomte de Mirabeau in *AP* VIII, 452/Baecque et al., *L'an 1*, 133.
33 18 August 1789, M. Gleizen in *AP* VIII, 454/Baecque et al., *L'an 1*, 142.
34 Cf. Edelstein, "A response to Jonathan Israel," 128.
35 For the numbers of the vote, see Rials, *La déclaration des droits*, 212.
36 The Sixth Bureau proposal is published in Baecque et al., *L'an 1*, 268–269.
37 Articles twenty and twenty-three of the Sixth Bureau proposal are thus identical to Articles twelve and fifteen of the final document.
38 27 August 1789, M. le Président [Comte de Clermont-Tonnerre], Baecque et al., *L'an 1*, 195.
39 Rials, *La déclaration des droits*, 155.
40 For Malouet's defense of slavery and colonialism, see Madeleine Dobie, *Trading Places: Colonization and Slavery in Eighteenth-Century French Culture* (Ithaca and London: Cornell University Press, 2010), 245–247.
41 1 August 1789, M. Delandine in *AP* VIII, 324/Baecque et al., *L'an 1*, 108.
42 See Dan Edelstein, "Enlightenment Rights Talk" in *The Journal of Modern History*, Vol. 86, No. 3 (2014): 530–565 for a discussion of the French eighteenth century sentimental varieties of natural rights thought.
43 Declaration of Independence, 1776. Quoted from Hunt, 216.
44 1 August 1789, M. le compte Mathieu de Montmorency in *AP* VIII, 320/Baecque et al., *L'an 1*, 100.
45 Gauchet, *La révolution des droits de l'homme*, 50.
46 1 August 1789, Pierre-Victor de Malouet in *AP* VIII, 322/Baecque et al., *L'an 1*, 105.
47 1 August 1789, Pierre-Victor de Malouet in *AP* VIII, 322/Baecque et al., *L'an 1*, 105.
48 Susan Maslan, "Nature and Society in Revolutionary Rights Debates" in *The Routledge Companion to Literature and Human Rights*. Edited by Sophia A. McClennen and Alexandra Schultheis Moore. (London and New York: Routledge, 2016), 261.
49 Jean-Jacques Rousseau, *Discourse on the Origin and the Foundations of Inequality among Men* in Jean-Jacques Rousseau, *The Discourses and other early political writings*. Ed. V. Gourevitch (Cambridge: Cambridge University Press, 2012), 132.
50 Rousseau, *Discourse on the Origin* in Rousseau, *The Discourses*, 125.
51 Paul de Man, *Allegories of Reading: Figural Language in Rousseau, Nietzsche, Rilke, and Proust.* (New Haven and London: Yale University Press, 1979), 149.

The Unfinished Declaration 47

52 de Man, *Allegories of Reading*, 155.
53 Maslan, "Nature and Society" in McClennen, Moore, *The Routledge Companion*, 266.
54 Jacques Rancière, *Le partage du sensible. Esthétique et politique*. (Paris: La fabrique, 2000), 12–26.
55 1 August 1789, M. Malouet in *AP* VIII, 323/Baecque et al., *L'an 1*, 106.
56 1 August 1789, M. Delandine in *AP* VIII, 325/Baecque et al., *L'an 1*, 110.
57 4 August 1789, M. l'abbé Grégoire in *AP* VIII, 341/Baecque et al., *L'an 1*, 123.
58 18 August 1789, M. le baron de Jessé in *AP* VIII, 452/Baecque et al., *L'an 1*, 134.
59 Mounier quoted from Fauré, *Les déclarations des droits de l'homme de*, 326.
60 Rials, *La déclaration des droits*, 162.
61 1 August 1789, M. Grandin in *AP* VIII, 321/Baecque et al., *L'an 1*, 103. On 4 August by M Duport; M. le marquis de Sillery; M. l'abbé Grégoire; M. de Lubersac and others.
62 4 August 1789, M. de Lubersac in *AP* VIII, 341/Baecque et al., *L'an 1*, 124.
63 4 August 1789, M. de Clermont-Lodève in *AP* VIII, 341/Baecque et al., *L'an 1*, 124.
64 Jaucourt, *Devoir* (*Droit nat. Relig. nat. Morale.*), 4: 915, available online: http://artflsrv02.uchicago.edu/cgi-bin/philologic/getobject.pl?c.3:2329. encyclopedie0513 [page last visited 11 April 2017].
65 4 August 1789, M. l'abbé Grégoire in Baecque et al., *L'an 1*, 123. This exact part of Grégoire's speech is absent from the version in *AP* VIII, 340–341.
66 On this topic, see my "Representation and Taxation: Fiscality, Human Rights, and the French Revolution" in Mikkel Thorup (ed.), *Intellectual History of Economic Normativities*. (New York: Palgrave MacMillan, 2016), 107–123.
67 Baecque et al., *L'an 1*, 158.
68 *Projet de déclaration des droits de l'homme et du citoyen. Discuté dans le sixième bureau de l'Assemblée nationale* in Baecque et al., *L'an 1*, 268–269.
69 Jean-Jacques Rousseau, *Of the Social Contract* in Jean-Jacques Rousseau, *The Social Contract and other later political writings*. Ed. V. Gourevitch. (Cambridge: Cambridge University Press, 2012), 60.
70 Rousseau, *Of the Social Contract* in Rousseau, *The Social Contract*, 115.
71 21 August 1789, M. de Talleyrand-Périgord in *AP* VIII, 465/Baecque et al., *L'an 1*, 158.
72 For Abbé Sieyès's views on political representation, see Murray Forsyth, *Reason and Revolution: The Political Thought of Abbé Sieyes* (New York: Leicester University Press 1987), 128–150; Keith Michael Baker, *Inventing the French Revolution: Essays on French Political Culture in the Eighteenth Century*. (Cambridge: Cambridge University Press, 1990), 244–250; Michael Sonenscher, "Introduction" in Emmanuel-Joseph Sieyès, *Political Writings* (Indianapolis/Cambridge: Hackett Publishing Company, Inc., 2003), vii–lxiv.
73 21 August 1789 in Baecque et al., *L'an 1*, 158.
74 Baecque et al., *L'an 1*, 159.
75 21 August 1789, M. de Lally-Tollendal in *AP* VIII, 466/Baecque et al., *L'an 1*, 159.
76 Edelstein, "A Response to Jonathan Israel" in *Self-Evident Truths?*, 131.
77 Emmanuel Joseph Sieyès, *What Is the Third Estate?* In Emmanuel Joseph Sieyès, *Political Writings*. Ed. M. Sonenscher. (Indianapolis/Cambridge: Hackett Publishing Company, Inc., 2003), 95.

48 *The Unfinished Declaration*

78 Sieyès, *What Is the Third Estate?* In Sieyès, *Political Writings*, 94–95.
79 William H. Sewell Jr., *A Rhetoric of Bourgeois Revolution: The Abbé Sieyès and* What Is the Third Estate? (Durham and London: Duke University Press, 1994), 57.
80 Sieyès, *What Is the Third Estate?* In Sieyès, *Political Writings*, 96n3.
81 Emmanuel Joseph Sieyès, *An Essay on Privileges* in Sieyès, *Political Writings*, 75; 83.
82 *Declaration of the Rights of Man and Citizen* in Hunt, *Inventing Human Rights*, 222.
83 Balibar, *Equaliberty*, 121.
84 Cf. Antoine-Nicolas Caritat de Condorcet, *Declaration of Rights/Déclaration des droits: Traduite de l'Anglois, avec l'original à coté* (Londres: [n.p.], 1789), 78–79), reprinted in Marquis de Cordorcet, *Œuvres de Condorcet*. Eds. A. Condorcet O'Connor and M. F. Arago (Paris: Firmin Didot Frères, 1847–1849), 9: 207. For a bibliographical comment on this text see Rials, *La déclaration des droits*, 282n15.
85 Emmanuel-Joseph Sieyès, *Préliminaire de la constitution. Reconnaissance et exposition raisonnée des droits de l'homme et du citoyen* in Fauré, *Les déclarations des droits de l'homme de*, 101. I have used the translation of this passage from Forsyth, *Reason and Revolution*, 117–118.
86 The question of active/passive citizenship has been heatedly debated by historians. See, e.g., Forsyth, *Reason and Revolution*, esp. Chapter. 8; William H. Sewell, Jr., "Le citoyen/la citoyenne: Activity, Passivity and the Revolutionary Concept of Citizenship" in Colin Lucas (ed.), *The French Revolution and the Creation of Modern Political Culture* vol. 2 (Oxford: Pergamon Press, 1988), 105–125; Sonenscher, "Introduction" in Sieyès, *Political Writings*, xxxi. I outline and partake in this debate in my "The inequality of common utility: active/passive citizenship in French revolutionary human rights" in Karen-Margrethe Simonsen and Jonas Ross Kjærgård (eds.), *Discursive Framings of Human Rights: Negotiating agency and victimhood* (Oxon and New York: Birkbeck Law Press/Routledge, 2017), 43–59.
87 Thouret in *AP* 9:203.
88 First chapter, Section II, Article 2, "Constitution Française du 3 Septembre 1791" in Léon Duguit and Henry Monnier (eds.), *Les constitutions et les principales lois politiques de la France depuis 1789* (Paris: Librairie générale de droit et de jurisprudence, 1908), 8. English translation taken from the website: https://web.archive.org/web/20140227131055/http://ic.ucsc.edu/~traugott/hist171/readings/1791-09ConstitutionOf1791. Page last visited 20 December 2017.
89 First chapter, Section II, Article 5. Ibid., 9; for the gender aspects of active/passive citizenship, see Sewell, "Le citoyen/la citoyenne."
90 Philologically, the speech has been surrounded by some controversy. The *Archives parlementaires* presents it as an appendix to the deliberations on 25 January 1790 (*AP*, 11:320–325). This dating is criticized convincingly by the editors of *Œuvres de Maximilien Robespierre* who argue, first, that the speech was in fact never delivered in the National Assembly but only sent to various clubs and popular societies for discussion and, second, that they received and discussed it in late March 1791. Only in April 1791 was the speech published officially. The editors also acknowledge, however, that Robespierre had criticized the active/passive schism at various occasions in 1790. Cf. their notes and introduction to the speech.

91 Thouret, 29 September 1789, in *AP*, 9:205. For Sieyès's role in writing this proposal, see Forsyth, *Reason and Revolution*, 159–161.
92 Maximilien Robespierre, *Œuvres de Maximilien Robespierre* vol. 7 (Paris: Presses Universitaires de France, 1950), 161. Maximilien Robespierre, "On the Silver Mark" in Maximilien Robespierre, *Virtue and Terror*. Trans. J. Howe. (London and New York: Verso, 2007), 6.
93 In *Of the Social Contract* (1762) Rousseau defines moral freedom in the civil state as "obedience to the law one has prescribed to oneself." Jean-Jacques Rousseau, *Of the Social Contract* in Jean-Jacques Rousseau, *The Social Contract and other later political writings*. Ed. V. Gourevitch. Cambridge: Cambridge University Press, 2012), 54.
94 Robespierre, *Œuvres*, 7:162. Robespierre, "On the Silver Mark" in Robespierre, *Virtue and Terror*. 7.
95 Maximilien Robespierre, *Projet de Déclaration des droits de l'homme et du citoyen* in *Pour le bonheur et pour la liberté*. (Paris: La fabrique, 2000), 236. Robespierre, "Draft Declaration of the Rights of Man and of the Citizen" in Robespierre, *Virtue and Terror*. 70.
96 Robespierre, "Draft Declaration of the Rights of Man and of the Citizen" in Robespierre, *Virtue and Terror*. 70.
97 Maximilien Robespierre quoted from Dan Edelstein, *The Terror of Natural Right: Republicanism, the Cult of Nature, & the French Revolution* (Chicago and London: The University of Chicago Press, 2010), 195.
98 Robespierre, "Draft Declaration of the Rights of Man and of the Citizen" in Robespierre, *Virtue and Terror*, 72.
99 Edelstein, *The Terror of Natural Right*, 18.
100 For the *longue durée* history of the *hostis humani generis*, see Edelstein, *The Terror of Natural Right*, 26–42.
101 Denis Diderot, "Droit naturel, (*Morale*.)." Online: http://artflsrv02.uchicago.edu/cgi-bin/philologic/getobject.pl?c.4:258:2.encyclopedie0416.1304602.1304608 [page last visited 19 April 2017]. Online: https://quod.lib.umich.edu/cgi/t/text/text-idx?c=did;cc=did;rgn=main;view=text;idno=did2222.0001.313. [page last visited 20 December 2017].
102 *La Marsaillaise* fifth verse. Online in both French and English: https://en.wikipedia.org/wiki/La_Marseillaise [page last visited 19 April 2017].
103 Gail Bossenga, *The Politics of Privilege: Old Regime and Revolution in Lille* (Cambridge: Cambridge University Press, 1991), 206–207.

Literature

Archives parlementaires de 1787 à 1860. Paris: Librairie administrative de P. Dupont, 1862–.

Baecque, Antoine de, Wolfgang Schmale, and Michel Vovelle (eds.): *L'an 1 des droits de l'homme*. Paris: Presses du CNRS, 1988.

Baker, Keith Michael: *Inventing the French Revolution: Essays on French Political Culture in the Eighteenth Century*. Cambridge: Cambridge University Press, 1990.

Baker, Keith Michael: "The Idea of a Declaration of Rights" in Dale Van Kley (ed.), *The French Idea of Freedom: The Old Regime and the Declaration of Rights of 1789*. Stanford, CA: Stanford University Press, 1994.

Balibar, Étienne: *Equaliberty: Political Essays*. Trans. J. Ingram. Durham, NC and London: Duke University Press, 2014.

Bossenga, Gail: "Financial Origins of the French Revolution" in Thomas E. Kaiser and Dale K. Van Kley (eds.), *From Deficit to Deluge: The Origins of the French Revolution*. Stanford, CA: Stanford University Press, 2011.

Bossenga, Gail: *The Politics of Privilege: Old Regime and Revolution in Lille*. Cambridge: Cambridge University Press, 1991.

Condorcet, Antoine-Nicolas Caritat de: *Declaration of Rights/Déclaration des droits: Traduite de l'Anglois, avec l'original à coté*. Londres: [n.p.], 1789.

Cordorcet, Marquis de: *Œuvres de Condorcet*. Eds. A. Condorcet O'Connor and M. F. Arago. Paris: Firmin Didot Frères, 1847–1849.

Diderot, Denis: "Droit naturel, (*Morale*.)" in D. Diderot and J. l. R. d'Alembert (eds.), *Encyclopédie ou Dictionnaire raisonné des sciences, des arts et des métiers, par une Société de Gens de lettres*. Available online: http://artflsrv02.uchicago.edu/cgi-bin/philologic/getobject.pl?c.4:258:2.encyclopedie0416.1304602.1304608 [page last visited 19 April 2017].

Diderot, Denis: "Natural Rights." Trans. S. J. Gendzier. Available online: https://quod.lib.umich.edu/cgi/t/text/text-idx?c=did;cc=did;rgn=main;view=text;idno=did2222.0001.313 [page last visited 20 December 2017].

Dobie, Madeleine: *Trading Places: Colonization and Slavery in Eighteenth-Century French Culture*. Ithaca, NY and London: Cornell University Press, 2010.

Douzinas, Costas: *Human Rights and Empire: The Political Philosophy of Cosmopolitanism*. London: Routledge-Cavendish, 2007.

Duguit, Léon and Henry Monnier (eds.): *Les constitutions et les principales lois politiques de la France depuis 1789*. Paris: Librairie générale de droit et de jurisprudence, 1908.

Edelstein, Dan: "Enlightenment Rights Talk." *The Journal of Modern History*, Vol. 86, No. 3 (2014): 530–565.

Edelstein, Dan: *The Terror of Natural Right: Republicanism, the Cult of Nature, & the French Revolution*. Chicago, IL and London: The University of Chicago Press, 2010.

Fauré, Christine: "Les déclarations des droits de l'homme" in Christine Fauré (ed.), *Les déclarations des droits de l'homme de 1789*. Paris: Éditions Payot, 1988.

Forsyth, Murray: *Reason and Revolution: The Political Thought of Abbé Sieyes*. New York: Leicester University Press, 1987.

Gauchet, Marcel: *La Révolution des droits de l'homme*. Paris: Gallimard, 1989.

Hunt, Lynn: *Inventing Human Rights: A History*. New York and London: W. W. Norton & Company, 2008.

Hyslop, Beatrice F.: *French Nationalism in 1789 According to the General Cahiers*. New York: Columbia University Press, 1934.

Ishay, Micheline R.: *The History of Human Rights: From Ancient Times to the Globalization Era*. Berkeley: University of California Press, 2004.

Israel, Jonathan: *Democratic Enlightenment: Philosophy, Revolution, and Human Rights 1750–1790*. Oxford: Oxford University Press, 2011.

Jaucourt, Louis de: "Devoir (Droit nat. Relig. nat. Morale.)" in D. Diderot and J.l.R. d'Alembert (eds.), *Encyclopédie ou Dictionnaire raisonné des sciences, des arts et des métiers, par une Société de Gens de lettres*, 4: 915. Available online […].

Kaiser, Thomas and Dale Van Kley (eds.): *From Deficit to Deluge: The Origins of the French Revolution*. Stanford, CA: Stanford University Press, 2011.

Kjærgård, Jonas Ross: "Representation and Taxation: Fiscality, Human Rights, and the French Revolution" in M. Thorup (ed.), *Intellectual History of Economic Normativities*. New York: Palgrave MacMillan, 2016.

Kjærgård, Jonas Ross: "The Inequality of Common Utility: Active/Passive Citizenship in French Revolutionary Human Rights" in K.-M. Simonsen and J. R. Kjærgård (eds.), *Discursive Framings of Human Rights: Negotiating Agency and Victimhood*. Oxon and New York: Birkbeck Law Press, Routledge, 2017.

Kwass, Michael: *Privilege and the Politics of Taxation in Eighteenth-Century France: Liberté, Égalité, Fiscalité*. Cambridge: Cambridge University Press, 2000.

Man, Paul de: *Allegories of Reading: Figural Language in Rousseau, Nietzsche, Rilke, and Proust*. New Haven, CT and London: Yale University Press, 1979.

Marsaillaise, La. Available online: https://en.wikipedia.org/wiki/La_Marseillaise [page last visited 19 April 2017].

Maslan, Susan: "Nature and Society in Revolutionary Rights Debates" in Sophia A. McClennen and Alexandra Schultheis Moore (eds.), *The Routledge Companion to Literature and Human Rights*. London and New York: Routledge, 2016.

Rancière, Jacques: *Le partage du sensible. Esthétique et politique*. Paris: La fabrique, 2000.

Rials, Stéphane: *La déclaration des droits de l'homme et du citoyen*. Paris: Hachette, 1988.

Robespierre, Maximilien: *Œuvres de Maximilien Robespierre*. Vol. 7. Paris: Presses Universitaires de France, 1950.

Robespierre, Maximilien: *Pour le bonheur et pour la liberté*. Paris: La fabrique, 2000.

Rousseau, Jean-Jacques: *The Discourses and Other Early Political Writings*. Ed. V. Gourevitch. Cambridge: Cambridge University Press, 2012a.

Rousseau, Jean-Jacques: *The Social Contract and Other Later Political Writings*. Ed. V. Gourevitch. Cambridge: Cambridge University Press, 2012b.

Sewell Jr., William H.: "Le citoyen/la citoyenne: Activity, Passivity and the Revolutionary Concept of Citizenship" in Colin Lucas (ed.), *The French Revolution and the Creation of Modern Political Culture*. Vol. 2. Oxford: Pergamon Press, 1988.

Sewell Jr., William H.: *A Rhetoric of Bourgeois Revolution: The Abbé Sieyès and What Is the Third Estate?* Durham and London: Duke University Press, 1994.

Sieyès, Emmanuel Joseph: *Political Writings*. Ed. M. Sonenscher. Indianapolis, IN and Cambridge: Hackett Publishing Company, Inc., 2003.

Sieyès, Emmanuel-Joseph: "*Préliminaire de la constitution. Reconnaissance et exposition raisonnée des droits de l'homme et du citoyen*" in Christine Fauré (ed.), *Les déclarations des droits de l'homme de 1789*. Paris: Éditions Payot, 1988.

Sonenscher, Michael: "Introduction" in Emmanuel-Joseph Sieyès (ed.), *Political Writings*. Indianapolis, IN and Cambridge: Hackett Publishing Company, Inc., 2003.

Sonenscher, Michael: *Before the Deluge: Public Debt, Inequality, and the Intellectual Origins of the French Revolution*. Princeton, NJ and Oxford: Princeton University Press, 2007.

Tackett, Timothy: *Becoming a Revolutionary: The Deputies of the French National Assembly and the Emergence of a Revolutionary Culture (1789–1790)*. Princeton, NJ: Princeton University Press, 1996.

Tunstall, Kate E. (ed.): *Self-Evident Truths? Human Rights and the Enlightenment*. New York and London: Bloomsbury Academic, 2012.

Whitman, Walt: *Leaves of Grass and Other Writings*. New York: W. W. Norton & Company, Inc., 2002.

Zuber, Valentine: *Le culte des droits de l'homme*. Paris: Gallimard, 2014.

2 What Was Literature?

What is literature? This deceptively simple question has, somewhat embarrassingly to some, haunted literary theory for decades.[1] To the distress of many, literature is an elusive concept whose definition changes over time. Must writing adhere to strict poetological rules in order to qualify as literature, or is literature that particular kind of writing that departs from all preconceived codes of conduct? Is literature per definition fictive, or does it reflect structures of the social reality? Must it be pleasurable and useful, beautiful or ugly? Is it a relevant criterion that literature investigates existential questions of general interest, or is it sufficient for it to use language in a new and self-reflective manner? Proponents of an essentialist definition of literature have sought to establish a set of stable criteria that must be met in order for a particular piece of writing to count as literature. Others have proposed a functional definition that sees literature as whatever kind of narrative readers and listeners from time to time and place to place have recognized as literature. And some have opted for an institutional definition, claiming that whatever a set of texts, schools, libraries, academies, and expert readers recognize as literary *is* in fact literary.

There are two reasons for which I wish to reraise the question of what literature is. I argue that literature intervened in and even cocreated that social imaginary within which the Declaration of Rights came into being. From the perspective of political history, this hypothesis necessitates an analysis of the *kind* of intervention literature had to offer. Were there types of claims or arguments that could be made in literature but not in pamphlets or through political deliberation? Could some kinds of arguments be made more compelling through literature than through other kinds of discourse? If so, what kinds of arguments were particularly suited to be put forth through literature, and how would authors do this? From the perspective of literary history, the political commitment of much late eighteenth-century French literature and its relationship to different aesthetic developments invites a different set of questions. How did authors of fiction understand their particular role in this historical period? Did they write in continuation of or in opposition to their historical predecessors? What kind of literary styles, genres, and tropes did they develop and pass on to later generations of writers?

I believe in historicizing the concept of literature. As theorists from Sartre to Eagleton have readily acknowledged,[2] readers and writers have spoken about different things over time when they spoke of literature, and this fact suggests that it could be useful to pose the question of literature in the past tense: What was literature? In his *Naissance de l'écrivain*, literary sociologist Alain Viala emphasizes the importance of analyzing what agents from a given period meant when they used "the names of 'author' and of 'literature'" because, he continues, "the hierarchy of genres, of notoriety, and even the definition of what is designated as literature is the object of incessant conflicts."[3] Like Viala, Christian Jouhaud invokes Pierre Bourdieu's concept of the *literary field* and defines this as an intellectual space giving direction to discussions of "what it means to be a writer."[4] Viala and Jouhaud attempt to historicize literature by bringing to life the conflicts authors were engaged in to get their writings accepted as literature and, by extension, to be themselves recognized *as* authors. Their historical focus is seventeenth-century France, the period in which the academies, the rights of authors, and the codification of language intensified and crystallized into recognizable "literary institutions."[5] As will become apparent in this chapter, Louis-Sébastien Mercier (1740–1814), Choderlos de Laclos (1741–1803), and Marie-Joseph Chénier (1764–1811) each in their way struggled to redefine literature and approach it to politics, but naturally, their late eighteenth-century context set up historically singular lines of conflict different from the seventeenth-century ones analyzed by Viala and Jouhaud. By placing my set of authors in their conflictual space, in their discussions of what literature was or should become, I try to answer the justified questions raised from both political and literary history. I hope to show how and why authors believed literature could be used for political purposes.

Viala insists that the literary field must be considered within a larger intellectual field to which it simultaneously belongs and seeks to break away.[6] This, I believe, is an important point because politicians, philosophers, and artists, like authors of fiction, contributed to the task of reimagining French society. In order to understand these similar, but different, efforts, I begin – somewhat surprisingly perhaps – by revisiting Alexis de Tocqueville's claim that no one incarnated the spirit of the French revolution better than the Physiocrats, that peculiar branch of French political economists spearheaded by the doctor François Quesnay. "The economists," Tocqueville wrote,

> have left less of a mark on history than the philosophers. They may not have contributed as much to the advent of the Revolution. Yet I believe that the true nature of the event is best studied in their works.[7]

I shall argue that my set of authors incarnate that spirit or "true nature" of the revolution, which Tocqueville finds characteristic of the Physiocrats. I relate his analysis to a general discussion of the figure of the author-politician before I present and analyze Mercier, Laclos, and Chénier, and their different views on the potential social effects of literature. I conclude by juxtaposing my understanding of literature and its relation to contemporary political developments with influential positions in the research field, including that of Lynn Hunt.

The Author-Politician and the Code of History

The Physiocrats preferred reasoned and philosophical expositions of their political and economic ideas. The head figure of the Physiocratic movement was the court physician François Quesnay, who was highly critical, not only of fictional literature but also of the mercantilism of his day.[8] According to Quesnay, the mercantilist politics held back the economic growth of the nation, and as an alternative, he proposed a far less regulated state financial legislative strategy. Physiocracy means *rule of nature*, and nature should here be taken in a double sense. The Physiocrats believed that all wealth derives from the earth and that the state counters its own best interests when it overregulates agricultural production and commerce through taxation. While nature, first, means agriculture to the Physiocrats, it also refers to that *natural order*, which Quesnay believed would materialize if agriculture and, more broadly, the economic market was allowed to regulate itself. As such, Physiocracy is a precursor to what we would later recognize as a liberalist, free market ideology but one focused primarily on growth in the agricultural sector secured through political deregulation. What is important here is not the philosophy of Physiocracy but more specifically Tocqueville's interpretation of the argumentative style of the Physiocrats and their scorn of all things past. In *The Old Regime and the Revolution*, Tocqueville writes,

> For the Economists, the past was an object of boundless contempt. 'The nation has for centuries been governed by false principles,' Letrosne wrote. 'Everything seems to have been left to chance.' Starting from this idea, they set to work. There was no institution, no matter how old or seemingly well founded, whose abolition they did not seek if it even slightly hindered their plans or disturbed their symmetry.[9]

Historians have recently revisited Tocqueville's argument and questioned whether everyone associated with Physiocracy actually partook in the condemnation of all things past, but for Tocqueville, no one prefigured the revolutionary mistrust of history more than Quesnay and his followers.[10] Like the later revolutionaries, the Physiocrats wanted to sever the bond with the past and instill a new society. When the past is the problem, one would of course not look back to find the way forward. Influential revolutionaries such as Mirabeau, Condorcet, and the abbé Sieyès were never wholly convinced by Physiocracy in its totality, but they were all influenced by it and approved of it in part.[11] And if his embrace of Physiocratic principles was only partial, Sieyès fully shared the Physiocrats' view on history. He described his intellectual method in the *Vues sur le moyens d'exécution dont les Représentants de la France pourront disposer en 1789* (1789), and his method not only resembles that of the Physiocrats but also resonates with the stylistic ambitions of my set of authors. Sieyès discusses the degree to which a politician should base his suggestions on existing facts and goes on to compare the legislator with the architect:

> It is of course the case that genuine policy and genuine politics involve combinations of facts, not combinations of chimeras, but they still involve combinations. Like an architect who, in his imagination, designs and, in some measure, prepares his plan before carrying it out, the legislator conceives of and, in his mind, realizes both the details and the whole of the social order which is fit for a people. When he presents us with the fruit of his meditations, we should assess its utility, not ask for factual proofs of its existence. Nothing would exist if it had to be brought into existence along with the facts, so to speak, attesting to its existence. Never has it been more urgent to restore reason to all its force and to rid the facts of a power that they have usurped to the misfortune of the human race.[12]

Facts hold back the legislator from inventing anything truly new. Instead of worrying about facts and details, the politician should use his imagination, like the architect does, and create a plan of the ideal social order. The people can then decide whether the suggested plan is useful and worth realizing or not. When Sieyès thus urges politicians and legislators to use the imagination to create visions of alternative and better worlds, could he not in fact equally well have described the task of the author? Certainly, Mercier and Chénier, as I will demonstrate, thought about literature in terms similar to the ones used by Sieyès. Among the revolutionaries, however, Sieyès was not alone in attacking the wisdom of history. In his pamphlet *Considérations sur les intérêst du tiers-état adressés au peuple des provinces par un propriétaire foncier* (1788), the Protestant Girondist Jean Paul Rabaut de Saint-Etienne expressed a similar suspicion toward facts and historical precedence. As a way of criticizing the historically based arguments of conservatives, Rabaut de Saint-Etienne wrote, "We rely on history; but our history is not our code. We must distrust the mania of proving what must be done, by what has been done; because what we contest is precisely what has been done."[13] Both Rabaut de Saint-Etienne and Sieyès opposed the ways of the past and tried to think society anew, and I agree with Alain Pons when he writes that "for Mercier, as for Rabaut, the past is disqualified, without consistence, and without richness."[14] In the double movement of attacking the past and dreaming about the future, there is a distinct similarity between literature and politics, between the role revolutionaries and fictional authors assumed as theirs. This similarity, however, does not make literature and politics one. As Viala insisted, authors of fiction simultaneously belong to a larger intellectual field, in this case, a political and philosophical one, *and* try to break free from it.

In the decades preceding the revolution, the Enlightenment movement "lost its fire."[15] The generation of *philosophes* who succeeded Diderot, Voltaire, and Rousseau became absorbed in the elitist *monde* and lived off pensions and held lucrative positions. This created a closed world of wealthy writers, but it also produced an excluded group of authors struggling to make ends meet. These Grub Street authors, Robert Darnton suggests, struggled to enter the closed circuits of the high Enlightenment, and when they were denied entrance, they began producing a libelous literature that fiercely attacked all established authorities. I find Darnton's description of the sociology of the literary market persuasive, but I think he overlooks the degree to which some authors reacted creatively, and not destructively, when confronted with the closed doors of the elite. Mercier, Laclos, and Chénier all attempted to develop what they considered a new kind of literature. Their frustration with tradition came out not as slander and *libelles* but as visions of social alterity and complex investigations of the wrongs of society. All three of them could have said, with Rabaut de Saint-Étienne, "history is not our code" and, especially Mercier and Chénier, could just as easily have signed up to Sieyès's architectural methodology.

It might seem strange that Mercier, Laclos, and Chénier thought about their roles as authors in terms similar to the ones revolutionary politicians used to describe their code and methodology. Authors and politicians, after all, pursue different aims and through dissimilar means. But in this specific historical period, revolutionary politicians wanted to think imaginatively, and authors wanted to contribute to the task of reimagining society. The authors I consider in this study all belong to the revolution's remarkably numerous crossover figures between literature and politics.[16] Mercier and Chénier were elected members of the National Convention, and Laclos worked closely with the Duc d'Orléans and helped develop and disseminate his political reform programs. The sheer number of figures active as both politicians and writers invites an examination of the interrelation between politics and literature in the revolutionary decade. In his *Political Actors*, Paul Friedland has taken up this task but with a particular emphasis on theater and politics.

Friedland suggests the existence of a "general merging of the theatrical and political stages," and argues that theater and politics were "mixed so familiarly that they had become virtually indistinguishable."[17] The reason theater and politics merged in this period, he writes, is that both responded to an "underlying revolution in the conception of representation itself."[18] To explain this revolution underlying the revolution, Friedland introduces the theological term *corpus mysticum*. Before the revolution, the French nation was thought to *be* such "a living communal body." In contrast to that sacred entity, every individual body was simply considered "a relatively meaningless abstraction of the communal whole."[19] 1789 changed that logic. Now, the *corpus mysticum* became a meaningless abstraction of the past, whereas the individual was posited as concrete reality. Earlier, the sovereign, in the form of the king, *was* the nation – "*L'État, c'est moi*," as Louis XIV is rumored to have said. After 1789, sovereignty became an abstraction that could be represented only by deputies elected by concrete individuals. Or in Friedland's theatrical terms,

> [T]he French Revolutionaries ushered in an era in which the legitimacy of representation depended not upon the physical identity between the actor and the object of representation but upon the political audience's willingness to accept the representative body as vraisemblable.[20]

I fail to see the necessity of introducing the concept of the *corpus mysticum*, and I think Friedland overstates the *coupure épistémologique* between monarchical absolutism and representative democracy. In general terms, he is surely right to interpret the revolution as a move from absolutism to representative democracy, but I prefer to think of the period between 1770 and 1799 as an ongoing struggle between different political anthropologies or, to speak with Charly Coleman, between different cultures of personhood. Some believed, as Friedland claims, in the concrete reality, or self-possessive nature, of the individual, but others adhered to different conceptions of communal bodies that entailed dispossessive notions of the self. As the National Assembly deputies said when they temporarily put a halt to the Declaration Debate, their work on the Declaration of Rights was "unfinished." I interpret this unfinishedness as an indication of the fact that the problem of the two contesting political anthropologies remained open, and this openness, I think, is what we need to understand.

I am furthermore skeptical of Friedland's thesis that theater and politics, and, more generally, literature and politics, were "virtually indistinguishable" during the revolution. Following Viala and Susan Maslan, I believe the challenge is to understand the shifting relations between literature and politics.[21] Authors and politicians had similar, but not identical or indistinguishable, ambitions, and it is precisely the contested relationship between the one and the other that is important to understand because it can explain why literature, as literature, could be used to pursue political goals. It is also the simultaneous differences and similarities between political and literary discourse that can help bring alive the period's *literary field* and its struggles to determine what literature was.

Louis-Sébastien Mercier and the Reawakening of Patriotic Virtue

Louis-Sébastien Mercier was a lifelong admirer of Jean-Jacques Rousseau, but unlike his intellectual role model, Mercier only rarely and unwillingly left Paris. He was born into an artisan family, "halfway between the poverty of ordinary workers and the prosperity of those who had risen into the ranks of the true bourgeoisie."[22] The family lived in an apartment in the Quai de l'école, the mother died just three years after Mercier's birth, and the father made a living as a weapons-maker. True to these socially middling origins, Mercier's education seems to have been somewhat fragmented, but M. Cupis, who would later feature prominently in Mercier's multivolume prose work, the *Tableau de Paris* (1782–1788), did teach him to dance, and Père Toquet, another home teacher, gave Mercier valuable lessons in Latin and writing.[23] He also attended the Collège des Quatre-Nations as an *élève externe* in 1749, and, judging by the fact that he held a teaching post in Bordeaux between 1763 and 1765,[24] the scattered educational efforts seem to have been successful.[25]

At age twenty, Mercier began publishing heroic poems, and after his return to Paris, he became a professional Grub Street writer, publishing texts in a variety of genres, including epistles, oriental tales, theatrical plays, and discourses on theater and literature. He achieved his major breakthrough in 1771 with *L'an 2440*, a novel that became the single best-selling book on the French clandestine literary market of the late eighteenth century, but because of his fear of royal authorities, it was not until 1791 that he officially admitted to having written the book.[26] The political topics and occasional religious criticism of his writings made him a constant target for royal censors, and after the 1781 publication of a pirated first edition of the *Tableau de Paris*, Mercier felt compelled to flee the country and take up residence in the Swiss city of Neuchâtel. He returned to Paris in the mid-1780s, and a police record from this period describes him as a "fierce, bizarre man" that has taken the "title of lawyer," even though he "hasn't been admitted to the bar."[27]

After his return to Paris, and after the completion of the *Tableau de Paris*, his fame increased, and according to Riikka Forsström, he became friends with influential revolutionary politicians such as Marat, Robespierre, Camille Desmoulins, Condorcet, Clootz, and Brissot in this period. At this time, he was also associated with a circle of pre-romantic writers, counting "personages such as Restif, Grimod de la Reynière, and Olympe de Gouges."[28] Jeremy Popkin writes that Mercier at this point was an atypical Enlightenment writer, skeptical of the faculty of reason and highly attracted to "illuminist speculations about reincarnation, spirits, and truths beyond the reach of science."[29] Reincarnation, in fact, is a central element of his imaginary future society and its religious beliefs.[30]

After twenty years of clandestine publications, Mercier entered politics in 1792 when he became a member of the Convention. He had always written about politics but together with Jean-Louis Carra he founded the *Annales patriotiques* in 1789, which became an important Paris daily, and gave Mercier the prominence needed to become elected. After entering politics, his views grew more moderate. He thus voted against the death penalty of Louis XVI and suggested perpetual detention instead,[31] and he spoke out against the Jacobins and particularly Robespierre, whom he referred to as a "*sanguinocrate* (bloodocrat)" and held responsible for the "worst excesses and failures of the revolution."[32] Because of his political views, Mercier was imprisoned during the Terror but was released after the fall of Robespierre on 9 Thermidor 1794 and resumed his place in the Convention. Mercier remained a highly productive writer in the latter years of the revolution, publishing the multivolume *Le Nouveau Paris* in 1798 and an alternative dictionary, the *Néologie*, in 1801. As a legislator, however, he seems to have been rather unsuccessful. His friend Reynière thus termed him a political "nonentity" and when he died in 1814, he was already half forgotten.

Today, Mercier is known primarily as an author of prose fiction but in the early years of his career, his ambition was to become a successful dramatist. Denis Diderot and his mid-eighteenth-century attempt to invent a new intermediary genre, *le drame*, between tragedy and comedy inspired him greatly and like Diderot, Mercier placed great faith in the potential of the theatrical tableau. Mercier's theatrical production of at least thirty-three plays has recently been republished in four dire volumes,[33] and the first place to look for his understanding of the role of the author is in his early reflections on theater. The theatrical treatise, *Du Théâtre, ou nouvel essai sur l'art dramatique* (1773), is a lively intervention in the struggle between the ancients and the moderns and an engaged attempt to present a new form of political theater.[34] His scorn for historical precedence, when it comes to the future of theater, is every bit as uncompromising as the Physiocratic and the revolutionary criticism of the "code of history." In *Du Théâtre*, Mercier writes that he would like to "remove and make disappear all these models that deceive and mislead" and continues to write, "[T]o make discoveries in an art, it is more advantageous to have learned nothing in advance and to walk alone, than to be led and directed by the march and the example of others. [...] That's why the methods, the rules, the poetics have spoiled and every day keep spoiling the most inventive minds."[35]

A servile spirit, Mercier claimed, had caused the French to imitate the Greeks, the Romans, and the French classicists instead of developing

What Was Literature? 61

new theatrical genres that could be both useful and pleasurable. The statement of these anticlassical claims provoked the satirical drawing of Figure 2.1 in which Mercier is depicted as a donkey treading upon various classical figures. There is of course a potential contradiction in the fact that Mercier wrote a poetological treatise whose main object was to criticize all kinds of poetics. Mercier himself raised this question in an early example of a true avant-gardist spirit:

> You will say: why do you present your code then? My motive is very different. It is to recommend to any young man who feels some genius for composition, to start by throwing all the poetics into the fire, beginning with this one.[36]

This anticlassicist spirit mirrors the Physiocratic scorn of historical precedence, but Mercier's connection with the Physiocrats actually went further.[37]

Figure 2.1 M ... r l'ane comme il n ' y en a point: peu m'importent les chefs d'oeuvres de tous les arts, pourvu que j'écrase, que je m 'élève, et que le chardon ne me manque pas. Ô gens de goût reconnaissez la bête!: inspiré par Crémier: [estampe]/[non identifié]. (Paris: [s.n.], 1798). Bibliothèque nationale de France.

Paul Cheney and Liana Vardi have both shown that Pierre Samuel Du Pont de Nemours (1739–1817), in his journalistic attempt to popularize Physiocracy, drew upon all kinds of textual genres, including theater and *belles lettres*.[38] In 1771, Du Pont wrote a series of articles in the Physiocratic journal *Éphémérides du citoyen*, on literature and the political potentials of art. Without giving the precise reference, Mercier in fact cites approvingly from one of these articles in *Du théâtre*. "The surveyor," Mercier writes,

> who after reading a tragedy asked what does this prove? said an extreme word, but (as the *Éphémérides du citoyen* says very well) there is a profound meaning hidden under these words: [The surveyor] felt confusedly that there was not a definite purpose in this enormous expense of spirit and talents; he explained himself ridiculously, but his feelings were those of a philosopher.[39]

It was Du Pont who wrote the article about the anonymous surveyor and like Du Pont, Mercier wanted theater to be "good for something."[40] Theater should be useful and have a moral goal and in his explanation of how theater could attain that goal, Mercier wrote:

> What is the dramatic art? It is the one who par excellence exerts all our sensibility, puts into action those rich faculties which we have received from nature, opens the treasures of the human heart, fills its pity, its commiseration, teaches us to be honest and virtuous; for virtue is learned, and it takes quite some effort. If left to sleep, the precious faculties of man will perhaps be annihilated; man will harden from inertia, from habit; wake them up and he will be tender, sensitive, compassionate. That is how a much used voice acquires lightness, flexibility, gentleness, strength, and expanse.[41]

Mercier here reveals himself to be a sensationalist, believing in the ability of theater to influence the morals of the spectators through the senses. He considers morals a sensory question because virtue depends on human faculties that fall into "inertia" unless they are regularly massaged. Theater is the art form capable "par excellence" of awakening human sensibility and thus of producing morals. In Chapter 5, I revisit this argument in my analysis of Chénier's sentimental play but here I want to emphasize the proximity between Mercier's sensationalist argument and Lynn Hunt's similar, albeit neurological, argument from *Inventing Human Rights*. Hunt explains that her argument depends on the assumption that

> reading accounts of torture or epistolary novels had physical effects that translated into brain changes and came back out as new concepts about the organization of social and political life. New kinds of reading (and viewing and listening) created new individual

experiences (empathy), which in turn made possible new social and political concepts (human rights).[42]

Hunt draws upon a different and more modern form of psychology but her basic idea that morals are produced through the senses and, in turn, give way to the development of new political concepts is very similar to Mercier's understanding of the politics of theater. Mercier, however, goes a step further when he suggests that the true purpose of theater resembles that of the legislator.

> [T]he most active and prompt means of invincibly arming the forces of human reason and of suddenly throwing upon a people a great mass of enlightenment [lumières], would certainly be the theater [...]. But so far, the true purpose of the dramatic art has been misunderstood. The poet, instead of being legislator, with that legitimate pride which suits his rank, has vainly obeyed the frivolous and petty taste of the aristarchists of his age.[43]

Dramatists should not follow the rules set by their predecessors but rather be legislators in their own right. By *throwing* enlightenment on the public, dramatists can steer the direction of society in a way that resembles the work of the legislator. In his own conception, the development of a new theatrical genre was an explicitly *political* task leading towards the goal of a happy society:

> "The sublime of politics would be to render pleasure advantageous, and to offer, at little expense, innocent and recreational spectacles to the middle class [la classe médiocrement riche]. Such spectacles would polish its manners, diminish its pains, prevent sentiments of virtue from being extinguished in the spectator's heart, and perhaps day by day make society softer, quieter and happier."[44]

Like Laclos and Chénier would later do too, Mercier here draws upon an old Horatian assumption about literature and its ability to be at once pleasurable and useful.

But one thing is theater – what about prose fiction? In his poetological writings, Mercier tends to prioritize theater, but he actually makes no sharp distinction between prose, drama, and poetry. In his 1778 reflections on literature, *De la littérature et des littérateurs*, he revisited the questions of historical precedence and the morality and politics of literature but from the perspective of a broader understanding of literature, encompassing different kinds of writing. "Our tragedies," he wrote, "are mechanical [...] Why this slow [...] and straight march laid out by Aristotle? Why the same protocol?"[45] In addition to this repeated intervention in the struggle between the ancients and the moderns, Mercier offered a strong defense of the social utility of the arts.

> Who, at a first glance, would think that discoveries, useful inventions, the mechanical arts, and the best political systems depend on the culture of the *belles Lettres*? They have always preceded the deep sciences [les sciences profondes]; they have decorated their surface, and it is by the ingenious artifice of the arts that the nation first adopted and later cherished the deep sciences. Everything comes from the resort of imagination and feeling; even the things that seem the most distant.[46]

In *Du théâtre*, Mercier emphasized the importance of feelings, but the imaginary dimension of art receives a different kind of attention here. What Mercier suggests is that art has a privileged connection with the imagination and, hence, with different visions of scientific and political alterity. This imaginary dimension of literature is what Mercier explores in his futuristic novel, but it is also this feature of literature, which, according to Susan Maslan, creates a special bond between literature and the development of human rights. In explaining why it is necessary to study literature in order to comprehend the development of human rights thought, she writes, "That I turn to literature is not incidental because it is *only* in literature, only by way of the imagination, that 'man' can be made real."[47] Even though I believe Mercier uses the imagination for his own singular, and different, ends in his futuristic novel, it is important to note that Mercier argues for the social usefulness of literature with a reference to the imagination.

In addition to *L'an 2440*, Mercier wrote one more bestseller, the *Tableau de Paris*. Here, Mercier collected hundreds of short depictions of everyday events in Paris with the aim of painting "this gigantic capital's moral physiognomy" and in the hope of placing the inhabitants of Paris in a position, wherefrom they again would be able to get a "precise view of scenes that they have seen so often that they no longer notice them."[48] The content of this twelve volume work is by nature heterogeneous but a recurring characteristic is the interest in the secondary characters of the Parisian social hierarchy. The *Tableau de Paris* also contains poetological reflections that offer the last clue to understanding Mercier's redefinition of the author role and of the politics of literature.

> I give fair warning that all I have done in this work is wield the painter's brush, and that I have indulged very little in philosophical reflection. I could easily have made this *Tableau* into a satire, but I have strictly limited myself. Each chapter could have designated a specific individual; I have refused to do so each time. Satire directed at particular individuals is always bad, because it doesn't make anyone change, it irritates, makes people stubborn, and doesn't lead them back to the straight path. My pictures are generalizations [peintures générales], and even devotion to the public welfare hasn't made me stray.

> I sketched this *Tableau* from living models. Enough others have dwelt on the centuries of the past; I have concerned myself with those alive today and with the appearance of my century, because it interest me much more than the little we know of the Phoenicians or the Egyptians. I owe special attention to what is going on around me. [...] My contemporary, my compatriot, that is the person I really need to understand, because I need to communicate with him, and as a result, every nuance of his character takes on a special importance for me.[49]

The focus upon his Parisian contemporaries resonates well with Mercier's general wish to depart from the ways of the literary tradition but the crux of the quote, I believe, is the distinction between the satire and the "peintures générales." Whereas the satire, according to Mercier, is solely directed at individuals, his *Tableau* is meant to paint a general picture because only hereby can he affect his reader as opposed to simply irritating him or her. He does not, however, develop a literary theory parallel to Sieyès's political philosophy and the latter's wish to do away with real life objects in favor of philosophical, architectural plans. Mercier instead sought to offer general pictures but based on individuals and living models. I interpret this strategy as a wish to avoid the philosophical abstraction of politics without falling into what he considered the trap of satire. In the *Tableau de Paris*, Mercier unties this knot by generalizing particular observations in two complementary ways; first, he presents literally hundreds of everyday occurrences hereby making general patterns visible, and second, he interprets these particular incidents in a generalizing way. A traffic mishap is not just an occasional accident. In Mercier, such an accident is seen to be emblematic of the indifference some rich Parisians demonstrate toward their lesser privileged fellow citizens.

What is striking about Mercier's understanding of literature and politics in this latter case is his reliance on concrete reality and his will to understand and depict familiar, everyday scenes. Here, I think, is an additional example of what literature does differently from political pamphleteers. What distinguishes Mercier and the author-politicians from political pamphleteers – in addition to their reliance upon feelings and the imagination – is the wish to create general depictions of social reality based on everyday scenes. The images of social alterity in Mercier's *L'an 2440* have a general or even architectural ambition but they differ from the theoretical abstraction of Sieyès's pamphlets because of their will to engage directly with ordinary co-citizens. In his struggle to define his author role and function, Mercier opts for a politically engaged literature that seeks to build the moral foundation of society. As shown earlier, he sometimes suggests that the author is like the legislator but at other times, he presents theater and literature simply as a way of disseminating existing legislation, something that would seem to relegate art to political propaganda.[50] Despite this contradiction in his aesthetic philosophy, it is clear that literature in Mercier's opinion should strive to build the morals of the nation. Laclos, as I will show, took a wholly different approach to the moral and political function of literature.

Choderlos de Laclos's Reinterpretation of *Dulce et Utile*

Pierre Ambroise François Choderlos de Laclos (1741–1803) was born into a newly ennobled family in Amiens in Northern France. When Laclos was born, his father, Jean-Ambroise, worked as an assistant to the intendant of the generality of Picardy.[51] At age ten he moved with his family to Paris where they settled in the Temple district, a mixed neighborhood mainly inhabited by members of the lower nobility and the bourgeoisie at this time. The father was unable to buy a position for Laclos and his brother and that basically meant that they could choose between three different career paths: the clergy, the colonies, and the army.[52] None of the brothers were particularly religious and while the older brother entered the Compagnie des Indes, the future author enrolled in the La Fère artillery school in 1760. Two years later he was promoted to second lieutenant but before he really had the chance to partake in battle, the Seven Years' War (1756–1763) ended and a relatively peaceful thirty-year period began. Laclos held various positions during his military career and began the work on *Les Liaisons dangereuses*, his only novel, in 1778.[53] It was a *succès de scandale* when it appeared in 1782, something which gave Laclos a libertine reputation. He married Marie-Soulange Duperré in 1786 with whom he had had a child a couple of years before and their marriage, according to Laclos's biographers, was happy and devoid of all libertine adventures. After having worked with the Duc d'Orléans in the early years of the revolution and after having spent a year in prison in 1793–1794, he reentered the army, now headed by Napoleon Bonaparte, in 1800 and died three years later in Tarente from dysentery and perhaps also malaria.[54] The invention of *le boulet creux*, an explosive projectile for canons, was presumably invented by Laclos in 1795.[55]

Unlike Mercier and Chénier, Laclos was never an elected parliamentary deputy and that makes him an atypical example of the author-politician. His direct involvement in politics culminated in the years between 1788 and 1792 when he worked as a secretary or assistant to the duc d'Orléans (1747–1793). Political historian George Armstrong Kelly has described the person and politics of this Prince of the Blood as a "riddle wrapped inside an enigma."[56] He was one of the richest men in late eighteenth-century France but adopted the name Philippe-Egalité to signal his Jacobin views in 1792 only to be sent to the guillotine by the revolutionary tribunal a year later.[57] To complete the picture of this contradictory figure, he was also, McMahon writes, "flamboyant, disaffected from the court of Louis XVI, an outspoken proponent of the English political system and an unabashed libertine."[58] From the mid-1780s, the duc d'Orléans assembled a group of intellectuals and writers around him and invented what Kelly calls a "'machine' vaguely designed for the requirements of the new politics."[59] With the usage of his wealth and his connections, he and his cohorts developed a political strategy of directing public opinion through the production and dissemination of pamphlets, propaganda, and *libelles*. Royalist observers feared that the duc d'Orléans plotted against the king and personally instigated insurrections in the countryside but while Kelly finds the "extraordinary circulation" of propaganda "striking" he also mirrors other historians in maintaining that the actual results of the duke's political attempts remain "somewhat nebulous."[60]

Madame de Genlis (1746–1830), author of fictional and pedagogical works, was associated with the duke's group and she also served as the *gouverneur* of his sons. She learned of Laclos's position as advisor to the duke in early 1789 and was highly displeased. She had read *Les Liaisons dangereuses* and found its morals "execrable" and considered it a "bad work" in terms of literary quality.[61] She also observed, however, that Laclos "pleased" the duc d'Orléans, that they formed an "intimate liaison," and that Laclos was consulted on "many important subjects during the revolution."[62] In Kelly's interpretation, Laclos entered the duke's group "for power and the joy of the game,"[63] but according to Georges Poisson, Laclos had more genuine ambitions too:

> He believed that the regime could be reformed from within, and that the struggle against the 'establishment' could be waged by one of its principle representatives [...] that is by one of the princes, more lucid and more determined than the king, and capable of regenerating the monarchy.[64]

This ambition would be naïve if the totality of the duke's politics were expressed in a line he delivered shortly after he was elected to the Estates General. The oft-cited line is quoted in a contemporary memoir:

> I don't give a damn what the Estates-General accomplish, but I wanted to be there at the moment when they took up the matter of individual liberty, so as to give my vote to a law that would assure me [...] that whenever I wanted to leave for London, Rome, or Peking, nothing could get in my way. I couldn't care less about the rest.[65]

Besides from expressing this privileged version of negative liberty, however, the duke did fight other political battles.

In November 1787, the duc d'Orléans famously challenged monarchical authority when he provocatively responded "Sir, that is illegal" to a

68   *What Was Literature?*

proposal presented by the king, something which resulted in him being momentarily exiled from Paris.[66] He also tried to strategically influence the design of the *Cahiers des doléances*. When the king summoned the Estates General he invited all regions of France to equip their representatives with lists of grievances (the *Cahiers des doléances*). These lists should detail the problems of all French regions and would function as a political program for the summoned representatives. If anyone could influence the wordings of the lists of grievances, they would have a real advantage in the coming political discussions. At least this was the assessment of the duc d'Orléans and of Laclos who set out to write a guide on what to mention in the lists of grievances. According to the memoir of Talleyrand, Laclos persuaded the duke to let him be in charge of this "political manual for the agents of d'Orléans."[67] Like the success of d'Orléans's political efforts, though, the details of Laclos's involvement in this process remains quite nebulous.

If the Duc d'Orléans is a "riddle wrapped inside an enigma," as Kelly claimed, that would make Laclos a puzzle placed within a riddle wrapped inside an enigma. While scholars lack the sources to gain full knowledge of his precise involvement in politics, Laclos qualifies as an author-politician because his will to engage with society prompted him to move between the roles of soldier, policy-maker, and author. Like Mercier and Chénier, Laclos was drawn toward politics and felt that he could contribute to politics through his actions as well as through his fictional writings. His exact political role was different from that of the deputies Mercier and Chénier and so too was his understanding of literature and of his societal role as an author. In describing his principled theory of the politics of literature, I draw upon two main sources: (1) an untitled essay presumably from 1783 known as "On the Education of Women" that deals with the importance of literature and reading in women's education and (2) an epistolary correspondence between Laclos and Madame de Riccoboni on the topic of the morals (or lack thereof) of *Les Liaisons dangereuses*. The correspondence was originally published in the two volume 1787 edition of the novel.[68]

In the essay, Laclos addresses the difference between novels and historical writings:

> One cannot read a historian, and particularly of the modern history, without noticing that he makes known only the public events and character of men. This means that nothing brings the reader into contact with the habits and affections of the men portrayed and that only very few readers can draw any rules of conduct [règles de conduit] and none any knowledge about men [connaissance des hommes] from their reading. It's up to the novels to supplement this insufficiency of history and from this point of view novels can be of great use [être d'une grande utilité]. But here the choice needs to be

rigorous on all points. For if the works of this genre lack in talent, reason, or morals there is nothing better suited than novels to spoil the taste, the spirit, or the heart. Perhaps there is not a single novel that a young woman can read without a degree of danger unless she is guided in her understanding.[69]

Laclos here makes two points that I consider particularly interesting. First, Laclos is less aggressive in his attack upon the legitimacy of history than Mercier was but he nonetheless describes the usefulness of literature as that which distinguishes it from history. Its usefulness resides in its capacity to represent ordinary people in their everyday actions. The sentimental epistolary novels of Rousseau and Richardson, which is what Laclos has in mind here, succeeded in making the experiences of regular men and women relevant and moving to its readers. *Les Liaisons* is not a sentimental novel but Laclos inscribes his own work in this tradition when he emphasizes the importance of the drama of everyday life.[70] Second, Laclos points to the novel's ability to affect its reader. His phrasing is less bombastic than that of Mercier who wanted to "throw" Enlightenment at the theatergoers, but Laclos had a similar belief in literature's ability to move its reader. The force of literature, in fact, is so strong that it can even be dangerous particularly for unsupervised young female readers. The novelist's everyday interests in combination with literature's ability to affect its reader explain the belief Laclos had in the potential moral, and by extension: political, usefulness of novels. Many were the critics, however, who failed to see the moral usefulness of *Les Liaisons*.

One of Laclos's fiercest critics was Madame de Riccoboni (1713–1792).[71] Marie-Jeanne Riccoboni, according to Diderot, was "the author of a great number of charming works, filled with spirit, honesty, finesse, and grace" but also "one of the worst actresses to ever appear on stage."[72] She was a playwright, a novelist, an intellectual, and an occasional participant in the salons of d'Holbach and Helvétius and at age sixty-nine she responded critically to *Les Liaisons* in a number of letters to Laclos. "A distinguished author, such as M. de Laclos," she wrote, "must have two aims when he publishes anything: that of pleasing and that of being useful [celui de plaire, et celui d'être utile]. It is not enough for an honest man to fulfill only one of them."[73] In invoking the terms *plaire* and *utile*, Riccoboni refers to the classic Horatian ideal of combining the sweet and pleasurable (*dulce*) with the useful (*utile*) in poetry.[74] She readily acknowledges that "M. de Choderlos writes well" but she chastises him for "ornamenting vice" with the invention of the libertine figure of Madame de Merteuil.[75] She admits that vice exists in society (not, however, on the scale suggested by Laclos) but expands on her criticism with the use of a painterly metaphor: "not all parts of the countryside offer a beautiful scenery but it's up to the painter to choose the scenes that he draws."[76] In order to be a good writer, the author needs to combine the pleasurable with the useful and for Riccoboni that means depicting the beautiful instead of dwelling on the uglier parts of nature or society. The selection of what to represent is crucial in her understanding of artistic responsibility.

Twenty-five years before her correspondence with Laclos, Riccoboni was involved in another critical correspondence, this time with Diderot on the topic of his recently published *Le fils naturel* (1757) and *Entretiens sur le fils naturel* (1757). What is interesting about this earlier correspondence is not only that Riccoboni here develops a criticism similar to the one she later directs at Laclos but also that Diderot's answer takes a different direction from that of Laclos's later retort. Together the two correspondences bring forth three different conceptions of what an author is or should be at this time and hence help outline that literary field within which the author-politicians maneuvered.

In his writings about theater, Diderot fiercely attacked what he regarded as the unnaturalness of the staged plays of his day. Why, he asked, should actors stand lined up next to each other, face toward the audience, when they delivered their lines? Why not let them talk to each other and thus mirror an ordinary conversation? Why not let actors sit down at times instead of always having them stand? In opposition to such dramaturgical renewals, Riccoboni warned against imitating nature too closely.

> Not all natural actions should be performed, but only those which express criticism or teach a lesson. Nature is beautiful, but it must be shown from the angles that make it useful and pleasant [utile et agréable]. There are defects one cannot eliminate and a naturalness that is revolting rather than touching. [...] The stage can never become as simple as a room and, to be truthful on the stage, one must renege on nature a bit [pour être vrai au théâtre, il faut passer un peu le naturel].[77]

As in her later correspondence with Laclos, Riccoboni here too invokes the Horatian ideal combination of pleasure and usefulness. And here too she suggests that the writer must deselect parts of the natural world, must "renege on nature a bit," to accomplish that ideal. Diderot's position was different, and in his self-conception, he worked for a more natural and truer form of theater:

> Does it mean nothing to you to have the variety and the naturalness of movements when the characters, in a conversation of some length, rise, rest, approach each other, move away from each other, embrace, or sit in accordance with the various feelings that occupy them? Isn't that how it happens at your place? But everything that's not exaggerated, forced, or slobbish is cold to those who have already lost the taste of truth. The most delicate details tire them.[78]

On the cover page of *Le fils naturel*, Diderot quoted Horace, the selfsame authority that Riccoboni referred to in her criticism of both Diderot and Laclos.[79] In *Ars Poetica*, Horace suggested that the artist should pay close attention to "the model of life and manners" and to the "commonplaces" of lived life as these could offer "keener pleasure[s]" to the audience than other topics and modes of speech.[80] The correspondence between Diderot and Riccoboni centers on the craftsmanship of theater, a central concern of the Horatian poetics, but Diderot's claim is that it is necessary to revolutionize prevalent performance strategies and theatre infrastructure in order to represent the truth and naturalness of lived life. "Forget your rules," Diderot writes to Riccoboni, "leave behind the technique: it's the death of the genius."[81] Riccoboni in her appropriation of horatian aesthetics emphasizes the *dulce et utile* combination in addition to an established tradition of performance techniques. Diderot likewise refers to Horace but prioritizes the idea of lived life and manners and argues that new kinds of performance, less bound up with traditional techniques, are necessary in order to achieve truth and naturalness on stage.

Laclos is less concerned with the technical side of art than with its moral aspects in his letters to Riccoboni. Riccoboni's criticism of both Diderot and Laclos was based on the Horatian principle of *Dulce et Utile*. Diderot's position was not in opposition to Horace but emphasized different aspects of the *Ars Poetica*. The same could be said for Laclos when he, referring to himself in the third person, wrote, "his primary goal was to *be useful* and it is only to attain that goal he *desired to please*."[82] Even though the grammatical use of third person singular produces a distance between Laclos and the ideas expressed in his letter, he does nonetheless argue consistently that his novel was meant to be morally useful. He acknowledges that the libertine figures of Valmont and particularly Merteuil are worse than any living figures, but they have a degree of reality akin to that of Molière's Tartuffe. "No of course," Laclos writes of Tartuffe, "this man never existed. But twenty or a hundred hypocrites have separately committed equal horrors. Molière united them in a sole figure and gave him up for public indignation."[83] With the figure of Merteuil, he continues, "I have thus painted, or at least I've wanted to paint, the darkness that depraved women got away with by hiding their vices behind the hypocrisy of morals."[84]

Riccoboni was completely unpersuaded by Laclos's moral defense of his work.

> So much depravation does not instruct; it only irritates. On every page one cries out: that's not true, that cannot be! [...] It's the sweet and simple truths that slip easily into the heart; it's impossible to put up defences against being moved.[85]

In his last attempt to convince his critic, Laclos pointed to the benefits of the public indignation raised by his novel:

> But how useful is it not to awaken this salutary public indignation that seems to have been released by the vices [of my book]! That's what I wanted to do. At this moment Madame de Merteuil and Valmont excite a general clamor.[86]

The politics of literature resides not only in its ability to produce virtuous feelings but also in its presentation of immoral figures from which the reader feels compelled to loudly distance him- or herself.

> The picture is a sad one, I admit it, but it's true. The merit, which I acknowledge, of mapping out *sentiments that one desires to imitate* does not, I believe, annul the usefulness of painting those sentiments one should defend oneself against.[87]

Laclos's position in this correspondence is an atypical one but it is important to notice that the politics of late eighteenth-century French literature resides not simply in its praise of virtue but can also be found in the depiction of immorality. Reading this correspondence, however, one must remember that Laclos – and his sole novel is the greatest proof imaginable – excelled in presenting arguments that were not necessarily sincerely held. The Laclos-Riccoboni exchange reminds us of the complexity of the politics of literature but as Chapter 4 will demonstrate it does not necessarily explain Laclos's position in the difficult discussion of politics and literature. Let me now turn to the most influential dramatist of the revolutionary decade, Marie-Joseph Chénier.

Marie-Joseph Chénier and the Author-Legislator

Marie-Joseph Chénier was born in Constantinople in 1764, two years after his poet brother André Chénier. He was raised by an aunt in Languedoc and began to write theatrical pieces in the mid-1780s after he had come to Paris. Early plays such as *Edgar, ou le Page supposé* and *Henriette d'Aquitaine* were unsuccessful but in 1789 he rose to the pinnacle of French revolutionary tragedy. In the tellingly titled pamphlets *De la liberté du théâtre en France* (1789) and *Dénonciation des inquisiteurs de la pensée* (1789) he argued for greater theatrical freedom and emphasized the necessity of a polemical literature: "Woe to the writer who speaks only half the truth, who composes, so to speak, with the errors, and who only quietly accuses the revolting absurdities!"[88] These pamphlets were received as attempts to include the institution of theater in the period's political revolution and they caught the attention of Parisian theatergoers. Chénier had submitted his play *Charles IX* to the

Comédie-Française in September 1788 but he was informed that it would be impossible to stage because the censorship would in all likelihood fail to appreciate the portrait of a murderous king. In the summer of 1789, however, it became a matter of revolutionary principle to see the play staged, which finally happened with great success in November 1789.[89] To revolutionary leader Georges Danton there was no doubt that "if *Figaro* had killed the nobility, *Charles IX* would kill the monarchy."[90]

In the 1790s Chénier had numerous plays staged, the most successful of which were *Henri VIII* (1791, 21 appearances), *Caïus Gracchus* (1792, 29 appearances), and *Fénelon* (1793, 141 appearances). Sometimes alone, sometimes in collaboration with composers such as François-Joseph Gossec (1734–1829) and Étienne Nicolas Mehul (1763–1817), Chénier wrote popular odes, revolutionary hymns, and chants. These were used in the state funded revolutionary festivals that Chénier helped organize together with painter Jacques-Louis David (1748–1825) and others.[91] Chénier's civil engagement culminated when he was elected to the national Convention in September 1792 as a deputy of Seine-et-Oise. As a politician he partook in the *Comité d'instruction publique* and even though he voted for the death of Louis XVI in January 1793, radicals would accuse him of being a moderate after *Fénelon* was staged.[92] The brother of Marie-Joseph, André Chénier, was guillotined in 1794 for crimes against the state but Marie-Joseph lived on and wrote a history of French revolutionary literature, *Tableau historique de l'état et des progrès de la littérature française depuis 1789* (1808) before he died in 1811.

Working as both playwright and politician, Chénier meets the criteria of an author-politician. In the poetological preface to *Fénelon*, Chénier looked into the future and reflected upon the differences and similarities of the fields of theater and parliamentary politics:

> But completely occupied with the indispensable task of founding the public teaching and the national education in France, after participating with all my weak means to this great charity which the French people has the right to expect from its representatives, I will return to the silence of the cabinet; and, encouraged by the memory of having sat in an assembly which presided over the cradle of the republic, I shall once more use the theater to attack any kind of prejudice that raises its head; I will provoke some tears over the heroes who are no more; and I will perhaps contribute, on this kind of tribune, to perfect the social mores, and to unnoticeably form new men for the new laws [et je contribuerai peut-être, dans cette espèce de tribune, à perfectionner les mœurs sociales, et à former insensiblement des hommes nouveaux pour les lois nouvelles].[93]

Being busy as a deputy of the Convention, Chénier in 1793 felt he had no time for theater. This was a truth with modifications since not only

Fénelon but also *Timoléon* (1794) were staged while he was a Convention deputy. The politician, in his description, is a representative of the people charged with watching over what is metaphorically described as the infant Republic. Working with national education Chénier was especially prone to thinking about politics as a caretaking and educational duty as is implied by his cradle metaphor. But while he initially distinguishes politics from theater, the quoted passage ends by reuniting the two professions, using yet another pedagogical metaphor. The playwright is charged with *forming* new men for the new laws. The playwright is not a member of an assembly but uses his particular "kind of tribune" to pursue the task of educating the people. Politics and theater, to Chénier, were not "virtually indistinguishable" as Friedland claims.[94] They operated within each their institutional frameworks, developed each their opportunities, and the political potential of theater resided in its difference from the parliamentary institution and from its ability to engage with audiences in its own particular ways.[95]

The differences between theater and politics, however, did not silence the ambition to use theater propagandistically as a way of educating the people, as a "school for the people."[96] The monarchy had privileged three Parisian theaters – the Comédie-Française, the Comédie-Italienne, and the Opéra – and given them the sole right to stage the classical repertory and the "high" theatrical genres.[97] Theater, then, was no different in its institutional organization than other professions and production sectors that were equally ordered by the Old Regime system of privileges. After 1789 and after the Declaration of Rights had sanctioned freedom of opinion (art. 10) and freedom of the press (art. 11), it was a logical next step to attack the theatrical system of privileges and censorship. Chénier did this in his *De la liberté du théâtre en France* (1789) as he, based on the premise that the new nation wanted to "recover its imprescriptible rights," wrote, "We must not imagine that we think freely in a nation where theater is still subject to arbitrary laws."[98] The Chapelier Law from 13 January 1791 was the legislative fulfillment of the demand voiced by Chénier and others. With a stroke it did away with the privileges of the three old theaters: "Any citizen may erect a public theater, and stage all kinds of pieces of any genre there, as long as he declares it to the Municipality before the theater's establishment."[99]

The Chapelier Law helped make the Parisian theater of the French revolution a candidate for "the most vital theater in the history of the West."[100] More than a thousand new plays were written and performed in the revolutionary decade, around fifty new theaters opened in the metropole, and Parisian theatergoers could choose between approximately twenty-five different plays every day. The Chapelier Law and its strike against theater privileges was a political event but given the popularity of revolutionary theater, politicians wanted to further explore the political potentials of theater. Thus, on 2 August 1793,

Georges Couthon, on behalf of the *Comité du Salut public*, addressed the Convention: "They [the theatres] have too often served tyranny; it's about time they serve liberty as well."[101] The Committee decreed two different strategies to promote the cause of liberty. In the month of August, three times a week, designated Parisian theaters should stage the tragedies *Brutus* (Voltaire, 1730), *Guillaume Tell* (Antoine-Marin Lemierre, 1768), and *Caïus Gracchus* (Marie-Joseph Chénier, 1792) free of change. This was a way of promoting "the glorious events of the Revolution, and the virtues of the defenders of liberty."[102] The second strategy was less edifying: "Any theater that plays pieces trying to deprave the public spirit, and to awaken the shameful superstition of royalty, will be closed, and the directors arrested and punished according to the rigor of the laws."[103]

The decree presented by Couthon marked a shift in the institutional political history of revolutionary theater. Whereas the 1789 struggle had opposed the Old Regime privileges and censorship, the August 1793 decree sought to use theater as political propaganda and effectively reintroduced theatrical censorship. The decree was put to use a month later when the *Comité de Salut public* hit down on what they described as the insults experienced by a number of patriots who had been struck by the "incivility" of François de Neufchâteau's *Paméla*, a theatrical version of Samuel Richardson's 1740 novel.[104] In punishment of having staged such an "antipatriotic piece" the Théâtre-Français should be closed and its troupe arrested along with the playwright Neufchâteau who was imprisoned until the fall of Robespierre.[105] French revolutionary theater was incredibly vibrant but changing legislation, informed by the shifting tides of power and ideology, also made the field of theater difficult and dangerous to navigate.

Despite being promoted in the August 1793 law, and despite being subsidized with 188,000 livres, the state-favored genre of heroic tragedy was largely unsuccessful with the public.[106] The failure of these ideologically acceptable plays is particularly striking when seen in comparison with the much more popular sentimental genres of *drame*, *mélodrame*, and *comédie*. As Cecilia Feilla has argued, the liberty of theaters occasioned a great genre diversity in Parisian theaters that makes it difficult to formally distinguish one genre from another.[107] The resulting blend of genres, I think, explains why important work on this period's literature has focused, not on genre, but on "the rhetorical practice" and "literary form" of sentimentality,[108] on the desired "*effects* that a work of art had on its reader or beholder,"[109] or on the interdisciplinary "centrality of sentimentalism in the cultural patterns of the period."[110] This scholarly literature focuses on rhetoric, style, and the desired effects of literature and theater, a focus which heeds the ambition of eighteenth-century playwrights who sought to take advantage of theater's special "kind of tribune" in their effort to emotionally affect their spectators. These efforts

76 *What Was Literature?*

differed from the Jacobin support of national and revolutionary tragedies, but they were nonetheless political for that matter. Subsidized tragedies offered positive depictions of historical moments considered crucial in the preparation of the French revolution, while sentimental theater explored and developed morals, *mœurs*, and new forms of interaction between rational and emotionally capable citizens.

Chénier's *Caïus Gracchus* was among the state subsidized tragedies but *Fénelon* is an example of the popular sentimental drama. In the *Discours préliminaire* (1793) to *Fénelon* Chénier offered his views on the politics of theater and emphasized the importance of morals. Theater, he wrote, "must not only follow the march of the national spirit but determine its progress" and went on to claim that his work had "a political and moral goal."[111] He clearly considered theater a potentially political institution but the politics of theater was intimately connected with morals and his understanding of morals, I think, is crucial for grasping how theater could be political in its own right and in a way different from that of the National Convention. In the preface, Chénier goes on to develop the idea of morals as a foundation of politics.

> Two successive revolutions, bringing along with them the feudal and monarchical ruins, have leveled the ground on which the edifice of the constitutional laws must be raised. But this building will crumble if it is not based on the foundations of public morality. It is therefore this morality that must be created; this is the aim of the legislators, the philosophers, the poets, the orators, those true teachers of the nations; that is the object I had especially in view when I composed the tragedy of *Fénelon*.[112]

The two revolutions of the quote are 4 August 1789 and 10 August 1792; dates representing, respectively, the elimination of feudal privileges and the end of the monarchy. Having removed these Old Regime structures, the terrain was now ready for the edifice of new constitutional laws; laws that should be anchored in sound morals. This idea of a moral foundation of politics appears outside of theatrical circles as well. Thus, in *What Is the Third Estate?*, the abbé Sieyès wrote that

> [m]orality is what should regulate all the ties binding men to one another, both in terms of their individual interests and their common or social interests. Morality ought to tell us what should have been done and, when all is said and done, it alone is able to do so.[113]

Morals, in their close alignment with natural law, Sieyès goes on to explain, serve to "form" a nation, which is afterward directed by the "*positive* laws" that all emanate from "the nation's will."[114] Morals, in the understanding of both Chénier and Sieyès, designate behavioral norms and ways of interaction that should guide the parliamentary legislative process. This alignment of morals and natural law reactualizes the exponential logic of the Declaration Debate explored in Chapter 1. There, Mounier and others considered the Declaration of Rights the foundation of the constitution which, in turn, laid out the principles of all further positive legislation. Chénier's theater targets what revolutionaries perceived as the basis or foundation of politics.

In the previous quote, Chénier was open to the idea that not only philosophers and authors could found morals but that this task could also be assumed by politicians. In *De la liberté du théâtre en France*, however, he had underscored the particular strength of theater in solving this task: "in a beautiful theatrical play, pleasure brings instruction to the spectator without him being aware of it, or able to resist it [...] The dramatic poet, by intensifying the passions, directs those of the spectator."[115] Like Mercier and Laclos before him, Chénier here invokes the Horatian *dulce et utile* ideal. He also emphasizes that the practical side of theater makes it especially suited to pursue this double goal. The collective consumption of theater in combination with its sensational appeal makes it an ideal medium for influencing the morals of the spectators, an idea he expanded on in the preface to *Charles IX*:

> A book, no matter how good it is, cannot act on the public mind in a manner as prompt and vigorous as a beautiful play. Scenes of great significance, luminous thoughts, truths of feeling, that are expressed in harmonious verse are easily engraved in the minds of most spectators. The details are lost on the multitude, the intermediate threads of reasoning escapes it; it only captures the results. All our ideas come from our senses; but the isolated man is moved only moderately: when men are assembled they receive strong and lasting impressions.[116]

In his antitheatrical treatise *Lettre à D'Alembert* (1758), Rousseau had famously complained that theaters were mere means of entertainment and that they turned spectators "fearful and motionless in their silence and inaction."[117] Rousseau's critique of the moral corruption of theater sparkled much debate in the following years and in the quote, Chénier follows in the wake of authors who attempted to develop a morally useful theater in answer to the critique raised so effectively by Rousseau. The collective consumption of theater made it better suited to affect the public spirit than any book read in solitude. Chénier expresses the sensationalist idea that feelings are contagious and will spread from stage to spectators and grow in strength in the crowd of the parterre. If a simple transportation of ideas and feelings from actor to audience seems naïve, historical sources show that the eighteenth-century theater audiences were much more verbal and participating than suggested by Rousseau.[118] Maslan even suggest that the theaters accommodated a version of direct democracy where spectators claimed the right to determine what was performed before them.[119] In order to affect or educate this unruly audience, however, it was necessary to develop a new theater. This was the task Chénier took upon himself, inspired in part by the similar attempts made by Diderot and Mercier a generation or two earlier. In *Entretiens sur le fils naturel* (1757), Diderot lets Dorval say,

> They say that there are no great tragic passions left to move us, and that it is impossible to portray elevated feelings in a new and striking way. That may be so of the kind of tragedy which has been written by the Greeks, the Romans, the French, the Italians, the English and every people on earth. But domestic tragedy will have a different kind of action, a different tone, and a sublimity all its own.[120]

Diderot's essay intervened in *la querelle des anciens et des modernes* on the part of the moderns. If theater wanted to be able to awaken the grand passions and stimulate sentiments, it had to develop a tone of its own. It needed, Diderot argued, to abandon classical and classicist aesthetic rules and begin to develop new ways of affecting its audience. As René Tarin has argued this wish to regenerate theater met a particularly favorable conjuncture during the revolution when new theaters opened and the repertory expanded.[121] In his *Fénelon* preface, Chénier too partook in the *querelle* as he mockingly wrote, "Do not invent, since Corneille, Racine and Voltaire invented. Each of these illustrious men opened new roads; so you shouldn't open any. [...] All three tried to be models; so you must be imitators."[122] The dramatic style of Chénier differs from that of Diderot and Mercier because he preferred to write in verse as opposed to the "barbarous prose" favored by the others.[123] But like them he wanted to open new roads for theater to investigate. He wanted to emulate not the aesthetics of his predecessors but their inventive spirit.

From a critical point of view, Chénier's biographer Adolphe Liéby is no doubt right to insist that

> from 1789 to 1792, the poet who flattered himself that he instructed and guided his co-citizens had simply followed the general movement that carried the France of Louis XVI to overthrow the monarchy and to the proclamation of the Republic.[124]

But in Chénier's social diagnosis and in his understanding of his own political and literary role, the new French laws demanded new men and in order to produce them, a new moral theater had to be invented. To accomplish this task demanded the ability to maneuver a constantly changing ideological and legislative reality in which today's hero could easily become tomorrow's villain. Chapter 5 analyzes how Chénier handled that task aesthetically and politically in his most performed play *Fénelon, ou les religieuses de Cambrai*.

* * *

So what was literature and how did it contribute to the political task of reimagining France? Based on my analysis of what three select authors wanted literature to be, it is possible to draw some preliminary conclusions and sketch what they counted as literature. Mercier, Laclos, and Chénier believed in the Horatian ideal of a pleasurable and useful literature and their interpretation of this ideal can be concretized with a reference to literature's *attack upon history, usage of the imagination*, and ability to *produce sound morals*.

The attack upon the authority of history was not particular to literature. Tocqueville found that the scorn of all things past was characteristic of the revolutionaries and he argued that no one incarnated this anti-historical spirit better than the Physiocrats. For the authors of fiction, the critical engagement with history was premised on the quarrel between the ancients and the moderns. Why, my set of authors (and particularly Mercier and Chénier) asked, should they follow the rules of Aristotle and other authors and critics of the past? Instead of repeating the solutions of the ancients, why not copy their inventive spirit and develop a literature suited to the modern times? Laclos was also critical of historical writing but for him, the problem, and hence his proposed solution, was a different one. He wanted to present recognizable figures in their everyday interactions because he believed readers could learn more from this than from heroes of the history books. Unlike Mercier and Chénier, he was moreover reluctant to present social ideals in his novel. The politics of *Les Liaisons*, based on Laclos's poetological reflections, lay in his creation of scare examples of moral corruption as opposed to ideal figures of virtue. This entailed a condemnation of Old Regime social practices but not a detailed reflection upon the new France. Despite their debt to Horace, my set of authors refused to copy the solutions found in history books and ancient poetics in their search for artistic and political progress.

Literature had important affinities with the human capacity to imagine social and political alterity. It was characteristic of the revolutionary and prerevolutionary era that the potential for political change seemed great and for some even inevitable. Abbé Sieyès welcomed this change and urged legislators to think of their task as equivalent to the imaginary effort of the architect. Forget about the past, forget about existing realities, he urged his contemporary legislators, and try to imagine society anew. According to Susan Maslan, the imaginary element of literature made it political because authors from the seventeenth and eighteenth centuries used it to present new forms of subjectivity. "*[O]nly* in literature, only by way of the imagination," she writes, could the man-citizen gain any kind of credence, could he "be made real."[125] It is important to note, however, that Mercier insists that the literary imagination works through "living models."[126] Like Laclos, Mercier sought to write about persons and scenes that were not identical but familiar to his readers because he believed that would be a way for them to see their surroundings and compatriots anew. Seeing society and its social forms anew, both Laclos and Mercier believed, was the first step toward change.

Literature, finally, had a rare ability to produce morals. Lynn Hunt has argued that the literary presentation of moving figures from unfamiliar social contexts produced empathetic readers disposed to accept the rights and autonomy of others. This conception resembles that of Mercier and Chénier who both believed that literature, and particularly theater, could be used to produce virtuous citizens. Laclos, however, took a different approach to the relationship between literature and morals in his correspondence with Madame Riccoboni. He argued that it was morally valuable for literature to present immoral scare examples, as these would provoke virtuous reactions from frightened readers. It is unclear whether his moral hopes were genuinely held but his argument does invite a critical reconsideration of Hunt's thesis. After all, as Chartier writes about the libelous pamphlets of the period, the opinions voiced in literature "were not graven into the soft wax of their reader's minds, and reading did not necessarily lead to belief."[127] Furthermore, and this will become particularly clear in the analyses of Mercier and Chénier, sentimental literature does not always encompass visions of universal equality. Most often, it operates with dehumanized villains and there is no guarantee that villains will be accepted in the sentimental communities of happy citizens.

In their reflections upon morals, Mercier and Chénier, like Sieyès, refer to the function of the legislator. Sieyès claims that the body of social laws is established on a foundation of morals and natural law. Part of his ambition is to affect that prelegal morality (we might also call it public opinion) because it sets the premises for the work of the legislator. Especially in revisionist studies, the late eighteenth-century rise of *l'opinion publique* has been studied as an important example of the changes in Old Regime political culture; changes that made the French revolution "thinkable."[128] To Keith Michael Baker, public opinion was not something expressed by a localizable sociological set of people. Rather, it was a new source of invocable political authority that contrasted with the figure of the monarchical king.

> 'Public opinion' took form as a political or ideological construct, rather than as a discrete sociological referent. It emerged in eighteenth-century political discourse as an abstract category, invoked by actors

in a new kind of politics to secure the legitimacy of claims that could not longer be made binding in the terms (and within the traditional institutional circuit) of an absolutist political order. The result was an implicit new system of authority, in which the government and its opponents competed to appeal to 'the public' and to claim the judgement of 'public opinion' on their behalf.[129]

I acknowledge that this rhetorical and non-sociological kind of public opinion is important in revolutionary discourse but my set of authors seem to share the belief that their writings are in fact able to influence public morality and public opinion. For that reason, their conception of morals seems closer aligned with what philosopher Charles Taylor calls *social imaginaries* than with Baker's understanding of public opinion. "By social imaginary, I [...] am thinking [...]," Taylor writes, "of the ways people imagine their social existence, how they fit together with others, how things go on between them, and the deeper normative notions and images that underlie these expectations."[130] Morals, in the conception of my set of authors, operate on this level and it is the task of politicians to pass laws in accordance with, as Chénier wrote, "the foundations of public morality."[131] As author-politicians they shared a keen awareness of the importance of public opinion and part of their political effort was the attempt to influence the prelegal moral foundation of society.

The aforementioned conclusions are drawn on the basis of an analysis of what the authors themselves hoped and thought they were doing when writing literature. I find that there is much to learn from the self-understandings of these authors but it is of course perceivable and even likely that their novels and plays at times depart from the explicitly stated ambitions of their writers. In the three chapters that follow, I approach the relationship between literature and politics from the perspective of the texts themselves. The result is sometimes a confirmation of the assumptions of the authors but at others, I present a much more critical evaluation of what happened when authors sought to reimagine France and make individual rights balance with general happiness.

Notes

1 Jean-Paul Sartre famously set the tone for this discussion in his polemical 1948 classic *What Is Literature?* Trans. B. Frechtman (London and New York: Routledge, 2006). For recent engagements with the question, see, e.g., J. Hillis Miller, *On Literature* (London and New York: Routledge, 2002) and Terry Eagleton, *The Event of Literature* (New Haven and London: Yale University Press, 2012).
2 Cf. Sartre, *What Is Literature?*, 8; 17 and Eagleton, *The Event of Literature*, 51; 55.
3 Alain Viala, *Naissance de l'écrivain. Sociologie de la littérature à l'âge classique* (Paris: Les éditions de minuit, 1985), 9.

82 *What Was Literature?*

4 Quoted from Christian Jouhaud, "Power and Literature: The Terms of the Exchange 1624–42" in Richard Burt, (ed.), *Administration of Aesthetics: Censorship, Political Criticism, and the Public Sphere* (Minneapolis: University of Minnesota Press, 1994), 34. The notion of a field is taken from the sociology of Pierre Bourdieu and is discussed, e.g., in Pierre Bourdieu, "Champ intellectual et projet créateur" in *Les temps modernes* (November 1966): 865–906.
5 Viala, *Naissance de l'écrivain*, 10.
6 Viala, *Naissance de l'écrivain*, 14.
7 Alexis de Tocqueville, *The Ancien Régime and the French Revolution*. Ed. J. Elster (Cambridge: Cambridge University Press, 2011), 143.
8 Physiocrat Pierre Samuel Du Pont de Nemours discusses Quesnay's "exaggerated" criticism of literature in his *The Autobiography of Du Pont de Nemours*. Trans. E. Fox-Genovese (Wilmington, DE: Scholarly Resources Inc., 1984), 271–272.
9 Tocqueville, *The Ancien Régime and the French Revolution*, 144.
10 For recent reevaluations of Physiocracy, see, e.g., Michael Sonenscher, *Before the Deluge: Public Debt, Inequality, and the Intellectual Origins of the French Revolution* (Princeton, NJ and Oxford: Princeton University Press, 2007); John Shovlin, *The Political Economy of Virtue: Luxury, Patriotism, and the Origins of the French Revolution* (Ithaca, NY and London: Cornell University Press, 2006); Paul Cheney, *Revolutionary Commerce: Globalization and the French Monarchy* (Cambridge, MA & London, UK: Harvard University Press, 2010) and Liana Vardi, *The Physiocrats and the World of the Enlightenment* (Cambridge: Cambridge University Press, 2012).
11 Gabriel Honoré Riquetti comte de Mirabeau (1749–1791) was the son of Victor de Riqueti, marquis de Mirabeau (1715–1789). Their relation was hardly a happy one but Mirabeau nonetheless approvingly invoked the legacy of his father during the Declaration Debate and likened Sieyès's political philosophy to the Physiocrats on the same occasion (cf. Antoine de Baecque, Wolfgang Schmale, and Michel Vovelle (eds.), *L'an 1 des droits de l'homme* (Paris: Presses du CNRS, 1988), 139–140). Condorcet wrote that the principles and language of the Physiocrats had at times been too "obscure and dogmatic," but overall, their ideas, he believed, had had a "salutary influence." (Marquis de Condorcet, *The Sketch* in Marquis de Condorcet, *Political Writings*. Eds. S. Lukes and N. Urbinati (Cambridge: Cambridge University Press, 2012), 100–101). For Sieyès and Physiocracy, see also William H. Sewell Jr., *A Rhetoric of Bourgeois Revolution: The Abbé Sieyès and What Is the Third Estate?* (Durham, NC and London: Duke University Press, 1994), 69–94.
12 Emmanuel Joseph Sieyès, *Views of the Executive Means Available to the Representatives of France in 1789*. In Emmanuel Joseph Sieyès, *Political Writings*. Ed. M. Sonenscher (Indianapolits/Cambridge: Hackett Publishing Company, Inc., 2003), 16.
13 Jean Paul Rabaut de Saint-Etienne, *Considérations sur les intérêst du tiersétat adressés au peuple des provinces par un propriétaire foncier* ([n.p.]: [n.p.], 1788), 13. For an extended analysis of the shifting legitimacy of historical precedence in revolutionary and prerevolutionary political argumentation see Keith Michael Baker, *Inventing the French Revolution: Essays on French Political Culture in the Eighteenth Century* (Cambridge: Cambridge University Press, 1990), esp. 59–86.
14 Alain Pons, "Préface" in Louis-Sébastien Mercier (ed.), *L'an 2440* (Paris: France adel, 1977), 20.

15 Robert Darnton, *The Literary Underground of the Old Regime* (Cambridge and London: Harvard University Press, 1982), 15.
16 Other examples are Collot d'Herbois (member of the Committee of Public Safety and author of dramas and comedies), Charles-Philippe Ronsin (playwright and member of the revolutionary army), Jean-François Boursault-Malherbe (actor, theater director, and "supplementary" deputy to the National Convention), or for that matter Olympe de Gouges (outspoken pamphleteer and playwright).
17 Paul Friedland, *Political Actors: Representative Bodies & Theatricality in the Age of the French Revolution* (Ithaca, NY and London: Cornell University Press, 2003), 2; 196. Friedland cites Marie-Hélène Huet's *Rehearsing the Revolution: The Staging of Marat's Death 1793–1797* (1982) as a source of inspiration and is, in turn, paraphrased in Matthew S. Buckley, *Tragedy Walks the Streets: The French Revolution in the Making of Modern Drama* (Baltimore, MD: The Johns Hopkins University Press, 2006), e.g., 36.
18 Friedland, *Political Actors*, 3.
19 Friedland, *Political Actors*, 5.
20 Friedland, *Political Actors*, 295.
21 Susan Maslan, *Revolutionary Acts: Theater, Democracy, and the French Revolution* (Baltimore, MD: The Johns Hopkins University Press, 2005), 3.
22 Jeremy D. Popkin: "A City in Words: Louis-Sébastien Mercier's *Tableau de Paris*" in Louis-Sébastien Mercier, *Panorama of Paris*. Ed. J. P. Popkin (University Park: The Pennsylvania State University Press, 1999), 4.
23 M. Cupis features in Chapter MXII: "Messieurs Cupis père et fils" in Louis-Sébastien Mercier (ed.), *Tableau de Paris* (Paris: Mercure de France, 1994), II: 1479–1482. See Joanna Stalnaker, *The Unfinished Enlightenment: Description in the Age of the Encyclopedia* (Ithaca, NY and London: Cornell University Press, 2010), 184–185 for a discussion of the importance of M. Cupis for the development of Mercier's aesthetics.
24 Riikka Forsström, *Possible Worlds: The Idea of Happiness in the Utopian Vision of Louis-Sébastien Mercier* (Helsinki: Suomalaisen Kirjallisuuden Seura, 2002), 33.
25 For the biography of Mercier, see Léon Béclard, *Sébastien Mercier: sa vie, son œuvre, son temps* (Paris: Libraire de la ville de Paris et de la société de l'histoire de Paris, 1903), 2–12.
26 Robert Darnton, *The Forbidden Best-Sellers of Pre-Revolutionary France* (New York & London: W.W. Norton & Company, 1996), 63. For the publishing history of *L'an 2440*, see Everett C. Wilkie Jr., "Mercier's *L'an 2440*: Its Publishing History During the Author's Lifetime," *Harvard Library Bulletin* Vol. 32, No. 1 (1984): 5–35.
27 "Extraits de divers rapports secrets faits à la police de Paris dans les années 1781 et suivantes, jusques et compris 1785, concernant des personnes de tout état et condition [ayant] donné dans la Révolution." Qtd. from Darnton, *The Literary Underground*, 26.
28 Forsström, *Possible Worlds*, 43.
29 Popkin: "A City in Words" in Mercier, *Panorama of Paris*, 6. On this topic, see also Henry F. Majewski, *The Preromantic Imagination of L.-S. Mercier* (New York: Humanities Press, 1971), chap. 2.
30 Cf. Louis-Sébastien Mercier, *Memoirs of the Year Two Thousand Five Hundred*. Trans. W. Hooper (Philadelphia: Thomas Dobson, 1795), Chapter XIX: The Temple.
31 Forsström, *Possible Worlds*, 43.
32 Stalnaker, *The Unfinished Enlightenment*, 152.

84 *What Was Literature?*

33 Louis Sébastien Mercier, *Théâtre complet (1769–1809)*. 4 vols. Ed. J.-C.-Bonnet (Paris: Honoré Champion, 2014.
34 On *la querelle des Anciens et des Modernes* and its influence on the Enlightenment, see Dan Edelstein, *The Enlightenment: A Genealogy* (Chicago, IL & London: The University of Chicago Press, 2010), esp. 37–44.
35 Louis Sébastien Mercier, *Mon bonnet de nuit suivi de Du théâtre*. Ed. J.-C. Bonnet (Paris: Mercure de France, 1999), 1138.
36 Mercier, *Mon bonnet de nuit*, 1139.
37 For Mercier and Physiocracy, see also Marcel Dorigny, "Louis-Sébastien Mercier, lecteur et propagateur de l'économie politique," *Dix-huitième Siècle*, No. 26 (1994): 163–175. Dorigny focuses mainly on *Tableau de Paris*.
38 Paul Cheney and Liana Vardi have shown that the Physiocrats did not always adhere to these principles. Particularly Dupont de Nemours wrote in all kinds of journalistic and literary genres to get his message across. Cf. Cheney, *Revolutionary Commerce*, chap. 5 and Vardi, *The Physiocrats and the World*, chap. 6.
39 Mercier, *Mon bonnet de nuit*, 1182. In his "Idées sur la poésie," Du Pont wrote, "Everyone knows the story of the surveyor who, when leaving [the theater] after having attentively heard a tragedy, said *what does this prove?*" (Pierre Samuel Du Pont, "Idées sur la Poésie en général, & la Poésie dramatique en particulier, par l'Auteur des Ephémérides" *Ephémérides du citoyen*, Vol. XII (1771): 130).
40 Du Pont, "Idées sur la Poésie," 131.
41 Mercier, *Mon bonnet de nuit*, 1147.
42 Lynn Hunt, *Inventing Human Rights: A History* (New York and London: W. W. Norton & Company, 2008), 33–34.
43 Mercier, *Mon bonnet de nuit*, 1131–1132.
44 Mercier, *Mon bonnet de nuit*, 1327–1328.
45 Louis-Sébastien Mercier, *De la littérature et des littérateurs suivi d'un nouvel examen de la tragédie française*. (Genève: Slatkine Reprints, 1970), 25.
46 Mercier, *De la littérature*, 5.
47 Susan Maslan, "The Anti-Human: Man and Citizen before the Declaration of the Rights of Man and of the Citizen," *The South Atlantic Quarterly*, Vol. 103, No. 2/3 (2004): 363.
48 Louis-Sébastien Mercier, *Panorama of Paris*. Ed. J. D. Popkin (University Park: The Pennsylvania State University Press, 1999), 23; Louis-Sébastien Mercier, *Tableau de Paris*. Ed. J.-C. Bonnet (Paris: Mercure de France, 1994), I: 17.
49 Mercier, *Panorama of Paris*, 26.
50 Cf. *De la littérature*, 21:

> What would we not do with Dramatic Poetry, if the Legislator knew how to use it: if he delivered to the Poet his laws, by saying to him: color these holy effigies of virtue, and make everyone bow down before them; use the energy of your Art, to impress the majesty of all that a people must revere.

51 For information about the family and childhood history of Laclos, see Émile Dard, *Le general Choderlos de Laclos auteur des Liaisons Dangereuses* (Paris: Perrin, 1905), 1–33 and Georges Poisson, *Choderlos de Laclos ou l'obstination* (Paris: Bernard Grasset, 1985), 9–21.
52 Cf. Poisson, *Choderlos de Laclos*, 17.
53 For a successful attempt to understand Laclos's novel in connection with his military career, and particularly his years as *fortificateur*, see Joan

Dejean, *Literary Fortifications: Rousseau, Laclos, Sade* (Princeton, NJ: Princeton University Press, 1984), 191–263.
54 Poisson, *Choderlos de Laclos*, 456.
55 Knut Stene-Johansen, *Libertinske strategier 1620–1789: Cyrano, Don Juan, Casanova, Valmont, Sade* (Oslo: Spartacus Forlag, 1996), 194.
56 George Armstrong Kelly, "The Machine of the Duc D'Orléans and the New Politics," *Journal of Modern History* 51 (December 1979): 667–684, qtd. 667.
57 In 1787 he had an income of 7.5 million livres (Kelly, "The Machine of the Duc D'Orléans," 667). In comparison, the entire French state, according to the calculations of Jacques Necker, had a revenue of 10.2 million livres in 1781, cf. Jacques Necker, *Compte rendu au Roi* (Paris: de l'imprimerie royale, 1781), 10.
58 Darrin M. McMahon, "The Birthplace of the Revolution: Public Space and Political Community in the Palais-Royal of Louis-Phillippe-Joseph D'Orléans, 1781–1789," *French History*, Vol. 10, No. 1 (1996): 1–29, qtd. 7.
59 Kelly, "The Machine of the Duc D'Orléans," 684.
60 Kelly, "The Machine of the Duc D'Orléans," 681.
61 Madame de Genlis, qtd. from Poisson, *Choderlos de Laclos*, 214.
62 Madame de Genlis, qtd. from Poisson, *Choderlos de Laclos*, 214.
63 Kelly, "The Machine of the Duc D'Orléans," 675.
64 Poisson, *Choderlos de Laclos*, 207.
65 Duc des Cars, *Mémoires*, 2 vols. (Paris, 1890), 1: 73 qtd. from Kelly, "The Machine of the Duc D'Orléans," 668. Same quote is in Poisson, *Choderlos de Laclos*, 210.
66 The famous retort was delivered at the 19 November Assembly of the Chambers when the topic of taxation and the General Estates was debated. For the line, see, e.g., McMahon, "The Birthplace of the Revolution," 25. For a sustained presentation of the meeting and a discussion of its importance, see Jean Egret, *The French Prerevolution 1787–1788.* (Chicago, IL and London: The University of Chicago Press, 1977), 105–118.
67 Kelly, "The Machine of the Duc D'Orléans," 679.
68 For bibliographical information about this version, which is the edition used in the latest Pléiade edition of *Les Liaisons*, see Cationa Seth, "Notice," in Choderlos de Laclos, *Les Liaisons dangereuses*. Ed. C. Seth (Paris: Gallimard, 2011), 795–797.
69 Choderles de Laclos, "Sur l'éducation des femmes" in Choderlos de Laclos (ed.), *Œuvres complètes*. Ed. M. Allem (Paris: Librairie Gallimard, 1951), 454.
70 Laclos underscores his connection to the sentimental epistolary novel by calling *Clarissa* "the climax of the novel [le chef-d'æuvre du roman]" (Laclos, "Sur l'éducation" in Laclos, *Œuvres completes*, 454) and by quoting the phrase, originally from Rousseau's Julie, "I have seen the mores of my time and I have published these letters" on the cover page of the 1782 edition of *Les Liaisons* (Laclos, *Œuvres complètes*, 3).
71 Another was François Mettra who in a 1782 article from *Correspondance secrète, politique et littéraire* wrote, "What aims does such a work serve? What moral ends can it result in? I don't have the faintest idea." He concluded his review by suggesting that the censorship ought to strike down harder on such an immoral work. (François Mettra, "[Sur 'Les Liaisons dangereuse']" in Laclos, *Les Liaisons*, 526. To the influential critic La Harpe the problem was not the depicted immorality in itself but rather that the punishment of Merteuil came, not from within as a direct result of her actions, but from the

86 *What Was Literature?*

outside in the form of defiguration and ruination. (La Harpe, "[Nouvelles littéraires du printemps 1782]" in Laclos, *Les Liaisons*, 529–531.
72 Denis Diderot, *Paradoxe sur le comédien* in *Œuvres esthétiques*. Ed. P. Vernière (Paris: Garnier, 1959), 365–366.
73 Madame Riccoboni, "Correspondance entre Madame Riccoboni et l'auteur des *Liaisons dangereuses*" in Choderlos de Laclos (ed.), *Les Liaisons dangereuses* (Paris: Gallimard, 2011), 463.
74 Horace, *Ars Poetica* in *The Norton Anthology of Theory and Criticism*. Ed. V. B. Leitch (New York and London: W. W. Norton and Company, 2001), 132.
75 Riccoboni, "Correspondance" in Laclos, *Les Liaisons*, 463. Riccoboni's critical idea of 'ornamenting vice' could, to follow in the horatian vein, be interpreted as what Horace calls a "purple patch" (*purpureus pannus*), cf. Horace, *Ars Poetica* in *The Norton Anthology*, 124.
76 Riccoboni, "Correspondance" in Laclos, *Les Liaisons*, 471.
77 Madame de Riccoboni, "Lettre de madame Riccoboni, actrice du Théâtre Italien, auteur des lettres de Miss Fanny Butler et du Marquis de Crécy, à M. Diderot" in Denis Diderot *Œuvres de Denis Diderot tome XV* (Ed. Jacques-André Naigeon). Paris: Desray, Rue Hautefeuille, No. 36, et Deterville, Rue du Battoir, No. 16, 1798, 458. Richard Gardner's helpful English translation is incomplete but available online from the University of Minnesota webpage: http://tems.umn.edu/pdf/Diderot%20--%20Letters%20with%20Mme%20 Riccoboni.pdf [page last visited 19 October 2017].
78 Denis Diderot, "Réponse de Diderot" in Diderot, *Œuvres de Denis Diderot tome XV*, 473–474. Passage not included in Gardner's translated extract.
79 Diderot frequently did so in his writings about theater and paintings, e.g., *Salon de 1767* (1768) and *De la poésie dramatique* (1758).
80 Diderot cites (in Latin) the second sentence of the following passage:

> My advice to the skilled imitator will be to keep his eye on the model of life and manners, and draw his speech living from there. Sometimes a play devoid of charm, weight, and skill, but attractive with its commonplaces and with the characters well drawn, gives the people keener pleasure and keeps them in their seats more effectively than lines empty of substance and harmonious trivialities.
> (Horace, Ars Poetica in *The Norton Anthology*, 131)

Cf. Denis Diderot, *Le fils naturel, ou les épreuves de la vertu* (Amsterdam: Chez Marc Michel Rey, 1757), 1.
81 Denis Diderot, "Réponse de Diderot" in Diderot, *Œuvres de Denis Diderot tome XV*, 476. Passage not included in Gardner's translated extract.
82 Laclos, "Correspondance" in Laclos, *Les Liasons dangereuses*, 465.
83 Laclos, "Correspondance" in Laclos, *Les Liasons dangereuses*, 469.
84 Laclos, "Correspondance" in Laclos, *Les Liasons dangereuses*, 469.
85 Riccoboni, "Correspondance" in Laclos, *Les Liaisons dangereuses*, 472.
86 Laclos, "Correspondance" in Laclos, *Les Liasons dangereuses*, 477.
87 Laclos, "Correspondance" in Laclos, *Les Liasons dangereuses*, 478.
88 Marie-Joseph Chénier, *Dénonciation des inquisiteurs de la pensée* in Marie-Joseph Chénier, *Oeuvres de M. J. Chénier* (ed. M. Arnault). (Paris: Guillaume, 1823–26), vol. 4: 427. Also commented in Gauthier Ambrus and François Jacob, "Introduction" in Marie-Joseph Chénier, *Théâtre* (Paris: Flammarion, 2002), 11.
89 Cf. Maslan, *Revolutionary Acts*, 24–74. *Charles IX* ran a total of 62 times.
90 Georges Darnton qtd. in Ambrus and Jacob, "Introduction" in Chénier, *Théâtre*, 16.

What Was Literature? 87

91 On French revolutionary festivals, see Mona Ozouf, *La fête révolutionnaire 1789–1799* (Paris: Gallimard, 1976). She comments on the role of Chénier in Chaps. 1 and 7.
92 Cf. Cecilia Feilla, *The Sentimental Theater of the French Revolution* (Surrey and Burlington: Ashgate, 2013), 54.
93 Chénier, "Discours préliminaire (1793)" in Chénier, *Théâtre*, 253.
94 Friedland, *Political Actors*, 196.
95 In Maslan's wording,

> Revolutionary theater and revolutionary politics did not transform themselves one into the other. On the contrary, theater and politics were important to each other during the Revolution because both were distinct and powerful fields that had their own ambitions, dynamics, and history and that, in different ways, created new meanings, new practices, and new possibilities.
> (Maslan, *Revolutionary Acts*, 1–2)

96 From the title of René Tarin, *Le théâtre de la Constituante ou l'école du peuple* (Paris: Honoré Champion, 1998).
97 Jeffrey S. Ravel, *The Contested Parterre: Public Theater and French Political Culture, 1680–1791* (Ithaca, NY and London: Cornell University Press, 1999), 13; Feilla, *The Sentimental Theater*, 26.
98 Chénier, *De la liberté du théâtre en France* in Chénier, *Théâtre*, 167–168.
99 *Rapport fait par M. Le Chapelier* (Paris: de l'imprimerie nationale, 1791), 22.
100 Maslan, *Revolutionary Acts*, 15.
101 Georges Couthon, 2 August 1793 in *AP* LXX, 134. Feilla comments on this decree but erroneously makes a reference to vol. 73 of the *Archives Parlementaires*, cf. Feilla, *The Sentimental Theater*, 3.
102 Georges Couthon, 2 August 1793 in *AP* LXX, 135.
103 Georges Couthon, 2 August 1793 in *AP* LXX, 135.
104 Bertrand Barère, 3 September 1793, in *AP* LXXIII, 360.
105 Bertrand Barère, 3 September 1793, in *AP* LXXIII, 360.
106 For the failure of the state subsidized plays, see Emmet Kennedy, Marie-Laurence Netter, James P. McGregor, and Mark V. Olsen, *Theatre, Opera, and Audiences in Revolutionary Paris: Analysis and Repertory* (Westport, CT & London: Greewood Press, 1996), 51–58. To set the amount of 188,000 livres in perspective, the price of one parterre ticket to Comédie-Française was 1 livre which was also what a Parisian manual labor earned for a day's work in the late eighteenth century, cf. Ravel, *The Contested Parterre*, 27.
107 "Much like the early novel, the *drame* responded to market forces once the liberty of the theaters was declared, and it adapted to the demands and tastes of a changing and growing theater public by appropriating its competition, blending with other genres, and expanding into new sectors." Feilla, *The Sentimental Theater*, 32.
108 Lynn Festa, *Sentimental Figures of Empire in Eighteenth-Century Britain and France* (Baltimore, MD: The Johns Hopkins University Press, 2006), 3.
109 David Marshall, *The Surprising Effects of Sympathy: Marivaux, Diderot, Rousseau, and Mary Shelley* (Chicago, IL and London: The University of Chicago Press, 1988), 2.
110 David J. Denby, *Sentimental Narrative and the Social Order in France, 1760–1820* (Cambridge: Cambridge University Press, 1994), 3.
111 Chénier, "Discours préliminaire (1793)" in Chénier, *Théâtre*, 251.
112 Chénier, "Discours préliminaire (1793)," 252.

88   *What Was Literature?*

113 Emmanuel Joseph Sieyès, *What Is the Third Estate?* In Emmanuel Joseph Sieyès, *Political Writings*. Ed. M. Sonenscher (Indianapolits/Cambridge: Hackett Publishing Company, Inc., 2003), 133–134.
114 Sieyès, *What Is the Third Estate?* In Sieyès, *Political Writings*, 136.
115 Chénier, *De la liberté du théâtre en France* in Chénier, *Théâtre*, 168.
116 Chénier, "Discours préliminaire" in Chénier, *Théâtre*, 73. For alternative readings of this passage, see Graham E. Rodmell, *French Drama of the Revolutionary Years* (London and New York: Routledge, 1990), 62 and Maslan, *Revolutionary Acts*, 31.
117 Jean-Jacques Rousseau, *Lettre à M. D'Alembert sur les spectacles* in *Œuvres complètes*, vol. V. Ed. Bernard Gagnebin et Marcel Raymond (Paris: Gallimard, 1995), 114.
118 Ravel sums up his understanding of the eighteenth century French parterre, writing,

> The parterre audience did not resemble the crowd of rural riots or the urban marketplace, nor did it match the organized, disciplined polity of the modern, Western democracy. Rather, the parterre lay somewhere between early modern notions of crowd activity and modern representative political practices.
>
> (Ravel, *The Contested Parterre*, 65)

119 Maslan juxtaposes the theater with the National Convention as she writes, "direct popular participation was not only compatible with theatrical representation but was sustaining of it; political representation, however, displaced the empowering public." (Maslan, *Revolutionary Acts*, 66).
120 Denis Diderot, *Entretiens sur le fils naturel* in Denis Diderot, *Œuvres esthétiques*. Ed. Paul Vernière (Paris: Classiques Garnier, 1994), 148. English translation in Denis Diderot, *Selected Writings on Art and Literature*. Trans. Geoffrey Bremner (London : Penguin Books, 1994), 56.
121 "The theater of the revolutionary period may appear as the result of previous theoretical writings, an application of the theses of Diderot, Sébastien Mercier and Restif de la Bretonne. It begins a movement which, in the second half of the century, finds a particularly favorable conjuncture; the emergence of a new area of freedom and the deepfelt need for a profound renewal" Cf. Tarin, *Le théâtre de la constituante*, 158. See also Feilla, *The Sentimental Theater*, 31.
122 Chénier, "Discours préliminaire (1793)" in Chénier, *Théâtre*, 250. According to the notes of Gauthier Ambrus and François Jacob, the critics that Chénier mocks are Jean-Marie Bernard Clément and royalist Julien Louis Geoffroy. (411–412n12).
123 Chénier, "Discours préliminaire (1793)," 250.
124 Adolphe Liéby, *Étude sur le théâtre de Marie-Joseph Chénier* (Paris: Société française d'imprimerie et de librairie, 1902), 105.
125 Maslan, "The Anti-Human," 363.
126 Mercier, *Panorama of Paris*, 26.
127 Roger Chartier, *The Cultural Origins of the French Revolution*. Trans. L. G. Cochrane (Durham, NC and London: Duke University Press, 1991), 83.
128 Baker, *Inventing the French Revolution*, 199. See also Mona Ozouf, "L'opinion publique" in Keith Michael Baker, Colin Lucas, François Furet, and Mona Ozouf (eds.), *The French Revolution and the Creation of Modern Political Culture I–IV* (Oxford: Pergamon Press, 1987–1994), I: 419–435; Dena Goodman, *The Republic of Letters: A Cultural History of the French Enlightenment* (Ithaca, NY and London: Cornell University

Press, 1996), e.g., 235–242. An important and acknowledged source of inspiration for these studies is Jürgen Habermas, *The Structural Transformation of the Public Sphere: An Inquiry into a Category of Bourgeois Society.* Trans. T. Burger. (Cambridge and Oxford: Polity Press, 1989), 89–102.
129 Baker, *Inventing the French Revolution*, 172.
130 Charles Taylor, *Modern Social Imaginaries* (Durham, NC and London: Duke University Press, 2004), 23.
131 Chénier, "Discours préliminaire (1793)," 252.

Literature

Archives parlementaires de 1787 à 1860. Paris: Librairie administrative de P. Dupont, 1862-.
Baecque, Antoine de, Wolfgang Schmale, and Michel Vovelle, (eds.): *L'an 1 des droits de l'homme.* Paris: Presses du CNRS, 1988.
Baker, Keith Michael: *Inventing the French Revolution: Essays on French Political Culture in the Eighteenth Century.* Cambridge: Cambridge University Press, 1990.
Béclard, Léon: *Sébastien Mercier: sa vie, son œuvre, son temps.* Paris: Libraire de la ville de Paris et de la société de l'histoire de Paris, 1903.
Bourdieu, Pierre: "Champ intellectuel et projet créateur" in *Les temps modernes*, November 1966: 865–906.
Buckley, Matthew S.: *Tragedy Walks the Streets: The French Revolution in the Making of Modern Drama.* Baltimore, MD: The Johns Hopkins University Press, 2006.
Chartier, Roger: *The Cultural Origins of the French Revolution.* Trans. L. G. Cochrane. Durham, NC and London: Duke University Press, 1991.
Cheney, Paul: *Revolutionary Commerce: Globalization and the French Monarchy.* Cambridge, MA & London, UK: Harvard University Press, 2010.
Chénier, Marie-Joseph: *Dénonciation des inquisiteurs de la pensée* in Marie-Joseph Chénier: *Oeuvres de M. J. Chénier.* Ed. M. Arnault. Paris: Guillaume, 1823–26.
Chénier, Marie-Joseph: *Théâtre.* Eds. G. Ambrus and F. Jacob. Paris: Flammarion, 2002.
Condorcet, Marquis de: *Political Writings.* Eds. S. Lukes and N. Urbinati. Cambridge: Cambridge University Press, 2012.
Dard, Émile: *Le general Choderlos de Laclos auteur des Liaisons Dangereuses.* Paris: Perrin, 1905.
Darnton, Robert: *The Forbidden Best-Sellers of Pre-Revolutionary France.* New York & London: W.W. Norton & Company, 1996.
Darnton, Robert: *The Literary Underground of the Old Regime.* Cambridge and London: Harvard University Press, 1982.
Dejean, Joan: *Literary Fortifications: Rousseau, Laclos, Sade.* Princeton, NJ: Princeton University Press, 1984.
Denby, David J.: *Sentimental Narrative and the Social Order in France, 1760–1820.* Cambridge: Cambridge University Press, 1994.
Diderot, Denis: *Œuvres esthétiques.* Ed. P. Vernière. Paris: Garnier, 1959.
Diderot, Denis: *Le fils naturel, ou les épreuves de la vertu.* Amsterdam: Chez Marc Michel Rey, 1757.

Diderot, Denis: "Réponse de Diderot à la letter précédente" in Ed. J.-A. Naigeon (ed.), Denis Diderot: Œuvres de Denis Diderot. Paris: Chez Desrey et Deterville, 1798: XV: 459–481.
Diderot, Denis: *Selected Writings on Art and Literature*. Trans. G. Bremner. London: Penguin Books, 1994.
Dorigny, Marcel: "Louis-Sébastien Mercier, lecteur et propagateur de l'économie politique." *Dix-huitième Siècle*, No. 26 (1994): 163–175.
Du Pont, Pierre Samuel: "Idées sur la Poésie en général, & la Poésie dramatique en particulier, par l'Auteur des Ephémérides." *Ephémérides du citoyen*, Vol. XII (1771): 130.
Du Pont de Nemours, Pierre Samuel: *The Autobiography of Du Pont de Nemours*. Trans. E. Fox-Genovese. Wilmington, DE: Scholarly Resources Inc., 1984.
Eagleton, Terry: *The Event of Literature*. New Haven, CT and London: Yale University Press, 2012.
Edelstein, Dan: *The Enlightenment: A Genealogy*. Chicago, IL & London: The University of Chicago Press, 2010.
Egret, Jean: *The French Prerevolution 1787–1788*. Chicago, IL and London: The University of Chicago Press, 1977.
Feilla, Cecilia: *The Sentimental Theater of the French Revolution*. Surrey and Burlington: Ashgate, 2013.
Festa, Lynn: *Sentimental Figures of Empire in Eighteenth-Century Britain and France*. Baltimore, MD: The Johns Hopkins University Press, 2006.
Forsström, Riikka: *Possible Worlds: The Idea of Happiness in the Utopian Vision of Louis-Sébastien Mercier*. Helsinki: Suomalaisen Kirjallisuuden Seura, 2002.
Friedland, Paul: *Political Actors: Representative Bodies & Theatricality in the Age of the French Revolution*. Ithaca, NY and London: Cornell University Press, 2003.
Goodman, Dena: *The Republic of Letters: A Cultural History of the French Enlightenment*. Ithaca, NY and London: Cornell University Press, 1996.
Habermas, Jürgen: *The Structural Transformation of the Public Sphere: An Inquiry into a Category of Bourgeois Society*. Trans. T. Burger. Cambridge and Oxford: Polity Press, 1989.
Horace: "Ars Poetica" in V. B. Leitch (ed.), *The Norton Anthology of Theory and Criticism*. New York and London: W. W. Norton and Company, 2001.
Hunt, Lynn: *Inventing Human Rights: A History*. New York and London: W. W. Norton & Company, 2008.
Jouhaud, Christian: "Power and Literature: The Terms of the Exchange 1624–42" in Richard Burt (ed.), *Administration of Aesthetics: Censorship, Political Criticism, and the Public Sphere*. Minneapolis: University of Minnesota Press, 1994.
Kelly, George Armstrong: "The Machine of the Duc D'Orléans and the New Politics." *Journal of Modern History* Vol. 51 (December 1979): 667–684.
Kennedy, Emmet, Marie-Laurence Netter, James P. McGregor, and Mark V. Olsen: *Theatre, Opera, and Audiences in Revolutionary Paris: Analysis and Repertory*. Westport, CT & London: Greewood Press, 1996.
Laclos, Choderlos de: *Les Liaisons dangereuses*. Ed. C. Seth. Paris: Gallimard, 2011.

Laclos, Choderlos de: *Œuvres complètes*. Ed. M. Allem. Paris: Librairie Gallimard, 1951.
Le Chapelier, Isaac-René-Guy: *Rapport fait par M. Le Chapelier*. Paris: de l'imprimerie nationale, 1791.
Liéby, Adolphe: *Étude sur le théâtre de Marie-Joseph Chénier*. Paris: Société française d'imprimerie et de librairie, 1902.
Majewski, Henry F.: *The Preromantic Imagination of L.-S. Mercier*. New York: Humanities Press, 1971.
Marshall, David: *The Surprising Effects of Sympathy: Marivaux, Diderot, Rousseau, and Mary Shelley*. Chicago, IL and London: The University of Chicago Press, 1988.
Maslan, Susan: *Revolutionary Acts: Theater, Democracy, and the French Revolution*. Baltimore, MD: The Johns Hopkins University Press, 2005.
Maslan, Susan: "The Anti-Human: Man and Citizen before the Declaration of the Rights of Man and of the Citizen." *The South Atlantic Quarterly*, Vol. 103, No. 2/3 (2004): 357–374.
McMahon, Darrin M.: "The Birthplace of the Revolution: Public Space and Political Community in the Palais-Royal of Louis-Phillippe-Joseph D'Orléans, 1781–1789." *French History*, Vol. 10, No. 1 (1996): 1–29.
Mercier, Louis-Sébastien: *Memoirs of the Year Two Thousand Five Hundred*. Trans. W. Hooper. Philadelphia: Thomas Dobson, 1795.
Mercier, Louis-Sébastien: *De la littérature et des littérateurs suivi d'un nouvel examen de la tragédie française*. Genève: Slatkine Reprints, 1970.
Mercier, Louis-Sébastien: *Tableau de Paris*. 2 vols. Ed. J.-C. Bonnet. Paris: Mercure de France, 1994.
Mercier, Louis Sébastien: *Mon bonnet de nuit suivi de Du théâtre*. Ed. J.-C. Bonnet. Paris: Mercure de France, 1999.
Mercier, Louis-Sébastien: *Panorama of Paris*. Ed. J. D. Popkin. University Park: The Pennsylvania State University Press, 1999.
Mercier, Louis Sébastien: *Théâtre complet (1769–1809)*. 4 vols. Ed. J.-C. Bonnet. Paris: Honoré Champion, 2014.
Miller, J. Hillis: *On Literature*. London & New York: Routledge, 2002.
Necker, Jacques: *Compte rendu au Roi*. Paris: de l'imprimerie royale, 1781.
Ozouf, Mona: *La fête révolutionnaire 1789–1799*. Paris: Gallimard, 1976.
Ozouf, Mona: "L'opinion publique" in Keith Michael Baker, Colin Lucas, François Furet, and Mona Ozouf (eds.), *The French Revolution and the Creation of Modern Political Culture I–IV*. Oxford: Pergamon Press, 1987–1994, I: 419–435.
Poisson, Georges: *Choderlos de Laclos ou l'obstination*. Paris: Bernard Grasset, 1985.
Pons, Alain: "Préface" in Louis-Sébastien Mercier (ed.), *L'an 2440*. Paris: France adel, 1977.
Popkin, Jeremy D.: "A City in Words: Louis-Sébastien Mercier's Tableau de Paris" in J. P. Popkin (ed.), *Louis-Sébastien Mercier: Panorama of Paris*. University Park: The Pennsylvania State University Press, 1999.
Rabaut de Saint-Etienne, Jean Paul: *Considérations sur les intérêst du tiers-état adressés au peuple des provinces par un propriétaire foncier*. [n.p.]: [n.p.], 1788.
Ravel, Jeffrey S.: *The Contested Parterre: Public Theater and French Political Culture, 1680–1791*. Ithaca, NY and London: Cornell University Press, 1999.

Riccoboni, Madame de: "Lettre de madame Riccoboni, actrice du Théâtre Italien, auteur des lettres de Miss Fanny Butler et du Marquis de Crécy, à M. Diderot" in J.-A. Naigeon (ed.), *Denis Diderot, Œuvres de Denis Diderot*. Paris: Chez Desray et Deterville, 1798: 454–459.

Riccoboni, Madame de: "Letter, from Madame Riccoboni, Actress at the Italian Theater, authoress of Letters from Miss Fanny Butler and The Marquis of Cressy, to Monsieur Diderot, 1758, followed by Diderot's response." Trans. R. Gardner. Available online: http://tems.umn.edu/pdf/Diderot%20—%20Letters%20with%20Mme%20Riccoboni.pdf [page last visited 19 October 2017].

Rodmell, Graham E.: *French Drama of the Revolutionary Years*. London & New York: Routledge, 1990.

Rousseau, Jean-Jacques: *Lettre à M. D'Alembert sur les spectacles* in *Œuvres complètes*, vol. V. Eds. B. Gagnebin and M. Raymond. Paris: Gallimard, 1995.

Sartre, Jean-Paul: *What Is Literature?* Trans. B. Frechtman. London & New York: Routledge, 2006.

Sewell Jr., William H.: *A Rhetoric of Bourgeois Revolution: The Abbé Sieyès and What Is the Third Estate?* Durham, NC and London: Duke University Press, 1994.

Shovlin, John: *The Political Economy of Virtue: Luxury, Patriotism, and the Origins of the French Revolution*. Ithaca, NY and London: Cornell University Press, 2006.

Sieyès, Emmanuel Joseph: *Political Writings*. Ed. M. Sonenscher. Indianapolits/Cambridge: Hackett Publishing Company, Inc., 2003.

Sonenscher, Michael: *Before the Deluge: Public Debt, Inequality, and the Intellectual Origins of the French Revolution*. Princeton, NJ and Oxford: Princeton University Press, 2007.

Stalnaker, Joanna: *The Unfinished Enlightenment: Description in the Age of the Encyclopedia*. Ithaca, NY and London: Cornell University Press, 2010.

Stene-Johansen, Knut: *Libertinske strategier 1620–1789: Cyrano, Don Juan, Casanova, Valmont, Sade*. Oslo: Spartacus Forlag, 1996.

Tarin, René: *Le théâtre de la Constituante ou l'école du peuple*. Paris: Honoré Champion, 1998.

Taylor, Charles: *Modern Social Imaginaries*. Durham, NC and London: Duke University Press, 2004.

Tocqueville, Alexis de: *The Ancien Régime and the French Revolution*. Ed. J. Elster. Cambridge: Cambridge University Press, 2011.

Vardi, Liana: *The Physiocrats and the World of the Enlightenment*. Cambridge: Cambridge University Press, 2012.

Viala, Alain: *Naissance de l'écrivain. Sociologie de la littérature à l'âge classique*. Paris: Les éditions de minuit, 1985.

Wilkie, Jr., Everett C.: "Mercier's *L'an 2440*: Its Publishing History during the Author's Lifetime." *Harvard Library Bulletin* Vol. 32, No. 1 (1984): 5–35.

3 Louis-Sébastien Mercier and the Dream of a Happy Future

According to Robert Darnton's authoritative list of forbidden best sellers in prerevolutionary France, *the* most popular clandestine book of the period was Louis-Sébastien Mercier's *The Year 2440, a Dream if Ever There Was One* [*L'an deux mille quatre cent quarente, rêve s'il en fût jamais*] (1771).[1] The favored books of readers attracted to the temptations of the illegal book-market were libelous attacks on political and religious authorities, often in the form of pornography, Enlightenment philosophy, or some mixture thereof. Some authors of forbidden best sellers are still read today (d'Holbach, Raynal, Voltaire, Rousseau), while others still await their revival (Pidansat de Marirobert, Du Laurens, Coquereau, etc.). Mercier's utopian novel is devoid of explicit sexuality, but it contains an invitation even more alluring than naked skin: the invitation to join in the dream of a perfect society. A society in which all the moral and social miseries of eighteenth-century Paris were washed away and replaced with a well-ordered society and a happy citizenry. The decades-long popularity of the work shows that this invitation was too intriguing to pass up. As such, the book is a fundamental piece in the puzzle of late eighteenth-century French ideas of future social happiness.

In opposition to the book's highly complex bibliographical history,[2] the plot of *L'an 2440* is simple, almost nonexistent. A Frenchman receives a visit from an English friend, and when the Englishman has bid his *adieu*, the French protagonist falls asleep, only to wake up in a dream in the year 2440. In this future Paris, an anonymous man offers to be his guide, and as the now 700-year-old main character and narrator is shown around the city, the guide and other future citizens explain how everything from clothing to traffic, from theater to taxation, and from science to religion has undergone a complete change. Gone are all the abuses of the Old Regime, and in their stead is a perfectly ordered and rational society without social inequality, without enmity, and without excesses of any kind. Regarded as a futuristic novel, *L'an 2440* is different from modern genre examples because the future holds no Star Trek*ish* inventions: "no ray guns, no space machines, no time-warp television, no intergalactic gimmickry of any kind," to cite Darnton.[3]

Instead of a surplus, the utopian future is characterized by its lack of every evil that Mercier associated with Old Regime Paris. As different from present-day genre conventions as the lack of technological innovations is the novel's lack of narrative buildup. The protagonist simply moves around, and the titles of the chapters indicate his findings: "The Carriages," "The Temple," "The Theatre," and so on. Rather abruptly, the novel ends as the protagonist finds Louis XIV walking around the ruins of Versailles, grieving the public misery his reign has caused. As the narrator is about to engage in conversation with the reinvigorated Sun King, a snake "darted from a broken column, stung me on the neck, and I waked" (360/294).[4]

Mercier's forbidden best seller is a key example of the ambition to reimagine society through literature, but its importance does not necessarily reside in its literary qualities. Thus, Bronislaw Baczko finds it "rather mediocre" and insists that it is "far from being a masterpiece."[5] Darnton continues in this vein and suggests that Mercier's major works had a "formless character" that enabled him to expand his narrative and thereby attract buyers to the many new augmented editions of his work.[6] While this was a clever business strategy, "the result was never elegant."[7] Other scholars, myself included, have taken a liking to Mercier's writing and have appreciated its "fractured aesthetic,"[8] its "totalizing observation,"[9] or its "moving vantage point."[10] I want to bracket the discussion of literary quality, however, and focus on the politics of Mercier's novel, and this, as shall become clear, necessitates a combined focus on the commercial appeal *and* the aesthetic functions of Mercier's abrupt style of writing. The politics of the novel depends, I argue, to considerable extent on the invitation to join the dream of future perfection. From a business perspective, the allure of the novel's invitation came from the paratextual signaling of ever new and augmented editions, urging people to buy. From an aesthetic point of view, however, Mercier's fractured aesthetics functioned somewhat like a half-finished puzzle enjoining the reader to finish the picture of future perfection.

The abruptness or the "fractured aesthetics" of *L'an 2440* is achieved, first, through the constant narrative jumps from one topic to another and, second, through the very extensive footnotes that repeatedly pause the narrative progression. The running text offers descriptions of future perfection, and the notes expand upon the topic by giving detailed explanations of the eighteenth-century problem that has found a solution in the future. This means that the text oscillates between three different positions of enunciation: the old protagonist seeing the future and asking his questions; the guide of the future explaining their ways and ideas; and finally, the notes, whose main function is to expand on the subject discussed in the dialogue of the narrative. The unfairly distributed taxes of Mercier's time, to offer an example, are sharply condemned in the notes, while the narrative presents the future fiscal system through the explanations of the guide and the questions of the protagonist. These shifts in enunciation have two important consequences.

First, the shifts create the sense of a dynamic relationship between present and future. One of the criticisms typically mounted against eighteenth-century utopian thought was its speculative and hence irrelevant character. Baczko quotes from an eighteenth-century dictionary and notes how critics pejoratively compared utopias with unrealistic political dreaming. Utopias, or "philosophical novels," as they were sometimes called, were thus "works whose aim is to present a system of perfection applicable to men as they ought to be and not as they are, works where the prospect of happiness is discovered only in an *inaccessible distance*."[11] This definition of utopian thought is a variety of the "realist" criticism of the Declaration of Rights presented by the monarchist Antoine-François Delandine, among others. During the Declaration Debate, Delandine said, "Instead of returning to the origins of the social order, let us improve the situation we're placed in. Let us abandon natural man and spend our time on civilized man."[12] To conservative, "realist" critics, the idea that society could be fundamentally reorganized was frightening, and to describe ideas of social otherness as irrelevant dreaming was an attempt to strike down such ideas through ridicule. By continuously linking his utopianism to recognizable concerns about traffic mishaps or taxation, Mercier tried to increase the relevance of his dream future. The abrupt shifts from the future of the running text to the present of the footnotes serve to present his visions as responses to very "real" problems.

Second, the shifts between the footnotes and the running narrative build a forceful unhappiness/happiness dichotomy. This dichotomy recurs in different forms and to different effect in both Laclos and Chénier, and it is an integrated element of the 1789 Declaration preface, which distinguishes between "public unhappiness [malheurs publics]" and the "happiness of all [bonheur de tous]."[13] In Lynn Hunt's work on the relationship between fictional literature and human rights, she suggests that literature taught lessons of empathy and sympathy.[14] Literature, in other words, provided a training ground for emotions that were necessary for the idea of human rights to appear reasonable or, more strongly, for the universal extension of human rights to seem "self-evident."[15] The shared unhappiness/happiness dichotomy of literature and human rights politics suggests a different kind of relationship between the two spheres of thought. Authors and politicians observed a set of problems, and they thought up more or less imaginative alternative scenarios, but they did so within similar intellectual frameworks. The parliamentary deputies turned to the philosophy of Rousseau in their search for alternative visions of social life, and they eventually came up with the Declaration of Rights as a legislative foundation for the new France. Authors of fiction, and Mercier is an excellent example of this, equally turned to philosophical ideas of social otherness, but they blended these ideas with emotionally engaging examples from everyday life and with peculiar and sometimes contradictory visions of their own. As the sales-figures of *L'an 2440* prove, this was a popular blend in the case of Mercier, but the blend also invites numerous analytical questions: How do different writers and thinkers define unhappiness and happiness? How do they imagine the transition from the one to the other? How do they handle the potential contradiction between individual rights and collective happiness?

In my reading of Mercier, I focus on three sets of problems appertaining in equal measure to his novel and to the human rights thought that matured in the decades of his novel's popularity: temporality, form of government, and taxation. By *temporality*, I refer to Mercier's intervention in the political and philosophical discussions about human progress and perfection. I argue that he develops a singular prophetic voice in his novel, which he uses to pass judgment on his contemporary society. In my analysis of his proposed future *form of government*, I demonstrate the degree to which his future vision depends upon discussions in his own day. This could be interpreted as a sign of Mercier's "weak" imagination, but it also testifies to the fact that he sought to intervene in pressing concerns of his day through literature. In my analysis of the future *fiscal system*, I compare Mercier's ideas to circulating fiscal reform proposals in political debates and pamphlets, and I thus seek to supplement a current trend in French revolutionary historiography to return to economic issues from a cultural historical vantage point.

Temporality in Mercier's Utopian Thought

"[T]here is no utopia," writes Baczko, "*without a synthetic and disruptive representation of social otherness.*"[16] If anything, the utopian genre is defined by its creation of a different form of society, but as the conflictual etymology of utopia suggests, this different society is caught in a characteristic tension between happiness and the unreal. Does the "u" of utopia refer to the Greek "eu," meaning good or happy, or to the adverb "ou," meaning no or nonexistent? According to Miguel Abensour's reading of Thomas More's *Utopia* (1516), in whose work the schism originates, utopia is and has always been "a ludic concept [...] that permanently oscillates between Eu and Ou, between the place where everything is good, the place of happiness (Eutopie) and the place of nowhere (Ou-topie)."[17] This playfulness between happiness and the unreal is operative in *L'an 2440*, but Mercier had his own word for the act of writing imaginative descriptions of alternative societies: to *fictionize*. In his alternative dictionary, *Néologie, ou vocabulaire de mots nouveaux* (1801), the entry "Fictionner" reads,

> It is not to narrate, to tell a story, fabulize, but, rather to imagine political or moral characters in order to put over truths essential

to the social order. *Fictionizing* a plan of government on a distant island, among an imaginary people, for the development of several political ideas, is what several authors have done who have written fiction on behalf of the science that embraces the general economy of states and the felicity of peoples.[18]

In the *Néologie*, Mercier presented new words that he felt grasped some part of reality and lacked an appropriate linguistic sign. In the preface to this alternative dictionary, he explained his ambition in a miniature dialogue between himself and an imagined reader:

The mind [l'entendement] produces the sign and the sign affects the mind. Nothing could be more true. Bacon and Leibnitz have said so. 'So you want many signs,' you'll say. Yes. – 'But you'll degenerate [our language] into nonsense, you'll bring about confusion.' – That's not at all my wish. On the contrary, I want to support your thought, I want to give it the means to become more precise and more clear.[19]

Words can help ideas come forth, and the dictionary entry is doubly interesting in this sense. It explains that imaginative writing may contain essential truths and genuine political ideas, but it also emphasizes the importance of the utopian, or fictionizing, act in itself. Twentieth-century commentators have seen destructive elements in the Enlightenment rationality and its ideal of progress,[20] they have commented on the potential danger of utopias turning into dystopias (how far is it from Mercier's 2440 to Orwell's *1984*?),[21] but for Mercier and many of his contemporaries, images of social otherness called attention to social inequality and were necessary to improve the social world. Making new worlds and making new words were part of bringing a new reality into existence and, hence, part of developing political arguments cut loose from the authority of historical precedent.

In their search for images of social alterity, numerous Enlightenment authors presented imaginary visions of geographical otherness. In travel narratives, such as Montesquieu's *Persian Letters* (1721) or Voltaire's *The Ingenu* (1767), the enlightened Oriental despot, Usbek, and the Amerindian Huron, respectively, travel around France.[22] In these novels, the foreign gazes of the protagonists function as a strategy of estrangement and are used to critically examine and ridicule contemporary French politics and mores. Reversing this logic, Mercier follows the examples of Fénelon's *Telemachus, Son of Ulysses* (1699) and Voltaire's *Candide* (1759) to the extent that he lets a homely gaze fall upon something foreign. In these works, the estrangement is achieved not by letting a foreigner look upon the homely but by letting a homely gaze fall upon foreign *mœurs* and their political systems. Télémaque travels around the Mediterranean region in search of his father and learns much from the happy kingdom of Salente.[23] The encounters with varying kinds of geographical otherness in *Candide* contain dystopian *and* utopian elements because Candide meets war, prison, and the promised land of El Dorado.[24]

While Mercier adopted the second of the aforementioned strategies of estrangement, he departed from his precursors by letting his protagonist remain in Paris throughout the novel (with a short trip to Versailles).[25] The otherness of *L'an 2440* is of a temporal, rather than a geographical, nature, and this shift from place to time has inspired Manuel and Manuel to suggest the term "euchronian" fiction, whereas Baczko, rightly to my mind, prefers the term "*u-chronie*," which retains More's characteristic blend of *eu* and *ou*.[26]

What are the implications of the shift from place to time? Mercier offers no sustained reflection on this shift, but Marquis de Condorcet, another uchronian writer, does in his unfinished *Tableau historique des progrès de l'esprit humain* (1795), known sometimes simply as *Esquisse* or *The Sketch*.[27] *The Sketch* divides the history of humankind into ten epochs from the "Tribal men" and "Pastoral peoples" of the first epochs to the ninth epoch of the Enlightenment and the foundation of the French Republic. The tenth epoch is dedicated to the "future progress of the human mind." Condorcet's account is an optimistic one in which he seeks to "demonstrate how nature has joined together indissolubly the progress of knowledge and that of liberty, virtue and respect for the natural rights of man."[28] It is one in which "the friends of humanity [...] will work together for its [own] perfection and its happiness."[29] In the beginning of the tenth epoch, he explains why his uchronian vision is truthful and not pure guesswork:

> If man can, with almost complete assurance, predict phenomena when he knows their laws, and if, even when he does not, he can with high probability forecast the events of the future on the basis of his experience of the past, why, then, should it be regarded as a fantastic undertaking to sketch, with some pretence to truth, the future destiny of man on the basis of his history?[30]

There is, argues Baczko, something paradoxical about Cordorcet's tenth epoch. On the one hand, it contains the hallmarks of utopian thought: perpetual peace, greater equality, longer life spans, etc. On the other hand, Condorcet insists that his futuristic vision is grounded in truth and scientific probability. It is an "*anti-utopian utopia*" that sees the future as the necessary, or at least the most probable, outcome of conjunctions in his own time and in the past.[31] Rhetorically, this gesture serves to disarm the "realist" critics of utopian thought, but it also testifies to the force of the idea of progress. Even though Condorcet frequently comments on the setbacks of Enlightenment progress, setbacks caused

Louis-Sébastien Mercier and the Dream of a Happy Future 99

by prejudice and corruption, he maintains his optimistic belief in the happy *telos* of humanity.

Mercier used a quote from Leibnitz as epithet to his novel: "the present is pregnant with the future" (i/23).[32] The idea that the future is somehow *in* the present resonates well with Condorcet's scientific ambition to predict the future by analyzing history, but generally, Mercier offers only a very vague description of the process that led from the unhappy present to the happy future. "'Can you believe it?,'" the guide asks the protagonist before he continues: "'The revolution was effected without trouble, and by the heroism of one great man. A philosophical prince, worthy of a throne, because he regarded it with indifference'" (262/226). The brevity of this explanation is striking and telling of Mercier's novel, and Alain Pons rightly notes that the transitory ease is in fact one of the decisively utopian traits of the novel.[33] Mercier is not interested in developing a detailed plot or in explaining the hard-fought struggle to acquire happiness. He simply juxtaposes the present of the notes with the future of the general narrative and invites his reader to accept the dream of future prosperity. This unhappiness/happiness dichotomy is actually established even before the narrative begins, namely, in the opening epistle dedicated to the year 2440 and in the foreword. The function of these two prefaces is to set up the value-laden dichotomy, which will then be developed throughout the novel, but they also invite the reader to join the right side of history. I quote from the beginning of the epistle:

> August and venerable Year! thou who art to bring felicity upon the earth! thou, alas! that I have only in a dream beheld, when thou shalt rise from out the bosom of eternity, thy sun shall enlighten them who will tread upon my ashes, and upon those of thirty generations, successively cut off, and plunged in the profound abyss of death. The kings that now sit upon the throne shall be no more; their posterity shall be no more. Then shalt thou judge the departed monarch, and the writer who lived in subjection to his power.
> (ix/25)

The subjected writer of the quote (the French original uses the plural: *les écrivains*) quickly morphs into an "I" in the epistle as Mercier writes, "I have exercised that authority which nature gave me; I have cited before my solitary reason the laws, the customs, and abuses of the country in which I have lived obscure and unknown" (x/25). The subjected writer is a prophetic voice who has seen and speaks the future. But like the Old Testament prophets, Mercier's "I" is not satisfied with describing the future. Instead, he uses the vision of the future and its altered values to pass judgment on his present. In the Old Testament, the prophets would predict future catastrophes and explain how the moral corruption of the present would inevitably lead to future disaster and thus take on the function of "social critics."[34] Mercier's prophecy is not one of catastrophe, but like the Old Testament prophets, he uses his dream vision to criticize the kings' present abuse of power. He creates a rhetorical position for himself from which he can speak and judge with all the authority of future enlightenment. While Condorcet claimed to be able to predict the future based on his knowledge of history, Mercier develops a different kind of temporality. Instead of seeing the future through the lens of the past and the present, as Condorcet would do, Mercier sees the present in light of the envisioned future, and he uses the moral rectitude of the imaginary future to pass judgment on the falsity of the present. This maneuver is of course a rhetorical strategy, but Mercier builds on it by inviting his reader to partake in his enlightened vision. In the introduction, he writes,

> For me, concentrated with Plato, I dream like him. O my dear countrymen [mes chers concitoyens], whom I have so often heard groan under that load of abuses, of which we are wearied with complaining, when will our dream be realized? Let us then sleep on; for in that must we place our felicity [Dormir, voilà donc notre félicité].
> (2/28)

Mercier calls upon the future and asks it to "[c]ome, and pour down happiness upon the earth! [viens éclairer le bonheur du monde!]" (xi/26) but he also, as Darnton notes, invites the reader to join "a community of citizens bound together by a common dream and united against a common enemy."[35] His readers are rhetorically positioned as members of a communitarian "we" who suffer from oppression but find comfort and shared identity in the opinions expressed by the prophet. For the moment, this community must bear a "load of abuses" but future society will be reorganized around the values shared by Mercier's "we." In his *Du théâtre* (1773), Mercier argued that the dramatic art should excite the spectator's "sensibility" and should "open the treasures of the human heart, fill its pity, its commiseration."[36] There are elements in both *L'an 2440* and the *Tableau de Paris* that could be read as attempts to awaken pity but more often, these prose works invite the reader to share a particular outlook and use it to look upon Paris anew. In the *Tableau de Paris*, Mercier writes,

> Many of [Paris'] inhabitants are like foreigners in their own city: this book will perhaps teach them something or will at least place under a sharper and more precise point of view scenes that as a result of seeing them often they no longer notice: for the objects we see every day are not those we know the best.[37]

By turning the prophet's futuristic eye on present times, Mercier in *L'an 2440* too obtains a defamiliarizing perspective on the present.

The "we" of the novel's introduction is performative in the sense that it creates a bond between writer and reader. This "we," this invitation to join the dream, is not, however, established solely in the dual prefaces. Darnton emphasized the business potential of Mercier's fragmented style of writing (it was easy to add new episodes and thus present fresh, augmented versions of the work) but in her discussion of the *Tableau de Paris*, Joanna Stalnaker argues that the "fractured aesthetic" of the work was a deliberate choice motivated in part by Mercier's ambition to let the reader partake in his book.[38] Mercier, Stalnaker demonstrates, preferred sketches to finished paintings because of the former's "increased possibilities for imaginative participation."[39] Mercier's abrupt and fragmented style might have been economically motivated but it also had the aesthetic effect that it invited the reader to join the prefatory "we" or, phrased closer to the vocabulary of Darnton, that it established a "community of citizens" who shared one and the same Enlightenment mission.

The significance of Mercier's participatory aesthetics is far-reaching because it leads to the question of Mercier's politics or, more precisely, it leads to one of two ways of thinking about literature and politics in the case of Mercier. From a *representative* perspective, Mercier's politics lie in the nature of the community he depicts. What kinds of values are operative in his ideal society? Who are included and excluded from membership? Who has the authority to make decisions and who is left with the practical task of carrying them out? From a *performative* perspective, however, the politics of *L'an 2440* resides in the community it creates or attempts to create. Who belongs to Mercier's prefatory "we"? Through what means and to what effect are readers called upon to participate in the value judgments of the novel? This "we" is powerfully created in the preface and kept alive through the narrative and remembering that readers would have had to have knowledge and real-life connections in the network of underground book trading to obtain a copy of the book, it is not difficult to imagine the sense of community many readers must have felt when reading the book. As Roger Chartier has noted, however, books do not necessarily transmit their ideas into the "soft wax" of their readers' minds and it is notoriously difficult to determine the political impact of books.[40] But at the very least we can conclude that Mercier attempts to engage his readers and include them in a communitarian "we" whose members share a set of specific values. If we cannot establish causality between literature and politics, we can prove correlation and if correlations are strong and sufficiently numerous, causality becomes credible and even probable.

In what follows I focus explicitly on the *political* vision of Mercier in the representative and performative senses of the term. The analysis so far has shown that the prophetic voice of the narrative, its particular temporal organization, is intimately tied to the novel's politics in the sense that the image of the future is used to pass judgment on the present. This suggests that Mercier's vision of the future is strategically adjusted to the social critique he wishes to make and that there is a selective correspondence between the author's historical context and his vision of the future. This, as I will show, is very much the case in the chapter on the future form of government.

The Form of Government in *L'an 2440*

In his article about the architectural transformations of Mercier's future Paris, Anthony Vidler has helpfully drawn attention to the close proximity between Mercier's future and circulating eighteenth-century ideas about urban renewal. In fact, Vidler suggests that if

> all the ameliorations proposed by Mercier were represented on a map, the result would closely resemble the Paris engraved by the architect Pierre Patte on a composite plan published in 1765. A plan, on which appeared the projects, submitted by different architects in the middle of the century, for the construction of a place destined to accommodate the statue of Louis XV.[41]

The subtitle of Vidler's essay is "The Utopia of the Real," and the urban plans of Mercier, seemingly foreign from eighteenth-century realities but nonetheless very much grounded in this historical context, exemplifies what is meant by the paradoxical mixture of reality and utopianism in Vidler's subtitle. The strangeness of the future is heavily marked by the Old Regime present. This temporal blending reoccurs in Mercier's depiction of politics. But how and to what effect?

In Chapter 36, entitled "The Form of Government," the guide explains that governmental forms have completely changed since the time of the protagonist's youth. He uses two different metaphors to describe the societal organization of the future; a vessel plowing the ocean and the human body. The chapter opens with the protagonist asking his guide, "May I ask what is the present form of government? Is it monarchical, democratic, or aristocratic?" (256/223). Interspersed between the question and the beginning of the guide's lengthy answer, is a reference to a note at the bottom of the page. It reads,

> The genius of a nation does not depend on the atmosphere that surrounds it; the climate is not the physical cause of its grandeur or debasement. Force and courage belong to all the people of the earth; but the causes that put them in motion and sustain them, are derived from certain circumstances, that are sometimes sudden, sometimes slow in their operations; but, sooner or later, they never fail

Louis-Sébastien Mercier and the Dream of a Happy Future 103

to arrive. Happy are the people who, by information or by instinct, seize the crisis! [Heureux le peuple qui, par lumière ou par instinct, saisit l'instant!]

(256–257/223)

The quote begins with a critique of a popular idea associated with the philosophy of Montesquieu in this period, namely the idea that human societies are largely controlled by their respective climates.[42] A warm climate in combination with a vast territory, as found in Asia, produces certain *mœurs* that specific forms of government will be able to handle better than others; in the case of Asia, despotism will be the most suitable form of government.[43] Mercier accepts the premise that outside causes affect all human societies but he argues that "force and courage" enable people to steer the outside circumstances in a happy direction. Uncontrollable things never fail to occur, they may be sudden, or they may be slow, but sooner or later, they will happen, and the happy people is the one who seizes this moment and uses it for their own good. The precise nature of the envisioned moment of change is vague, but the general idea is clear enough: Change is inevitable, and the people's response should be to direct that change toward general happiness through the use of force and courage.

Once the guide of the future gets to explain their form of government, he uses the metaphor of a vessel plowing the ocean. This ship metaphor is solely present in the general narrative but whereas in most instances the narrative describes the solution to a problem voiced in the footnote, the running narrative here serves as an alternative way of presenting the selfsame idea introduced in the footnote; the idea, that humanity can control its own fate. The guide says,

> It is true, that pride, luxury, and self interest produce a thousand obstacles; but how glorious is it to discover the means of making those private passions subservient to the general good! The vessel that plows the ocean commands the elements at the same moment that it is obedient to their empire; submissive to a double impulse, it incessantly re-acts against them. You there see, perhaps, the most lively [fidèle] image of a state; borne up by tempestuous passions, it receives from them its movements, and at the same time resists the storm. 'The art of the pilot is all.' [...] If oppression thundered on your heads, you ought to have accused your own weakness only. Liberty and happiness appertain to those who dare to seize them. All is revolution in this world; the most happy of all has had its point of maturity, and we have gathered its fruits.

(258–259/224)

In this ship metaphor, there is a distinct Rousseauian influence, which is made more explicit on the novel's next page when the man from the future uses Rousseau's central concept of the general will to rhetorically ask, "Is not the law the voice of the general will of the people? [La loi n'est-elle pas l'expression de la volonté générale?]" (260/225). The ship metaphor illustrates the difference and simultaneous interdependence between the individual wills and the general will. The vessel gets its movements from the waves of the ocean, and yet, if the pilot is skillful, the vessel will not be thrown around but rather cruise through, taking advantage of the oceanic forces. Similarly, the general will of any society consists in the differing individual wills of its members. However, instead of a schizophrenic legislation, controlled by constantly shifting and opposing particular wills, the general will is a common denominator of the wills of society's members, and legislation should follow from this general will. Just as Rousseau's political philosophy raises the practical question: Do everyone take an equal part in making up the general will? – so too does Mercier's governmental ship metaphor. One answer to such a question of political membership and its limits is given when a future citizen says,

> The law being universal, no one can complain. The women have no other distinction than what is reflected on them by their husbands. Constantly submissive to the duties that their sex requires, their honour is to observe the strict laws that result from them, by which alone they can secure their happiness.
> (285/241–242)

Seemingly, the happiness of women resides in submission to the rules of men, and no one can complain since the law applies to everyone.[44]

In his political philosophy, Étienne Balibar uses the term "extensive universalism" to designate a geographically delimited space guided by a set of universally applicable positive laws.[45] As my analysis of passive citizenship in the Declaration Debate demonstrated (cf. Chapter 1), a society guided by universal positive laws could very well develop principles of internal political exclusion. In the happy future of *L'an 2440*, everyone, including the women, is subject to the same laws, but women are nonetheless excluded from political membership and individual distinction. This case raises the problem of the relationship between individual and society; a problem captured with great rigor by Rousseau. In *Of the Social Contract* (1762), he proposed that the social contract was the "solution" to precisely this "fundamental problem."[46] The problem, he wrote, was "[t]o find a form of association that will defend and protect the person and goods of each associate with the full common force, and by means of which each, uniting with all, nevertheless obey only himself and remain as free as before."[47] Writing about the future tenth epoch of human history, Condorcet revisits this problem, suggesting that the "perfection of laws and public institutions" resides

Louis-Sébastien Mercier and the Dream of a Happy Future 105

in "the reconciliation, the identification of the interests of each with the interests of all."[48] Mercier's ship metaphor expresses the same ideal of fusing particular wills with common ones but different examples, the subjection of women being a crucial one, testify to the problem of striking the right balance between individual and society. When the old protagonist sees a man in a mask and asks his guide who that man is, the reader finds another example:

> It is an author that has wrote a bad book. When I say bad, I speak not of the defects of judgment or style; an excellent work may be made by the aid of plain strong sense alone; I only mean that he has published dangerous principles such as are inconsistent with sound morality [la saine morale], that universal morality which speaks to every heart. By way of reparation, he wears a mask, in order to hide his shame, till he has effaced it by writing something more rational and beneficial to society. He is daily visited by two worthy citizens [deux citoyens vertueux], who combat his erroneous opinions with the arms of eloquence and complacency, hear his objections, confute them, and will engage him to retract when he shall be convinced. Then he will be re-established [réhabilité].
>
> (44/65)

The passage is particularly arresting because it is followed by the guide's reassurance that "the liberty of the press is the true measure of the liberty of the people;" a claim backed up in a footnote stating, "This is equivalent to a mathematical demonstration" (45/66). Other commentators too have seen a contradiction here between principled freedom and actual censorship.[49] It is worth repeating in this context, however, because Article Ten of the Declaration of Rights contains a similar contradiction: "No one should be disturbed for his opinions, even in religion, *provided that their manifestation does not trouble public order as established by law.*"[50] Religion was a sensitive topic in the debates about the freedom of opinion and in Mercier too, religion provides a particularly glaring example of the tension between what Rousseau calls "the person" and the "common force." Chapter 19, "The Temple," thus adds a religious dimension to the "sound morality" of the "virtuous citizens" as it suggests that an "all-piercing eye" will look after sinners and make them "incessantly subject to fresh tortures, that will renew their slavery and their misery" (110/117). To fulfill the dystopian image, the rare criminal of the happy future is even asked to pass judgment on himself: "'Do justice to society and condemn yourself.' The criminal bowed his head; by which he declared that he judged himself deserving of death" (81/96).

The future form of government is thus philosophically inspired by Rousseau and Mercier's depiction of it runs into problems of political membership and moral education reminiscent of the Genevan's political philosophy. Condorcet acknowledges that the perfect equilibrium between individual and society is an ideal and not a fact but in *L'an 2440*, this state of perfect equilibrium is a *fait accompli* even though the examples highlighted in the previous showcase the contradictions of Mercier's imagined future. Before drawing conclusions as to what this means, I want to consider the second metaphor Mercier uses to describe the society of the future: the body metaphor.

After having explained how a "philosophical prince, worthy of the throne, because he regarded it with indifference [roi philosophe, digne du trône puisqu'il le dédaignait]" (262/226), led the French people through its "revolution," the guide goes on to explain how this king

> offered to put the estates of the nation in possession of their ancient prerogatives; he was sensible that in an extensive kingdom there should be an union of the different provinces in order to its being well governed; as in the human body beside the general circulation, each part has one that is peculiarly adapted to itself; so each province, while it obeys the general laws, modifies those that are peculiar to it, agreeable to its soil, its position, its commerce and respective interests. Hence all lives, all flourishes. The provinces are no longer devoted to serve the court and ornament the capital. A blind order from the throne, does not carry troubles into those parts where the king's eye [l'œil du souverain] has never penetrated. Each province is the guardian of its own security and its own happiness; its principle of life is not too far distant from it; it is within itself, always ready to assist the whole, and to remedy evils that may arise.
>
> (262–263/226–227)

Mercier's body politics praises a society in which the provinces are allowed to adopt general laws to local particularities. Such a decentralized form of legislation has the benefit of allowing the nonmetropolitan regions to flourish in their respective ways, according to their soil, position, and commercial interests. The body metaphor is used to make an argument that is more politically poignant than anatomically accurate: Just as each separate part of the human body has its separate system of circulation while simultaneously functioning as part of the general circulation, so too should the political body allow the provinces a degree of self-determination because this will help them flourish and consequently allow the state as a whole to blossom. In other words, just as the hand is both distanced from and depends on the rest of the human body, so too should the provinces be allowed a portion of self-rule. In 1771, such a proposition is an unambiguous comment on the power struggle between the Crown and the regional *parlements*, a struggle culminating in the Maupeou coup of January 1771.

Prior to the coup of Chancellor René Nicolas Charles Augustin de Maupeou, there were twelve parlements throughout France with a total membership of approximately 1,000 magistrates.[51] The parlements were royal courts of final appeal to which cases came from lower courts. According to historian William Doyle, they were the most important intermediary political institutions between the people and the king in Old Regime France, and they had four main legally sanctioned prerogatives. First, they could promulgate *arrêts de règlement* (arrêts being official resolutions usually with the force of law) in matters deemed important for public order. This gave them large local power. Second, new national laws only became operative when they were officially registered by the parlements. Third, in connection with the power to register laws, the parlements had the right to write remonstrances. When the King and his officials would send out laws to be registered by the parlements, parlementary magistrates could reply with comments and criticism if they considered new laws problematical. In effect, this right of remonstrance was a legally sanctioned possibility of opposing royal policy. Fourth, the offices held by the magistrates performing the tasks of the parlements were lifetime appointments. These mainly legal offices had the character of property, meaning that the king could only abolish an office and office holder by buying the office and reimbursing the owner financially.[52] Using his atypical body politics metaphor, Mercier wanted to see precisely these regional political institutions strengthened.

After years of political conflict between the parlements and the crown, the chancellor Maupeou sought to definitively solve the ongoing power struggle by exiling magistrates, abolishing the lifetime ownership of parlementary offices, and restaffing the courts with men willing to accept the new judicial framework defined by the chancellor.[53] Contrary to Mercier's proposal of strengthening the local parlements, Maupeou thus consolidated the political and legislative power of the monarch by abolishing the only political institutions with any legally sanctioned "counterweight" to royal authority.[54] To many observers, this was a tyrannical act, and to Diderot it revealed something he had long suspected, namely that the parlementary check on royal power was nothing but a scam to create the illusion of political liberty. In *Entretiens avec Cathrine II* (1773), he wrote,

> Between the head of the despot and our eyes, there was a great spider's web upon which the multitude adored a great image of liberty. The clear-sighted among us had long since looked through the little holes in the web and knew exactly what was behind; [now] the web has been torn away, and tyranny stands openly revealed.[55]

Tyrannical as it seemed to some observers, the coup was also one among multiple attempts to streamline and simplify the French state. Despite their obvious political differences, both Mercier and Maupeou recognized that the French state apparatus was inefficient due to its complexity and randomness. They agreed that greater administrative simplicity was an important political goal. Nowhere is this ideal clearer in *L'an 2440* than in Chapter 39, "The Taxes." Before analyzing that chapter, however, I want to pause for a moment and reflect on the analysis thus far.

Regarded from the perspective of political philosophy, Mercier draws heavily upon the work of Rousseau. As was the case for the later parliamentary deputies, the Rousseauian heritage influences the particular formatting of the individual/society-problem he encounters. The analysis has demonstrated some of the ways in which this problem remains unsolved in *L'an 2440*, but the protagonist, along with the future guides, nonetheless treats it as a solved issue. Bearing in mind Mercier's particular usage of the prophetic voice, the postulate of the solved problem is understandable but in combination with the troublesome examples of women, criminals, and immoral writers, it suggests a political anthropology akin to what Charly Coleman calls the *culture of dispossession*.[56] Personhood is here not a matter of distinctive features or individual possessions. Instead, people receive their personhood from the larger body they belong to. In the case of religious mysticism, this could be the body of God but in Mercier's novel, the subjectivity of the characters stem from the moral collective of the general will. They are, and must remain, members of this social body and are hence strongly discouraged from developing unsound ideas of their own. What is most striking, perhaps, is not that the novel fails to reach a philosophically satisfying solution to the individual/society-problem but rather the persistence with which it insists upon having found a happy solution. In what follows, I will pursue this self-assured persistence of Mercier's novel into the perhaps surprising realm of taxation. In addition to being a heatedly debated topic in the prerevolutionary years, taxation also represents a possibility to approach the individual/society-dilemma from a different angle. I will prepare the analysis with a presentation of the period's fiscal system and debates.

Taxation and the Duty of Patriotism

In his reading of *L'an 2440*, Alain Pons suggests an interesting interpretation of Mercier's blend of utopian dream and present-day preoccupations. In Pons's vocabulary, Mercier arrives at a peculiar blend of ideology and utopia.

> In Mercier, then, the opposition that Mannheim establishes between utopia and ideology disappears almost completely. If ideology is a system of ideas that express and justify an existing order and the interests of a dominant class, and if utopia is 'an orientation that surpasses reality and simultaneously cuts off the links to the existing order,' then utopia and ideology arrive at a meeting point when

Louis-Sébastien Mercier and the Dream of a Happy Future 109

a new order is about to substitute an ancient one and when a new dominant class learns to assume power. Starting out as protesting and liberating, the utopia becomes justificatory. This explains the disconcerting blend in Mercier of bravery and timidity, of an innovative and a conservative spirit, of generosity and prudent realism.[57]

Behind the "contradictions" of Mercier, Pons finds a "perfectly coherent bourgeois spirit" that "speaks in advance in the voice" of the editors of the Declaration of Rights.[58] I agree that there is an affinity between Mercier and the Declaration of Rights but since the 1977 publication of Pons's article, numerous scholars have challenged the interpretative paradigm of the "bourgeois" revolution.[59] Within French revolutionary historiography, as elsewhere in the humanities, the attempts to explain societal change with references to class struggle, the "bourgeois spirit," or long-term economic transformations were criticized from the late 1960s and onward for being too crude and sometimes empirically incorrect. Actually, it was demonstrated, the revolution counted numerous clerics and nobles within its ranks and oftentimes members of the third estate would attempt to buy their way into the nobility instead of overthrowing it.[60] This is not the place to revisit the Marxist/revisionism-debate but in proposing a cultural and literary interpretation of taxation, I seek to complement the work of historians such as Gail Bossenga, Michael Kwass, and Michael Sonenscher who have attempted to bridge what has increasingly come to seem the insurmountable gap between social and cultural interpretations of the French revolution.[61] Pons is right to notice that ideology and utopia meet in Mercier but to explain this correspondence with a reference to an underlying bourgeois spirit is analytically unsatisfying. By revisiting the topic of taxation from a cultural historical perspective, I seek to add precision to the discussion about ideology and utopianism in Mercier.

The fact is often overlooked but the Declaration of Rights deals explicitly with taxation and state finances in two of its only seventeen articles.[62]

> 13. For maintenance of public authority and for expenses of administration, common taxation is indispensable. It should be apportioned equally among all the citizens according to their capacity to pay.
> 14. All citizens have the right, by themselves or through their representatives, to have demonstrated to them the necessity of public taxes, to consent to them freely, to follow the use made of the proceeds, and to determine the means of apportionment, assessment, and collection, and the duration of them.[63]

Taxation is often considered a technical and administrative concern – which it is – but in these articles taxation is clothed in the words of the human rights discourse: Taxes must be apportioned "equally," citizens have "rights," and everyone should consent "freely" to fiscal regulations. In a sense, this is unsurprising because taxation is a central means of regulating that core relation of the Declaration of Rights between the state and the people. In her study of the *Cahiers de doléances*, Beatrice Fry Hyslop has shown that the demand for greater fiscal equality was "well-nigh *unanimous*" in the cahiers of 1789 and the very public Necker/Calonne controversy of the 1780s brought the issues of taxation and state finances to the top of the public agenda.[64]

Jacques Necker (1732–1804) was Director General of Finances from 1777 to 1781 and again from 1788 to 1790. Charles Alexandre de Calonne was his replacement between 1783 and 1787 and from one perspective, their disagreement centers on a considerable, yet manageable amount from the 1781 account of the state finances. Whereas Necker claimed that the ordinary revenues exceeded the ordinary expenses from that year by 10.2 million livres in his *Compte rendu au roi* (1781), Calonne, in a speech before the King and the Assembly of the Notables on 22 February 1787, argued that Necker had in fact miscalculated a prior deficit of 37 million and failed to take into account the interests of a 440 million livres loan taken up in 1781.[65] In his 110 page answer to these allegations of bad accounting, Necker summed up that there was "a difference of sixty millions" between their calculations and that one of them "is gravely mistaken."[66] Naturally, sixty million livres is a large amount in a financial account that sets the total ordinary income of the year at approximately 264 million livres.[67] But in comparison with the fact that France, according to Calonne, in the years between 1776 and 1786 had borrowed a total of 1250 million livres, sixty millions would seem manageable, had the circumstances been less extraordinary.[68]

What is important here about the Necker/Calonne controversy is the public interest it generated, what Jacob Soll has called the rise of "financial literacy," and the revealing fact that even capable ministers like Necker and Calonne were fundamentally unable to calculate the French finances accurately.[69] At a time when the Seven Years' War (1756–1763) and the War of American Independence (1775–1783) had severely aggravated the state deficit, the combination of public interest and ministerial incapacity was a dangerous cocktail that helps explain why state finances and taxation would find their way into the Declaration of Rights. Before the Necker/Calonne controversy, however, Mercier had already proposed a novelistic solution to the problem.

In the future Paris, the protagonist is shown two coffers, one with the caption "Tribute due to the King representing the state" and the other with the heading "Free gifts." When he asks if these coffers really represent the future tax system, the men of the future answer collectively:

> That large coffer you see, they said, is our receiver-general of the finances. It is there that every citizen deposits his contribution for the

Louis-Sébastien Mercier and the Dream of a Happy Future

support of the state. We are there obliged to deposit the fiftieth part of our annual income. He that has no property, or what is only just sufficient for his maintenance, is exempt; for why should we take bread from him whose daily labour is but sufficient for his maintenance? In the other coffer are the voluntary offerings, intended for useful designs, for the execution of such projects as have been approved by the public [destinées à d'utiles fondations, comme pour l'exécution des projets proposés et qui ont l'agrément du public]. This sometimes is richer than the other; for we love liberality in our gifts, and no other motive is necessary to excite it than equity and a love for the state [la raison et l'amour de l'État]. Whenever our king sends forth an useful edict, that merits the public approbation, we run in crowds to the chest with our marks of acknowledgment; he has but to propose, and we furnish him with the means of accomplishing every important project.

(300–303/252–254)

Mercier's future fiscal system is structured around two kinds of taxes, a 2% mandatory tax and voluntary offerings. The idea of a *cinquantième* tax should be considered in the light of two of the actual eighteenth-century taxes; the *vingtième* and the *dixième*, respectively a 5% and 10% direct tax. The complicated Old Regime fiscal system did not operate with one universal and continuous tax. Instead, there were a number of direct and indirect taxes, some of the most important being the *taille* (a direct tax on land), the *gabelle* (a regionally differentiated tax on salt), the *capitation* (a direct tax aimed on every head in France, hence the name), and the *corvée* (a tax paid by way of mandatory unsalaried road maintenance).[70] As Kwass has shown, the persistent financial problems of the French state caused the king and his ministers to propose ever new temporary taxes throughout the long eighteenth century. Hereby, the monarch became involved in a political struggle with Third Estate members who already felt that the fiscal burden was too heavy but also with clerics and nobles who were used to being exempt from fiscal contributions due to the system of privileges. There was an especially large potential in taxing the privileged classes more because they, as opposed to the unprivileged classes, had much money and comparatively few fiscal obligations. Hence, the crown proposed new universal and more equally distributed taxes, and repeatedly relied on three recurring arguments to legitimize its demands, "[T]hat universal taxes would provide relief for the people; that they would strengthen the defense of the kingdom; and that they would fund the debt."[71] Hence, between 1695, when the *capitation* was first levied, and 1789, new taxes were proposed by the crown as a way of solving military and financial problems but also as a means of addressing social inequality. The problem, as Kwass stresses, was that even though the various universal taxes did in fact strike the nobility with considerable force, they did nothing to lighten the burden of the unprivileged, meaning that even though the relative fiscal equality between privileged and unprivileged increased, the fiscal politics simultaneously exerted "heavy fiscal pressure on commoners."[72]

The context of Mercier's future fiscal system is this eighteenth-century morass of different kinds of highly unpopular taxes. The argument underlying Mercier's chapter on taxation is that by simplifying the administrative measures of tax collection, state expenditures would decrease, and a 2% mandatory tax should be sufficient, especially if the increased fiscal liberty could simultaneously inspire the virtuous citizens to voluntarily offer more funds. Here, Mercier again places great faith in the general will or the collective morality of the people and he assumes that individuals will disregard their individual interests and act according to what Coleman calls "totalizing forces outside the self."[73] The idea of voluntary fiscal contributions may seem the most utopian of Mercier's ideas, but a number of late eighteenth-century observers made similar propositions all of them highlighting an unexploited link between voluntary fiscal contributions and the civic spirit of happy citizens. Thus, in her pamphlet *Lettre au peuple, ou projet d'une caisse patriotique; Par une citoyenne* (1788), Olympe de Gouges proposed to set up a box in which citizens could voluntarily offer whatever economic reserves they might have (Figure 3.1).

> All Citizens contributing a sum to this purse, according to their means, would inscribe their names on a register, below the sum they had remitted to the said purse. This precaution would protect us from corruption and give each contributor a chance to acknowledge the other; all Citizens would see themselves in the same mirror and this touching portrait would define both the soul, the heart and the spirit of the French.
> [...] As for Princes, Lords and the Wealthy, they will all compete to pay this voluntary tax; a suitable name is needed to better embody this tax; I would like it to be called The Patriotic Tax: no one, down to the Boarder in a Convent, would refuse to make savings and participate in this tax.[74]

Like Mercier, who was her personal acquaintance, Gouges saw unreaped economic potential in the patriotic morals of the French citizenry.[75] In her reasoning, citizens would voluntarily choose to help solve the financial problems of the state if the fiscal system was reformed. In the allegorical drawing that accompanied Gouges's proposal, the people is invited to see itself in a mirror. Similar to the case of Mercier's performative "we," there is a communitarian ambition in this image. Fénelon, and before him Machiavelli, had developed the "mirror of princes" genre with the aim of showing sovereigns an ideal

Louis-Sébastien Mercier and the Dream of a Happy Future 113

Figure 3.1 Projet de l'impot patriotique donné par Mad. e de Gouges, dans le mois de sept.re 1788: tout citoyen se verrait dans le même miroir ce portrait touchant caracteriseroit à la fois l'ame, le coeur et l'esprit français: [estampe] / Desrais inv.; Frussotte sculp. (Paris: [s.n.], 1788). Bibliothèque nationale de France.

to follow. Judith Shklar has noted that "the 'mirror of princes' has the same function as utopia: to judge the actual by confronting it with the perfect."[76] What she emphasizes is not the pedagogical side of the mirror of princes but its characteristic, and utopian, juxtaposition of reality and perfection. Gouges was an avowed monarchist and made no attempt to hide it and the community she invites her readers to join is a community of royal subjects. "The King is like a father," she writes, "whose affairs are in a mess; it is therefore an honour, a proof of love and a sign of respect for his children to willingly fly to his side to help this unfortunate parent."[77] Her understanding of patriotism is more overtly monarchical than Mercier's but they both appeal and seek to create a patriotic community.

The idea of voluntary fiscal contributions may seem "utopian" in the pejorative, unrealistic sense of the term but it actually made it all the way into the political elite. In a comment on an early version of the 1791 Constitution, the abbé Sieyès took up the interconnection between civic-mindedness and voluntary offerings. In fact, he regretted that the constitutional committee, of which he himself was a prominent member, had not dared to propose such voluntary contributions to the state as these would have demonstrated the public interest of the contributor. This again would have facilitated a distinction between those who deserved political rights and those who did not, or, in Sieyèsian terms, a distinction between active and passive citizens.

> It is nonetheless true that there are men who may be perfectly sound in a physical sense, but to whom all social ideas are remote, and who are hence not in a position to take an active part in the public weal. They should not be personally discriminated against: but who would dare to consider it wrong that they should be excluded to some extent, not, it must be repeated, from legal protection and public aid, but from the exercise of political rights? This exercise could be made to depend on a positive criterion which would be a direct voluntary contribution of a specific amount. The committee has not dared to propose such a thing to the Assembly; it has restricted itself to a direct forced contribution to the local value of three working days.
>
> If the time is not yet ripe for the general establishment of a voluntary and *civic* payment, it is nonetheless difficult not to feel that such a free gift could provide great help in a good constitution, as it could be of infinite use in defending it to some extent from dangerous influences in a situation where there is not yet a system of national education.[78]

In Sieyès, the aim is to use the voluntary contribution as a way of singling out citizens with an interest in public affairs as these are entitled to special rights. As in his reflections on active/passive citizenship, Sieyès here too pursues ways of determining who should take an active part in forming society and who should not. The "voluntary and *civic* payment" would be a way to draw the line between these two groups of people but it is also clear that Sieyès wishes to *create* this group of active

Louis-Sébastien Mercier and the Dream of a Happy Future 115

citizens. The forceful first lines of *What Is the Third Estate?* testify to the performative ambition of Sieyès.

1   What is the Third Estate? – *Everything.*
2   What, until now, has it been in the existing political order? – *Nothing.*
3   What does it want to be? – *Something.*[79]

Sieyès speaks here on behalf of the 99%, of the Third Estate, but in the earlier quotation, it is the smaller community of capable, active citizens he tries to create. Even though he is less optimistic than Mercier and Gouges about the political realism of voluntary gifts, he too thinks of them as a potential economic benefit of civic mindedness, should this virtue be allowed to blossom.[80]

As noted earlier, Michael Kwass identified three recurring ways of legitimating new universal taxes in eighteenth-century France: "[T]hat universal taxes would provide relief for the people; that they would strengthen the defense of the kingdom; and that they would fund the debt."[81] In Gouges, the proposed voluntary offerings depend partly on the third of these arguments but in general, the three suggestions take a different road. They aim to evoke a patriotic community. In the case of Gouges, this is a monarchical community brought together by the wish to aid the paternal king. Sieyès, contrarily, is a republican who tries to harvest the civic virtue and thus bring together a set of socially interested people with sufficient knowledge and capability to decide the organization of the state. Mercier lies somewhere in between in the sense that he, like Sieyès, attempts to create a learned "we" consisting of writers and readers who share a set of values and use them to fell judgment on the social miseries of his day. Like Gouges, on the other hand, Mercier, despite his revolutionary zeal, had more than a stint of royalism to him.[82] Thus, the men of the future come running in crowds whenever their "king sends forth an useful edict, that merits the public approbation." The keyword in that sentence is "useful," because it suggests that royalism is unproblematic as a form of government if only the king rules reasonably. In other words, Mercier seeks to propagate a set of values that he finds useful and reasonable and if these virtues blossom, the specific form of government matters less. Rhetorically, he uses the prophetic voice and the performative "we" of the preface to reach out to his readers and create a communitarian bond.

When he entered politics in the time of the revolution, Mercier returned to the problem of state finances. Prior to his 1792 election to the Convention, he published a public letter to the king entitled *Lettre au roi, contenant un Projet pour liquider en peu d'années toutes les dettes de l'Etat, en soulageant, dès-à-présent, le Peuple du fardeau des Impositions* (1789). It is a strange letter in which Mercier, presumably in order to position himself as a man of the people, makes the outrageous claim that he hardly knows how to read or write.[83] He also proposes the establishment of a national lottery; a lottery which, according to his sixty pages of calculations, would generate the fantastic amount of 1,045 million livres to the state. Here it bears remembering that Necker had estimated the 1781 state financial result at a surplus of mere 10.2 million livres but also that Mercier had been extremely critical of all kinds of lotteries in the *Tableau de Paris*, describing them as "bad intestines" and a contagious disease coming from Italy.[84] These oddities aside, Mercier also re-invoked his comparison between the state and a boat in stormy weather. This time, however, the competent steersman had a name:

> It is well known that the state is burdened and that the debt ties everyone together. Everyone must work to find ways of liquidating it. Nothing is simpler even though the finances right now resemble the figure of a man steering a boat that has received a bad gust of wind and is just about to sink. It is high time to come to its aid and to reassure everyone who is affected and live in incertitude. M. Necker has honorably committed himself to oblige the nation. Without any kind of self-interest, and more adroitly than any Frenchman, he takes control of the ship and steadies it.[85]

Alain Pons suggested that utopianism (the dream of a different society) collapsed into ideology (the justification of the existing society) in *L'an 2440* because Mercier embodied the "bourgeois spirit" that would crystallize in 1789 with the Declaration of Rights. In his celebration of Jacques Necker, Mercier reiterates his comparison of the state to "a vessel that plows the ocean" and he repeats the image of the competent pilot, originally summed up in the dictum "the art of the pilot is all" (258–259/224). The passage is interesting not only because it, like Figure 3.2, testifies to the popularity of Necker in 1789 but also because it reactualizes Pons's problem of utopianism and ideology in Mercier.

As the contrastive examples of Mercier, Gouges, and Sieyès show, there is no single "bourgeois spirit." Their texts are differently intoned interventions in the ongoing discussion about patriotism and taxation. Interpreting them as mere reflections of a bourgeois spirit is unsatisfying for at least two reasons. Their interventions, first, range from Gouges's explicit monarchism to Sieyès's elitist republicanism and these differences in themselves suggest that "bourgeois spirit" is too broad a term. Instead, I prefer to think of the arguments as competing claims in a struggle to set right the future of France. The different proposals, second, are characterized by a recurring ambition to performatively *create* communities bound together by differing sets of values. When Pons identifies a bourgeois spirit "behind" Mercier's contradictions, he suggests that the novel reflects a specific *Zeitgeist*, which was there in advance.[86]

Louis-Sébastien Mercier and the Dream of a Happy Future 117

Figure 3.2 Patience… ça ira : y n' faut qu' sentendre: [estampe] / [non identifié]. (Paris: [n.p.], 1789). Bibliothèque nationale de France. The angel at the bottom left is inscribing the name of Necker at the bust.

Such an interpretation misses an essential aspect of the politics of literature, an aspect especially important in the case of Mercier but also, as I shall demonstrate, in Chénier's case. These literary works aim to create communities tied together by particular sets of value. Through commercial and aesthetic strategies, they appeal to their readers and invite them to join a community founded in and through the book's outreach. This kind of literary politics has important consequences too for the relationship between literature and French revolutionary human rights, a topic I will turn to in conclusion.

* * *

L'an 2440 is clearly an imaginative piece of writing and according to Susan Maslan, it is literature's affinity with the imagination that made it an important medium in the history of human rights. Her focus is the literary genealogy of the double subject of the Declaration of the Rights of *Man* and of the *Citizen* and she explains that literature was important in making real the figure of the man-citizen: "That I turn to literature is not incidental because it is *only* in literature, only by way of the imagination, that 'man' can be made real."[87] The early modern period, she argues, generally operated with a distinction between the man of feeling and the reasonable and political citizen. Much of the importance of the Declaration of Rights lies in its juridical ratification of the feeling citizen and literature from the early modern period created visions of this figure, visions that preceded and framed the juridical work of the assembly deputies.

Mercier used the imaginary element of literature, I believe, to achieve a different goal. The political anthropology of *L'an 2440* is premised on a set of communitarian norms. In their political philosophy, Balibar and Foucault stress the intricate relationship between society and individuality and argue that social institutions model the forms of subjectivity just as the structures of society depend upon the wishes and the work of individuals and interest groups.[88] There is, in other words, an interrelation between the individual and the social and Coleman's concepts of possessive and dispossessive cultures of personhood can be regarded as the two opposite ends on a spectrum.[89] The political anthropology suggested by Mercier belongs on the communitarian side, meaning that the future citizens of Paris model their personhood on communitarian values. As the example of the bad writer (the man in a mask) suggests, Mercier's ideal citizens are discouraged from pursuing their own singular ideas and expected to abide by a set of communitarian norms. As the novel's examples of the caring woman of the *oikos* and the reasoned man of the *polis* suggest, Mercier's primary aim is not to unite the homely with the public. There are elements in Mercier's poetological writings that suggest an ideal combination of reason and sentiment but the imaginary element of his novel, I believe, lies primarily in his creation of the prophetic voice.

The prophetic voice appears first in the extradiegetic introductions to the novel but is continually developed through the narrative. The vision of the ideal future is used to cast critical light on Mercier's present and like Old Testament prophets, Mercier seeks to create a communitarian "we," a "we" that includes the reader and incarnates the Enlightened futuristic values. With the emphasis upon the prophetic voice and the performative "we," my interpretation of *L'an 2440* departs from Mercier's poetological writings. In *Du Théâtre*, Mercier argued that theater could "invincibly" arm the "forces of human reason" and throw Enlightenment on the spectators and he claimed that the dramatic art could "open the treasures of the human heart" and fill it with "pity."[90] His poetics suggest that drama should function as an intellectual and sentimental education of the spectator and these poetological ideals resonate well with Hunt's emphasis upon the empathetic education of the reader of epistolary novels.[91] His novel, however, does little to invite readers to sympathize with fictional strangers because all his characters are alike and are non-individualistic in the sense that their personhood is defined by communitarian ideals. For those reasons, I prefer to think of the politics of Mercier's novel, not as a sentimental education, and not as a vision of the imaginary man-citizen, but as an "interpellation" of the reader.[92] The performative "we" calls upon the reader and positions him or her as a subject who has understood and accepted the wisdom of the prophet. This act of interpellation differs from education because it presupposes a set of shared values between reader and book, a set of shared values whose importance and relevance of course are emphasized and developed through and with the book.

What does the rhetorical interpellation of the reader teach us about the politics of Mercier's novel? First, that the politics of literature lies not only in the development of psychological capacities or in the imaginary production of modes of subjectivity. Literature can also be political in its creation of communitarian bonds founded upon particular norms and ideals. Second, that the ideal virtues propagated by *L'an 2440* are strategically designed as interventions in current political and economic affairs. Despite its utopian, or *uchronian*, style, Mercier's novel is intended as a direct political intervention. Third, Mercier thinks and writes within an intellectual framework similar to the one that National Assembly deputies would later occupy in the Declaration Debate. His continuous dialogue with the political philosophy of Rousseau and his reliance on an engaging unhappiness/happiness dichotomy place his novel in an intellectual and artistic field that authors of fiction would often invoke and build upon in late eighteenth-century fiction. One of the writers who would explore this intellectual space to very different artistic effect was Choderlos de Laclos whose only novel is the object of the next chapter.

Notes

1 Robert Darnton, *The Forbidden Best-Sellers of Pre-Revolutionary France* (New York and London: W.W. Norton & Company, 1996), 63.
2 The authoritative source on the bibliographical aspects of *L'an 2440* is Everett C. Wilkie, Jr., "Mercier's *L'an 2440*: Its Publishing History during the Author's Lifetime" in *Harvard Library Bulletin*, Vol. 32, No. 1 (1984): 5–35 and the extended bibliography in no. 4: 348–400. Wilkie explains that Mercier, who only acknowledged his authorship of the book in 1791, repeatedly claimed that *L'an 2440* was published in 1770, despite the facts that the first known edition said 1771 on the cover and that there was no public mention of the work until 1771. The title page states London as place of publication but it was not uncommon for clandestine works to give false places of publication to throw off royal censors. Wilkie argues that the first edition was published in Amsterdam by Van Harrevelt in early 1771, meaning that Mercier either misremembered or consciously falsified the precise date of publication. Despite Wilkie's clarifying study, matters remain confusing because new, augmented, corrected, or revised editions of the work appeared frequently, with the most important textual variants being those of 1771, 1774, 1786, and 1799. By Mercier's death in 1814, Wilkie estimates that the novel had been printed in at least 63,000 copies and had been "spread thoroughly over Europe."
3 Darnton, *The Forbidden Best-Sellers*, 122.
4 In the running text, I quote from the 1795 English translation of *L'an 2440*: Louis-Sébastien Mercier, *Memoirs of the Year Two Thousand Five Hundred*. Trans. W. Hooper (Philadelphia: Thomas Dobson, 1795). Because of

the freedom of this translation, I also refer to the 1999 La Découverte/Poche French edition of the 1771 version of the book, edited by Christophe Cave and Christine Marcandier. The first page reference is to the English text, the second one to the French original.
5 Bronislaw Baczko, *Utopian Lights: The Evolution of the Idea of Social Progress*. Trans. J. L. Greenberg (New York: Paragon House, 1989), 28; 123.
6 Darnton, *The Forbidden Best-Sellers*, 118.
7 Darnton, *The Forbidden Best-Sellers*, 118.
8 Shelly Charles, "Écrivain journaliste" in J.-C. Bonnet (ed.), *Louis Sébastien Mercier: un hérétique en littérature* (Paris: Mercure de France, 1995), 102.
9 Anthony Vidler, "Mercier urbaniste: l'utopie du réel" in Bonnet (ed.), *Louis Sébastien Mercier*, 237.
10 Joanna Stalnaker, *The Unfinished Enlightenment: Description in the Age of the Encyclopedia* (Ithaca and London: Cornell University Press, 2010), 170.
11 M. Demeunier, *Encyclopédie méthodique. Economie politique et diplomatique* (Paris, 1784–1788), IV: 814. Quoted from Baczko, *Utopian Lights*, 23.
12 1 August 1789, M. Delandine in *Archives parlementaires de 1787 à 1860* (Paris: Librairie administrative de P. Dupont, 1862–),324/Antoine de Baecque, Wolfgang Schmale, and Michel Vovelle (eds.), *L'an 1 des droits de l'homme* (Paris: Presses du CNRS, 1988), 108.
13 *Déclaration des droits de l'homme et du citoyen* in Baecque et al. (eds.), *L'an 1*, 198.
14 Lynn Hunt, *Inventing Human Rights: A History* (New York and London: W. W. Norton & Company, 2008), 35–70.
15 Hunt, *Inventing Human Rights*, 19.
16 Baczko, *Utopian Lights*, 15.
17 Miguel Abensour, "Persistante utopie," *Moribus* 1 "Utopie de Marché" (2006), 38. Bazko makes a similar observation in Baczko, *Utopian Lights*, 17.
18 Louis-Sébastien Mercier, *Néologie* (Paris: Chez Moussard et Maradan, an IX), 266. Entry translated in Baczko, *Utopian Lights*, 23.
19 Mercier, *Néologie*, ix–x.
20 I am thinking here of Max Horkheimer and Theodor Adorno, *Dialectic of Enlightenment: Philosophical Fragments*. Trans. E. Jephcott (Stanford: Stanford University Press, 2002).
21 For discussions of utopia/dystopia see Baczko, *Utopian Lights*, 127; Darnton, *The Forbidden Best-Sellers*, 136; Riikka Forsström, *Possible Worlds: The Idea of Happiness in the Utopian Vision of Louis-Sébastien Mercier*. (Helsinki: Suomalaisen Kirjallisuuden Seura, 2002), 28.
22 Montesquieu, *Persian Letters*. Trans. M. Mauldon (Oxford: Oxford University Press, 2008); Voltaire, *The Ingenu* in Voltaire, *Candide and Other Stories*. Trans. R. Pearson (Oxford: Oxford University Press, 2008).
23 François de Fénelon, *Telemachus, Son of Ulysses*. Trans. P. Riley (Cambridge: Cambridge University Press, 1994).
24 Voltaire, *Candide and Other Stories*.
25 Mercier was not the first to write a temporal utopia Forsström 55–56; Baczko 122–123; Alain Pons, "Préface" in Louis-Sébastien Mercier, *L'an 2440* (Paris: France adel, 1977), 12–13.
26 Frank E. Manuel and Fritzie P. Manuel, *Utopian Thought in the Western World* (Oxford: Basil Blackwell, 1979), 458; Baczko, *Utopian Lights*, 123. Pons is critical of this genre label, cf. Pons, "Préface" in Mercier, *L'an 2440*, 13–14.
27 There is a large literature on *The Sketch*. A good place to begin is Keith Michael Baker, *Cordorcet: From Natural Philosophy to Social Mathematics* (Chicago and London: The University of Chicago Press, 1975), 343–383.

Louis-Sébastien Mercier and the Dream of a Happy Future 121

28 Marquis de Condorcet, *The Sketch* in Marquis de Condorcet, *Political Writings*. Eds. S. Lukes and N. Urbinati. (Cambridge: Cambridge University Press, 2012), 6.
29 Condorcet, *The Sketch* in Condorcet, *Political Writings*, 6.
30 Condorcet, *The Sketch* in Condorcet, *Political Writings*, 125.
31 Baczko, *Utopian Lights*, 144.
32 The epithet is taken from § 22 of Leibnitz' *Monadology*: "Et comme tout present état d'une substance simple est naturellement une suite de son état precedent, tellement le present y est gros de l'avenir." Gottfried Wilhelm Leibniz, *G. W. Leibniz's Monadology: An Edition for Students*. Ed. N. Rescher (Pittsburgh: University of Pittsburgh Press, 1991), 96.
33 Pons, "Préface" in Mercier, *L'an 2440*, 24–25.
34 For an inspiring discussion of the prophetic voice in literature, see Isak Winkel Holm, "Drawing the Line: zombies and citizens in Heinrich von Kleist's 'The Earthquake in Chile'" in K.-M. Simonsen and J. R. Kjærgård (eds.), *Discursive Framings of Human Rights: Negotiating Agency and Victimhood* (Oxon and New York: Birckbeck Law Press, 2017), 169–182. For the idea that the Old Testament Prophets are "social critics," see also Michael Walzer, *In God's Shadow: Politics in the Hebrew Bible* (New Haven and London: Yale University Press, 2012), 86.
35 Darnton, *The Forbidden Best-Sellers*, 133.
36 Louis Sébastien Mercier, *Mon bonnet de nuit suivi de Du théâtre*. Ed. J.-C. Bonnet (Paris: Mercure de France, 1999), 1147.
37 Louis-Sébastien Mercier, *Tableau de Paris* (Paris: Mercure de France, 1994), volume I: 14. Translation taken from Stalnaker, *The Unfinished Enlightenment*, 161.
38 Darnton, *The Forbidden Best-Sellers*, 118.
39 Stalnaker, *The Unfinished Enlightenment*, 169.
40 Roger Chartier, *The Cultural Origins of the French Revolution*. Trans. L. G. Cochrane (Durham and London: Duke University Press, 1991), 83.
41 Vidler, "Mercier urbaniste" in Bonnet (ed.), *Louis Sébastien Mercier*, 230.
42 Montesquieu presents his climate theory in books fourteen to seventeen of *The Spirit of the Laws* (1748). Diderot, among many others, expresses similar ideas, e.g., in Denis Diderot, *Observations sur le Nakaz* in Denis Diderot, *Political Writings*. Eds. J. H. Mason and R. Wokler (Cambridge: Cambridge University Press, 2005), 77–165.
43 The idea of Asian despotism and its dependence on climate and geography is expressed, e.g., in Book 17, Chapter 6:

> In Asia one has always seen great empires; in Europe they were never able to continue to exist. This is because the Asia we know has broader plains; it is cut into larger parts by seas; and, as it is more to the south, its streams dry up more easily, its mountains are less covered with snow, and its smaller rivers form slighter barriers. / Therefore, power should always be despotic in Asia. For if servitude there were not extreme, there would immediately be a division that the nature of the country cannot endure.
> Charles-Louis de Secondat Montesquieu, *The Spirit of the Laws*. Trans. A. M. Cohler, B. C. Miller and H. S. Stone (Cambridge: Cambridge University Press, 2011), 283

44 As is the case with his political philosophy, Mercier's view on women may be inspired by Rousseau who expressed similar ideas. E.g., in *Lettre à M. d'Alembert*: "Somewhere in the world there may be some women worthy of being listened to by an honest man; but is it from them, in general, that he must take counsel, and will there be no way of honoring their sex, unless we

degrade our own?" Jean-Jacques Rousseau, *Lettre à M. D'Alembert sur les spectacles* in *Œuvres complètes*. Vol. 5. Eds. B. Gagnebin and M. Raymond (Paris: Gallimard, 1995), 44. In opposition to Mercier's view on women's rights is Condorcet who, in his uchronia, writes,

> Among the causes of the progress of the human mind that are of the utmost importance to the general happiness, we must number the complete annihilation of the prejudices that have brought about an inequality of rights between the sexes, an inequality fatal even to the party in whose favour it works. It is vain for us to look for a justification of this principle in any differences of physical organization, intellect or moral sensibility between men and women. This inequality has its origin solely in an abuse of strength, and all the later sophisticated attempts that have been made to excuse it are vain.
> (Condorcet, *The Sketch* in Condorcet, *Political Writings*, 140–141)

45 Étienne Balibar, *Equaliberty: Political Essays*. Trans. J. Ingram (Durham and London: Duke University Press, 2014), 106.
46 Jean-Jacques Rousseau, *Of the Social Contract* in Jean-Jacques Rousseau, *The Social Contract and Other Later Political Writings*. Ed. V. Gourevitch (Cambridge: Cambridge University Press, 2012), 50.
47 Rousseau, *Of the Social Contract* in Rousseau, *The Social Contract*, 49–50.
48 Condorcet, *The Sketch*, 140. See also Baczko, 151–152.
49 Darnton, *The Forbidden Best-Sellers*, 135.
50 *Declaration of the Rights of Man and Citizen* in Hunt, *Inventing Human Rights*, 222. My italicization.
51 John Bosher, "Introduction" in Jean Egret, *The French Prerevolution 1787–1788*. Trans. W. D. Camp (Chicago and London: The University of Chicago Press, 1977), viii.
52 William Doyle, "The Parlements" in K. M. Baker, (ed.), *The French Revolution and the Creation of Modern Political Culture*. Vol. 1 (Oxford: Pergamon Press, 1987), 157–158.
53 Keith Michael Baker, *Inventing the French Revolution: Essays on French Political Culture in the Eighteenth Century* (Cambridge: Cambridge University Press, 1990), 139.
54 For the idea that parlements function as a "counterweight to despotic government in France," see Michael Kwass, *Privilege and the Politics of Taxation in Eighteenth Century France: Liberté, Égalité, Fiscalité* (Cambridge: Cambridge University Press, 2000), 194.
55 Denis Diderot *Œuvres politiques*. Ed. P. Vernière (Paris: Éditions Garnier Frères, 1963), 241. The quote is commented (and translated into English) in Baker, *Inventing the French Revolution*, 140.
56 Charly Coleman, *The Virtues of Abandon: An Anti-Individualist History of the French Enlightenment* (Stanford: Stanford University Press, 2014), 3.
57 Pons, "Préface" in Mercier, *L'an 2440*, 26. Pons refers to Karl Mannheim's classic *Ideologie und Utopie* (1929).
58 Pons, "Préface" in Mercier, *L'an 2440*, 28–29.
59 The paradigmatic shift from a Marxist, social, and economic interpretation to one centered on discourse and political culture has been repeatedly described in the research literature. For a good introduction to the shift, see, e.g., William Doyle, *Origins of the French Revolution*. 2nd edition (Oxford: Oxford University Press, 1990), 7–41.
60 For such spielverderber arguments see, e.g., George V. Taylor, "Types of Capitalism in Eighteenth-Century France" *English Historical Reviews*,

Vol. 79, No. 312 (1964): 478–497; George V. Taylor, "Noncapitalist Wealth and the Origins of the French Revolution" in *The American Historical Review*, Vol. 72, No. 2 (1967): 469–496 and David D. Bien, "Old Regime Origins of Democratic Liberty" in D. Van Kley (ed.), *The French Idea of Freedom: The Old Regime and the Declaration of Rights of 1789* (Stanford: Stanford University Press, 1994), 23–72.
61 Michael Kwass puts it well:

> The turn toward revolutionary political culture produced a rich body of literature, but there is mounting concern that the pendulum has swung too far from the question of capitalism and the everyday experiences of material life. Fundamental economic problems have been pushed aside, resulting in a 'separation of economic history from cultural and political history [that] is positively harmful to both.' It is time to reverse this process of fragmentation; to reintegrate economic, political, and cultural histories of the period; and to reconsider the conditions under which the old regime state collapsed.

Michael Kwass, *Contraband: Louis Mandrin and the Making of a Global Underground* (Cambridge and London: Harvard University Press, 2014), 6. See also Michael Sonenscher, *Before the Deluge: Public Debt, Inequality, and the Intellectual Origins of the French Revolution* (Princeton and Oxford: Princeton University Press, 2007), esp. 20–21; Gail Bossenga, "Financial Origins of the French Revolution" in T. E. Kaiser and D. K. Van Kley (eds.), *From Deficit to Deluge: The Origins of the French Revolution* (Stanford: Stanford University Press, 2011): 37–67.
62 I have addressed this issue in Jonas Ross Kjærgård, "Representation and Taxation: Fiscality, Human Rights and the French Revolution" in M. Thorup (ed.), *Intellectual History of Economic Normativities* (New York: Palgrave MacMillan, 2016), 107–123.
63 *Declaration of the Rights of Man and Citizen* in Hunt, *Inventing Human Rights*, 222.
64 Beatrice Fry Hyslop, *French Nationalism in 1789 according to the General Cahiers* (New York: Columbia University Press, 1934), 84.
65 Jacques Necker, *Compte rendu au Roi* (Paris: de l'imprimerie royale, 1781), 10; Charles-Alexandre de Calonne, *Discours prononcé de l'ordre du roi et en sa présence par M. De Calonne, contrôleur général des finances, dans l'Assemblée des notables, tenue à Versailles, le 22 février 1787* (Versailles: Ph.-D.- Pierres, 1787), 18–19.
66 Jacques Necker, *Réponse au discours prononcé par Mr. de Calonne a l'assemblée des Notables*. ([n.p.]: [n.p.], [1787]), 24.
67 Necker, *Compte rendu*, 114.
68 Calonne, *Discours prononcé*, 20. The Necker/Calonne-controversy has been described in great detail elsewhere, see, e.g., Égret, *The French Prerevolution*, 1–31; Jean Egret, *Necker: Ministre de Louis XVI 1776–1790* (Paris: Librairie Honoré Champion, 1975), 162–214; Robert D. Harris, *Necker: Reform Statesman of the Ancien Régime.* (Berkeley: University of California Press, 1979), 217–236; Kwass, *Privilege and the Politics of Taxation*, 213–252; John Shovlin, *The Political Economy of Virtue: Luxury, Patriotism, and the Origins of the French Revolution.* (Ithaca and London: Cornell University Press, 2007), Chapters 4 and 5, esp. 142–159; Jacob Soll, *The Reckoning: Financial Accountability and the Rise and Fall of Nations* (New York: Basic Books, 2014), 132–147.
69 Soll, *The Reckoning*, 146. Regarding the significance of the miscalculations, John Bosher writes,

Such able ministers as Necker and Calonne failed in the attempt to see clearly enough to plan properly, and they revealed the shortcomings of the system incidentally in their writings, especially in the course of their public quarrel in 1787 and the years following. One of the few sound conclusions to be drawn from that quarrel is that neither had been able to get a grip on the financial administration – 'cette immense machine', as they both described it with awe.

John Bosher, *French Finances 1770–1795: From Business to Bureaucracy* (Cambridge: Cambridge University Press, 1970), 43–44.
70 The best account of French eighteenth century taxation is Kwass, *Privilege and the Politics of Taxation*. Among other useful sources are: Richard Bonney, "The State and its Revenues in *ancien-régime* France," *Historical Research* 65, (1992): 150–176; Richard Bonney, "France, 1485–1815" in Richard Bonney, ed., *The Rise of the Fiscal State in Europe, c. 1200–1815* (New York: Oxford University Press, 1999), 123–177; Gail Bossenga, "Taxes" in François Furet and Mona Ozouf, *A Critical Dictionary of the French Revolution*. Translated by Arthur Goldhammer (Cambridge and London: The Belknapp Press of Harvard University Press, 1989), 582–591; Bossenga, "Financial Origins" in Kaiser and Van Kley (eds.), *From Deficit to Deluge*, 37–67.
71 Kwass, *Privilege and the Politics of Taxation*, 43.
72 Kwass, *Privilege and the Politics of Taxation*, 66.
73 Coleman, *The Virtues of Abandon*, 4.
74 Olympe de Gouges, "Lettre au peuple, ou projet d'une caisse patriotique; Par une citoyenne" *Écrits politiques 1788–1791* (Paris: côté-femmes, 1993), 42–43. I have used Clarissa Palmer's English translation available online: www.olympedegouges.eu/index.php [page last visited on 20 December 2017].
75 Forsström, *Possible Worlds*, 43. Gouges defends Mercier against critics in Olympe de Gouges, "Réflexions sur les hommes nègres" postface to Olympe de Gouges, *Zamore et Mirza; ou l'heureux naufrage* (Paris: [n.p.], 1788), 98.
76 Judith N. Shklar, *Men & Citizens: A Study of Rousseau's Social Theory* (Cambridge: Cambridge University Press, 1985), 4.
77 Gouges, *Lettre au peuple* in Gouges, *Écrits politiques 1788–1791*, 41.
78 Emmanuel-Joseph Sieyès, *Observations sur le rapport du Comité de constitution sur la nouvelle organisation de la France* in Emmanuel-Joseph Sieyès, *Écrits politiques* (Paris: éditions des archives contemporaines, 1985), 255. The translation of the quote comes from Murray Forsyth, *Reason and Revolution: The Political Thought of Abbé Sieyes* (New York: Leicester University Press 1987), 162–163.
79 Emmanuel Joseph Sieyès, *What Is the Third Estate?* In Emmanuel Joseph Sieyès, *Political Writings*. Ed. M. Sonenscher (Indianapolis/Cambridge: Hackett Publishing Company, Inc., 2003), 94.
80 As a final example of the interrelation between morals and voluntary taxes, Madame de Staël would claim, in her *De L'Allemagne* (1813–1814), that such a voluntary fiscal system had already been in place in Hamburg: "The charitable enterprises must prosper in the city of Hamburg. Morals are so high among its inhabitants that they have long paid the taxes in a kind of trunk without anyone has ever kept a record of how much people paid. These taxes were proportional to everyone's fortune and, when calculations have been made, payments have always been exactly right. Isn't it like hearing a story from the golden age if, that is, they had had any private wealth and public taxes in the golden age?" (Madame de Staël, *De l'Allemagne* (New York: Roe Lockwood & Son, 1860), 118.)

81 Kwass, *Privilege and the Politics of Taxation*, 43.
82 According to Darnton, "Mercier's text actually throbs with monarchist sentiment" (Darnton, *The Forbidden Best-sellers*, 126).
83 Louis-Sébastien Mercier, *Lettre au roi, contenant un Projet pour liquider en peu d'années toutes les dettes de l'Etat, en soulageant, dès-à-présent, le Peuple du fardeau des Impositions* (Amsterdam: les Marchands de Nouveautés, 1789), 3.
84 Louis-Sébastien Mercier, *Tableau de Paris*. Ed. J.-C. Bonnet (Paris: Mercure de France, 1994), vol. I: 690.
85 Mercier, *Lettre au roi*, 100–101.
86 Pons, "Préface" in Mercier, *L'an 2440*, 28.
87 Susan Maslan, "The Anti-Human: Man and Citizen before the Declaration of the Rights of Man and of the Citizen" in *The South Atlantic Quarterly*, Vol. 103, No. 2/3 (2004), 363.
88 Michel Foucault, "Le sujet et le pouvoir" in *Dits et écrits II. 1976–1988* (Paris: Gallimard 2001), 1041–1062; Étienne Balibar, *Equaliberty: Political Essays*. Trans. J. Ingram (Durham and London: Duke University Press, 2014), 107–108.
89 Coleman, *The Virtues of Abandon*, 1–17.
90 Mercier, Mon bonnet de nuit, 1131; 1131; 1147; 1147.
91 Hunt, *Inventing Human Rights*, 35–70.
92 The concept of interpellation was suggested to great effect by Louis Althusser in "Ideology and Ideological State Apparatuses" (1979). Available in English translation online: www.marxists.org/reference/archive/althusser/1970/ideology.htm [page last visited 11 January 2018].

Literature

Abensour, Miguel: "Persistante utopie," *Moribus* 1 "Utopie de Marché" (2006): 37–58.

Althusser, Louis: "Ideology and Ideological State Apparatuses." Available in English translation online: www.marxists.org/reference/archive/althusser/1970/ideology.htm [page last visited 11 January 2018].

Archives parlementaires de 1787 à 1860. Paris: Librairie administrative de P. Dupont, 1862–.

Baczko, Bronislaw: *Utopian Lights: The Evolution of the Idea of Social Progress*. Trans. by J. L. Greenberg. New York: Paragon House, 1989.

Baecque, Antoine de Wolfgang Schmale, and Michel Vovelle, (eds.): *L'an 1 des droits de l'homme*. Paris: Presses du CNRS, 1988.

Baker, Keith Michael: *Cordorcet: From Natural Philosophy to Social Mathematics*. Chicago and London: The University of Chicago Press, 1975.

Baker, Keith Michael: *Inventing the French Revolution: Essays on French Political Culture in the Eighteenth Century*. Cambridge: Cambridge University Press, 1990.

Balibar, Étienne: *Equaliberty: Political Essays*. Trans. James Ingram. Durham, NC and London: Duke University Press, 2014.

Bien, David D.: "Old Regime Origins of Democratic Liberty" in D. Van Kley, (ed.), *The French Idea of Freedom: The Old Regime and the Declaration of Rights of 1789*. Stanford: Stanford University Press, 1994.

Bonnet, Jean-Claude (ed.): *Louis Sébastien Mercier: un hérétique en littérature*. Paris: Mercure de France, 1995.

Bonney, Richard: "France, 1485–1815" in R. Bonney (ed.), *The Rise of the Fiscal State in Europe, c. 1200–1815*. New York: Oxford University Press, 1999: 123–177

Bonney, Richard: "The State and Its Revenues in *ancien-régime* France." *Historical Research*, Vol. 65 (1992): 150–176.

Bosher, John: *French Finances 1770–1795: From Business to Bureaucracy*. Cambridge: Cambridge University Press, 1970.

Bossenga, Gail: "Financial Origins of the French Revolution" in T. E. Kaiser and D. K. Van Kley (eds.), *From Deficit to Deluge: The Origins of the French Revolution*. Stanford: Stanford University Press, 2011: 37–67.

Bossenga, Gail: "Taxes" in F. Furet and M. Ozouf (eds.), *A Critical Dictionary of the French Revolution*. Trans. A. Goldhammer. Cambridge and London: The Belknapp Press of Harvard University Press, 1989.

Calonne, Charles-Alexandre de: *Discours prononcé de l'ordre du roi et en sa présence par M. De Calonne, contrôleur général des finances, dans l'Assemblée des notables, tenue à Versailles, le 22 février 1787*. Versailles: Ph.-D.-Pierres, 1787.

Chartier, Roger: *The Cultural Origins of the French Revolution*. Trans. L. G. Cochrane. Durham and London: Duke University Press, 1991.

Coleman, Charly: *The Virtues of Abandon: An Anti-Individualist History of the French Enlightenment*. Stanford: Stanford University Press, 2014.

Condorcet, Marquis de: *Political Writings*. Eds. S. Lukes and N. Urbinati. Cambridge: Cambridge University Press, 2012.

Darnton, Robert: *The Forbidden Best-Sellers of Pre-Revolutionary France*. New York and London: W.W. Norton & Company, 1996.

Diderot, Denis: *Œuvres politiques*. Ed. P. Vernière. Paris: Éditions Garnier Frères, 1963.

Diderot, Denis: "Observations sur le Nakaz" in *Political Writings*. Eds. J. H. Mason and R. Wokler. Cambridge: Cambridge University Press, 2005.

Doyle, William: *Origins of the French Revolution*. 2nd edition. Oxford: Oxford University Press, 1990.

Doyle, William: "The Parlements" in K. M. Baker (ed.), *The French Revolution and the Creation of Modern Political Culture*, vol. 1. Oxford: Pergamon Press, 1987.

Egret, Jean: *Necker: Ministre de Louis XVI 1776–1790*. Paris: Librairie Honoré Champion, 1975.

Egret, Jean: *The French Prerevolution 1787–1788*. Trans. W. D. Camp. Chicago and London: The University of Chicago Press, 1977.

Fénelon, François de: *Telemachus, Son of Ulysses*. Trans. P. Riley. Cambridge: Cambridge University Press, 1994.

Forsström, Riikka: *Possible Worlds: The Idea of Happiness in the Utopian Vision of Louis-Sébastien Mercier*. Helsinki: Suomalaisen Kirjallisuuden Seura, 2002.

Forsyth, Murray: *Reason and Revolution: The Political Thought of Abbé Sieyes*. New York: Leicester University Press 1987.

Foucault, Michel: "Le sujet et le pouvoir" in *Dits et écrits II. 1976–1988*. Paris: Gallimard, 2001.

Gouges, Olympe de: *Écrits politiques 1788–1791*. Paris: côté-femmes, 1993.

Gouges, Olympe de: "Letter to the People, or Patriotic Purse Project." Trans. C. Palmer. Online: www.olympedegouges.eu/index.php [page last visited on 20 December 2017].

Gouges, Olympe de: *Zamore et Mirza; ou l'heureux naufrage*. Paris: [n.p.], 1788.

Harris, Robert D.: *Necker: Reform Statesman of the Ancien Régime*. Berkeley: University of California Press, 1979.

Holm, Isak Winkel: "Drawing the Line: zombies and citizens in Heinrich von Kleist's 'The Earthquake in Chile'" in K.-M. Simonsen and J. R. Kjærgård (eds.), *Discursive Framings of Human Rights: Negotiating Agency and Victimhood*. Oxon and New York: Birckbeck Law Press, 2017.

Horkheimer, Max and Theodor Adorno: *Dialectic of Enlightenment: Philosophical Fragments*. Trans. E. Jephcott. Stanford: Stanford University Press, 2002.

Hunt, Lynn: *Inventing Human Rights: A History*. New York and London: W. W. Norton & Company, 2008.

Hyslop, Beatrice Fry: *French Nationalism in 1789 According to the General Cahiers*. New York: Columbia University Press, 1934.

Kjærgård, Jonas Ross: "Representation and Taxation: Fiscality, Human Rights and the French Revolution" in M. Thorup (ed.), *Intellectual History of Economic Normativities*. New York: Palgrave MacMillan, (2016): 107–123.

Kwass, Michael: *Contraband: Louis Mandrin and the Making of a Global Underground*. Cambridge and London: Harvard University Press, 2014.

Kwass, Michael: *Privilege and the Politics of Taxation in Eighteenth Century France: Liberté, Égalité, Fiscalité*. Cambridge: Cambridge University Press, 2000.

Leibniz, Gottfried Wilhelm: *G. W. Leibniz's Monadology: An Edition for Students*. Ed. N. Rescher. Pittsburgh: University of Pittsburgh Press, 1991.

Manuel, Frank E. and Fritzie P. Manuel: *Utopian Thought in the Western World*. Oxford: Basil Blackwell, 1979.

Maslan, Susan: "The Anti-Human: Man and Citizen before the Declaration of the Rights of Man and of the Citizen." *The South Atlantic Quarterly*, Vol. 103, No. 2/3 (2004): 357–374.

Mercier, Louis-Sébastien: *L'an 2440. Rêve s'il en fut jamais*. Eds. C. Cave and C. Marcandier. Paris: La Découverte/Poche, 1999.

Mercier, Louis-Sébastien: *Lettre au roi, contenant un Projet pour liquider en peu d'années toutes les dettes de l'Etat, en soulageant, dès-à-présent, le Peuple du fardeau des Impositions*. Amsterdam: les Marchands de Nouveautés, 1789.

Mercier, Louis-Sébastien: *Memoirs of the Year Two Thousand Five Hundred*. Trans. W. Hooper. Philadelphia: Thomas Dobson, 1795.

Mercier, Louis Sébastien: *Mon bonnet de nuit suivi de Du théâtre*. Ed. J.-C. Bonnet. Paris: Mercure de France, 1999.

Mercier, Louis-Sébastien: *Tableau de Paris I-II*. Paris: Mercure de France, 1994.

Mercier, Louis-Sébastien: *Néologie*. Paris: Chez Moussard et Maradan, an IX.

Mercier, Louis Sébastien and Restif de la Bretonne: *Paris le jour, Paris la nuit*. Eds. M. Delon and D. Baruch. Paris: Éditions Robert Laffont S. A., 2006.

Montesquieu, Charles-Louis de Secondat: *Persian Letters*. Trans. M. Mauldon. Oxford: Oxford University Press, 2008.

Montesquieu, Charles-Louis de Secondat: *The Spirit of the Laws*. Trans. A. M. Cohler, B. C. Miller and H. S. Stone. Cambridge: Cambridge University Press, 2011.

Necker, Jacques: *Compte rendu au Roi.* Paris: de l'imprimerie royale, 1781.

Necker, Jacques: *Réponse au discours prononcé par Mr. de Calonne a l'assemblée des Notables.* [n.p.]: [n.p.], [1787].

Pons, Alain: "Préface" in Louis-Sébastien Mercier, *L'an 2440.* Paris: France adel, 1977.

Rousseau, Jean-Jacques: "Lettre à M. D'Alembert sur les spectacles" in B. Gagnebin and M. Raymond (eds.), *Œuvres complètes,* vol. V. Paris: Gallimard, 1995.

Rousseau, Jean-Jacques: *The Social Contract and Other Later Political Writings.* Ed. V. Gourevitch. Cambridge: Cambridge University Press, 2012.

Shklar, Judith N.: *Men & Citizens: A Study of Rousseau's Social Theory.* Cambridge: Cambridge University Press, 1985.

Shovlin, John: *The Political Economy of Virtue: Luxury, Patriotism, and the Origins of the French Revolution.* Ithaca and London: Cornell University Press, 2007

Sieyès, Emmanuel-Joseph: *Écrits politiques.* Paris: éditions des archives contemporaines, 1985.

Sieyès, Emmanuel Joseph: *Political Writings.* Ed. M. Sonenscher. Indianapolis/Cambridge: Hackett Publishing Company, Inc., 2003.

Soll, Jacob: *The Reckoning: Financial Accountability and the Rise and Fall of Nations.* New York: Basic Books, 2014.

Sonenscher, Michael: *Before the Deluge: Public Debt, Inequality, and the Intellectual Origins of the French Revolution.* Princeton and Oxford: Princeton University Press, 2007.

Staël, Madame de: *De l'Allemagne.* New York: Roe Lockwood & Son, 1860.

Stalnaker, Joanna: *The Unfinished Enlightenment: Description in the Age of the Encyclopedia.* Ithaca and London: Cornell University Press, 2010.

Taylor, George V.: "Noncapitalist Wealth and the Origins of the French Revolution." *The American Historical Review,* Vol. 72, No. 2 (1967): 469–496.

Taylor, George V.: "Types of Capitalism in Eighteenth-Century France." *English Historical Reviews,* Vol. 79, No. 312 (1964): 478–497.

Voltaire: *Candide and Other Stories.* Trans. R. Pearson. Oxford: Oxford University Press, 2008.

Walzer, Michael: *In God's Shadow: Politics in the Hebrew Bible.* New Haven and London: Yale University Press, 2012.

Wilkie, Jr., Everett C.: "Mercier's *L'an 2440*: Its Publishing History during the Author's Lifetime." *Harvard Library Bulletin,* Vol. 32, No. 1 (1984): 5–35.

4 The Search for Order in Choderlos de Laclos's *Liaisons dangereuses*

True to eighteenth-century literary conventions, the narrative of *Les liaisons dangereuses* (1782) is preceded by a "Publisher's note" *and* an "Editor's preface."[1] More or less imaginatively, early modern authors used prefaces for multiple reasons, some of the recurring ones being fake claims of authenticity, recommendations from persons of authority, or self-positioning *vis-à-vis* the reading public. In *Les liaisons dangereuses*, Laclos inventively presents a fictional editor and plays him out against an equally fictional publisher. The publisher initially warns the reader of the feigned authenticity that he or she will confront in the narrative by stating that he has "compelling reasons to believe it is simply a novel" (3). According to this feigned publisher, the author has outright disproved the narrative's claim to "verisimilitude" by disingenuously placing persons of such "vicious habits [mauvaises mœurs]" in this "age of philosophy" (3 [13]). However, in immediate succession of the publisher's anti-authenticity note, the editor relates that in assembling the letters, his only mission was to "put in order" (4) the various letters. In other words, he has received an enormous written correspondence between actual people and has been charged with the task of publishing a work which is both useful and pleasurable. To accomplish this task, he has had to do what any author does, namely, omit certain unimportant details, insert notes wherever necessary, change the real-life names of the characters, and make sure that everything finds "its proper place [sa place]" (7 [11]). In this humorous and complex juxtaposition of feigned and contested authenticity claims, what exactly does it mean to place letters, people, events, and things in their right order?

I argue that the extradiegetic search for compositional order is paralleled by an intradiegetic search for social order. By social order, I mean a situation in which hierarchies and modes of interaction are transparent and in which the forms of subjectivity are stable and reliable. I mean, in other words, a durable social world very different from the scheming, lying, and manipulating *monde* of the novel. This search for the right order, however, remains fundamentally unsuccessful in Laclos's case, and there are good reasons for that. Whereas Mercier assumed the task of giving a full description of the perfect future society in his philosophical novel, the ambition of Laclos is different and, as the contradictory prefaces indicate, openly ambivalent. His aim is to diagnose the depravity of late Old Regime elite society by demonstrating its inability to procure a stable set of social norms. Different forms of social interaction, with each their own codes of conduct and each their own forms of happiness, are played out against each other throughout the narrative but in a way that makes their mutual destruction inevitable. In 1780s France, the elite society of the upper aristocracy was in crisis, but in the novel, the threat to elite society is not an external force (a rising bourgeoisie or an egalitarian philosophy) but rather an internal inability to live according to existing worldly mores.[2] I read the novel as a search for a stable form of sociality but as a fundamentally unsuccessful one. There is a longing but no solution in Laclos. He uses the epistolary novel to investigate the nature of sociality at a time when traditional forms of interaction are crumbling without new ones having gained ground, and he diagnoses – to great literary success – the systemic inability to establish a lasting social order.

With its focus on sociality and politics, my reading adds to the enormous literature on Laclos.[3] The formal complexity of the novel in combination with its piquant thematics has attracted scholars whose readings can be associated sometimes firmly, sometimes loosely with traditions influenced by phenomenology,[4] structuralism,[5] reader-response theory,[6] deconstruction,[7] and the tradition of *explication de texte*.[8] Feminist readings have examined gender relations in the novel;[9] genre historians have added a historical dimension to the study of Laclos's usage of the epistolary format;[10] and cultural historians have noted his invocation of, among other things, furniture, weights, and measures in the novel.[11] Most recently, these readings have been supplemented by translation studies and analyses of the novel's theatrical and filmic appropriations.[12] My reading takes particular inspiration from the studies of Peter Brooks and Susan Winnett, who have demonstrated the importance of manners and forms of interpersonal and amorous relations in the novel.[13] I want, however, to link the study of social relations to the historical and political problems that are treated throughout this book.

Because of its textual ambivalence and critical social diagnosis, Laclos's novel might seem a strange *case* in this study of literary attempts to reimagine a new, happy French society. The aim of Laclos, it seems to me, is not to construct society anew but to destroy what he feels to be already corrupted. The politics of literature, however, does not reside solely in imaginative creations of new worlds. *Les Liaisons* is more concerned with breaking down and with inviting the reader to reflect upon social corruption than with constructing society anew or with proposing alternative forms of subjectivity. That does not mean, though, that the agenda of the novel is unconcerned with the political discussions about happiness and human rights. Laclos's work repeatedly invokes the concepts of *bonheur* and *droit* in sometimes atypical and even perverse ways.[14] As I will demonstrate, his critical diagnosis of elite society uses the intellectual and discursive framework that parliamentary deputies would revisit during the 1789 Declaration Debate. By showcasing this proximity between the vocabulary of the deputies and that of Laclos, and by analyzing the political implications of his interest in social forms, I hope to add to the relatively understudied political dimensions of his novel and to the greater cultural historical question of the politics of intimate relations in the years preceding the French revolution.[15]

Before I turn to the different rhythms and hierarchies of various forms of social interaction in the novel, and before I zoom in on its search for social order, I want to begin by explaining my understanding of the novel's social interest and the politics of sociality in this period.

The Politics of Social Forms

The French revolution entailed all-encompassing changes in French society. While clear analytical distinctions between, say, the moral, political, and economic spheres of French revolutionary culture can create order in the messiness of history, such distinctions also run the risk of oversimplifying the interconnectedness of various social phenomena. In *The Family on Trial in Revolutionary France*, Suzanne Desan emphasizes the necessity of analyzing the questions of domesticity, family, and gender roles as these are shaped by, and, in turn, give shape to, the simultaneous changes in state politics. "The Revolution," she argues, "transformed the most intimate relationships and challenged the patriarchal structure of Old Regime families," but "remaking the family and gender relationships was [also] integral to forging the revolutionary state and politics."[16] State politics and family patterns were embedded in one another, and to analyze them separately is to miss the degree to which "the family acted as the crucial matrix – natural, moral, and legal – that linked each individual to the new nation-state."[17] The premise of my political reading of *Les liaisons dangereuses* is the existence of such an interconnection of politics, family formation, and forms of social interaction.

By forms of social interaction, I mean the recurring patterns that direct the actions of the novel's characters. The conduct of the protagonists is guided not simply by individual whims and wishes but by implicit and sometimes explicit rules and expectations. This tendency to manage oneself according to extra-individual social norms is particularly clear in the case of Merteuil and Valmont, whose correspondence unfolds as a candid discussion of their behavioral principles. The libertines are extraordinary in the sense that they continuously reason upon their chosen forms of interaction, but in the fact that they act according to nonindividual social patterns, they are very much like the rest of the novel's characters. In fact, as Brooks rightly claims, *Les liaisons* is a "novel about system, processes of systematization, man as a creature of system."[18] To understand the workings of this system, I distinguish between three kinds of competing social norms, and I argue that the novel's social diagnosis resides in its narrative juxtaposition of these forms of sociality. Because politics and social forms mutually depend upon one another in this period, so my argument continues, the social diagnosis of the novel entails a political one. The three social forms I distinguish between are *arranged marriages*, *libertinism*, and *love*, all of which are attached to questions of interpersonal behavior, gender roles, and family formation and all of which have larger histories, social and literary.

Arranged marriages were standard procedure in France among the Old Regime nobility. They were strategically and economically important because they linked powerful families to one another and because they structured the distribution of wealth through inheritance. As Matthew Gerber has emphasized, the primary function of marriage in the early modern period was not to celebrate love but to secure social and material interests: "Marriage safeguarded social stability by assuring the intergenerational transmission of power, property, and identity along patrilineal bloodlines, particularly those theoretically sanctified by the sacramental grace of God. Marriage helped to naturalize, legitimize, and even sanctify the traditional social order."[19] Marriage was an important political concern because it regulated society on a personal level, and whether they were profound or not, moral dogmas were essential means toward the goal of minimizing uncontrolled social mobility. Eighteenth-century libertinism was based on a naturalist philosophy according to which a multidirected sexual desire formed part of the human condition.[20] This belief was diametrically opposed to the conservative morals of arranged marriages, and from the libertine's perspective, marriages were nothing but obstacles to overcome in the pursuit of enjoyment. The virtuous clothing of marriages was equally false, frustrating, and repressive.

In *Les Liaisons dangereuses*, the topic of arranged marriages is present from Letter 1, in which the young Cécile informs her monastery friend, Sophie, that she has been taken out of convent because she is about to be married away to a man unknown to her. In his treatment of arranged marriages, Laclos takes full advantage of the "'stereoscopic' vision" for which he is rightly famous.[21] Readers are presented with the strategic ambitions of Madame de Volanges and with the anxious excitement of her daughter, Cécile; with Tourvel's desperate clinging to the hope of marital happiness; and with Merteuil's unsavory penchant for the predictability of arranged marriages. Michel Feher notes that the libertines were confronted with the obstacle of "an artificial moral system that promotes modesty and constancy" but what the different perspectives on the *marriages de convenances* demonstrate is that the institution of arranged marriages is as threatened as the philosophy of the libertines. The marriage institution is threatened by libertines who pursue their own pleasure instead of submitting to the plans of well-meaning parents; by increasingly popular ideas about personal inclination that tend to view arranged marriages as unjust and overly strategic; and, as has always been the case, by unreasonable and spontaneous feelings of love. The traditional marriage is a prime example of that Old Regime social order which is under heavy pressure in the novel. Arranged marriages used to be able to provide stability, but their legitimacy is at this point declining rapidly. The arranged marriage and the web of social norms it is embedded in is the first social form I am interested in.

The second one is *libertinism*, which follows a wholly different set of conventions than do the arranged marriages. The term libertine is etymologically linked with liberty and was invoked already in the sixteenth century by Jean Calvin in his "Contre la secte phantastique et furieuse des libertins qui se nomment spirituels" (1543). In this sixteenth-century theological context, *libertin* was a pejorative term and was used to designate opposition to and divergence from established forms of religion.[22] Through the sixteenth and seventeenth centuries, "libertinism" was appropriated in different contexts but was recurrently used to designate religious and scientific deviants, such as Giordano Bruno (1548–1600), Théophile de Viau (1590–1626), and Galileo Galilei (1564–1642). In eighteenth-century parlance, the libertine kept his role as freethinking outsider, but the term was increasingly associated with licentious sexuality and with the declining aristocracy.[23] The scientific and theologic past of *libertinage* remains important, however, in its distinction from hedonism because it carries a sense of systematic rationality which is most often absent from hedonism.[24] The libertine is a rational being whose logic is at odds with the conventional wisdom of society.

The libertines of Laclos's novel are unconventionally wise, aristocratic, and sexually energetic. Describing the successful seduction of Tourvel, Valmont uses a favored metaphor among the libertines and one that signals their self-understanding: He compares his libertine strategy to the maneuvering of a military general.[25] "[Y]ou will see that I have not diverged at all from the true principles of this art [of seduction], which we have often noticed is so very similar to the art of warfare. Judge me then as you would a Turenne or a Friedrich" (311). The military analogy, however, is not the only one used to describe the character of libertinism. Elsewhere, the libertine is described as a hunter searching "the finest woods in the world" (126) for prey or as a "[d]eity" who can control the desires and actions of "blind mortals" (132). In their differences, what these metaphors signal is the degree to which the superior libertine seeks to impose his or her will upon others. The libertine wants

134   *Choderlos de Laclos's* Liaisons dangereuses

control and attains it through minute planning and, if necessary, violent execution. In the words of Georges Poulet, the libertine is a "man of projects," a being whose existence relies on the next seduction.[26]

While the morals of libertines deviate markedly from those of Madame de Volanges and other defenders of arranged marriages, these two groups nonetheless share an ambition to plan and control the future. They have different projects but resemble each other in *having* projects. *Love*, the third social form, is wholly different. It takes its powers from the reservoir of irrational feelings, and it uses them to distract the lovers and hence makes all planning impossible. Toward the end of *Les liaisons*, Danceny, who is at this point Merteuil's lover, recapitulates an opposition between libertinism and love that runs throughout the narrative:

> It is only the seducer who never acts unless he plans in advance, co-ordinating his resources and his moves, and foreseeing events far ahead. True love does not permit meditation and reflection in this fashion. It uses our feelings to distract us from our thoughts. Its power is never stronger than when we are unaware of it. And it is in darkness and silence that it tangles us in a web equally impossible to perceive or to break.
>
> (358)

Danceny's arachnid description of love as an unknown force, silently tangling its victims in an unbreakable web, is not his perspective alone. His characterization of love summarizes a metaphorical pattern established throughout the narrative. Thus, love makes "blind" (14); it brings one into a "state of timid servitude [Déjà vous voilà timide et ésclave]" (28 [34]); it is a "talisman" (101), an "invincible power" (191); and it makes the lover "enslaved [subjugué]" (327 [368]). In being a mystical force that works unbeknownst to the subject and that tends to enslave it, love is everything that the libertine seeks to break away from. Merteuil's entire project is premised on the struggle to throw off her yoke, to avoid what she calls "the weight of her chains [le poids de sa chaîne]" (179 [203]). In other words, while libertinism seeks to corrupt love, love equally poses a threat to the rational planning of libertines and proponents of arranged marriages. This explains why Brooks suggests not only that *Les Liaisons* is a novel about systematization but also about man's incompatibility with systematization.[27]

Historically, the idea of love as a sudden force, stronger than any individual will, has deep cultural roots reaching back to the mythological figures of Eros and Cupid, who literally shot love into their defenseless victims. Closer to the context of *Les Liaisons*, Madame de Lafayette presented a similar vision of love in her 1678 novel *La Princesse de Clèves*.

Prefiguring the latter case of Tourvel, a young aristocratic woman there too was torn between her marital virtue and an uncontrollable extramarital love, and like Tourvel, Madame de Clèves sought refuge from her feelings in a convent only to die unhappy, presumably from a broken heart.[28]

But love was not only a literary phenomenon. During the French revolution, and culminating with the marriage legislation of the summer of 1792, love became part of two powerful political projects, namely, populationism and voluntarity. In the later years of Louis XIV's reign, the idea that France was losing population gained ground particularly among the critics of absolute monarchy. Historical studies have shown that the fear was unfounded, but it was a "fertile error" in the sense that it became a strong argument against not only unproductive monastery vows but also arranged marriages.[29] Arranged marriages were considered to lead to marital unhappiness and were thus procreatively problematic. In order to flourish, the state needed a large population, and the voluntary marriage was seen to be better able to perform on this parameter. "In the ideal marriage," Desan writes, "a free individual made a choice that simultaneously benefited himself or herself, society, and the state. Joining freedom of choice with social stability, marriage exemplified the reconciliation of the individual with the general good."[30] Love and reason, as Figure 4.1 demonstrates, were now seen to be potential partners. As I will demonstrate in Chapter 5, this revolutionary idea would later blossom in Chénier's play *Fénelon*, but in theorizing about love and in exploring its social consequences, Laclos too contributed to the period's growing politicization of love.

My point is not that any one of these social forms is more authentic than the others. I am interested in the way in which libertinism, arranged marriages, and love set out three different kinds of subjectivity and social interaction in the novel. I consider these social forms mutually destructive, and I believe that the novel's social diagnosis resides in its juxtaposition of these forms and in its display of their failure. The 1789 Declaration of Rights was an attempt to think society anew, to put a new form of subjectivity and a new relationship between the individual and society into words. In *L'an 2440*, the inventive aspect of literature was used to help lift this imaginative task. Laclos chose a different direction. Instead of building a new society, he located the contradictions of the old one and played them out against each other. His is an attempt not to build society anew but to demonstrate the internal contradictions of the old. To analyze this critical juxtaposition of social forms, I compare them according to two different criteria in what follows: their *rhythms* and their *hierarchies*. In doing this, it will become clear that these social forms entail considerably different and mutually undermining conceptions of happiness and subjectivity.

Figure 4.1 L'Amour et la Raison: [estampe] / Fr. Bartolozzy delineav.; Elisab. G. Herhan sculpsit. (Paris: Chez Joubert, 1794). Bibliothèque nationale de France.

The Rhythm of Social Forms

In her 2015 book *Forms*, Caroline Levine takes up what I consider an old discussion about the politics and historicity of literary form. This discussion guided much of the work of Marxist scholars such as Georg Lukàcs, Theodor Adorno, and later Fredric Jameson, but in reopening it, Levine makes the argument that social institutions – educational, penal, political – operate according to forms that literary scholars with their training in formal analysis might be well suited to understand.[31] In concentrating on forms such as rhythm, hierarchy, and network, her analytical focus closer resembles that of Georges Poulet and other literary phenomenologists than that of traditional Marxist scholars.[32] Following Levine, I understand rhythm as a temporal formatting of a social community, and I believe there are different and competing rhythms, different types of temporal formatting, at work in *Les Liaisons*. The novel operates with a particularly sharp distinction between the libertine's fixation on future conquest and the lovers' momentary enjoyment.

The libertines are not alone in being oriented toward the future. In planning her daughter's marriage, Madame de Volanges share this particular temporality. In speculating that *mariages de convenance* are "the most fertile ground for these scandals which are becoming more and more common every day?" (233), Madame de Volanges expresses a suspicion that arranged marriages are beneficial neither for the individuals involved nor for society. But, as she admits in the same letter to Merteuil, "Monsieur de Gercourt is a better party than I might have hoped for my daughter. I even admit that I was extremely flattered that his choice fell upon her" (232). In an analysis of the "economic system" of the novel's "exchange in women," Anne Deneys-Tunney emphasizes the economic aspects of love and sex in the novel.[33] These are present in the reflections of the mother who states that the only thing that keeps her from giving her daughter to Danceny, the awkward music teacher, is "financial [considerations]" (232). From the perspective of Cécile, the fact that she is destined to marry a stranger for reasons of family power and wealth is in itself unproblematical. To her convent confidante, she writes about Gercourt that "[h]e is rich, he is aristocratic, colonel of the regiment of ... So far so good. But he is *old*: just image, he is at least thirty-six years old!" (83)[34] Even more depressing than Gercourt's old age, however, is the prospect of not seeing Danceny again once she is married. In her – as Merteuil will later claim – naïve conception, marriage is a lifelong commitment that sets strict limitations on women's sexual liberty.

The rhythm of arranged marriages is divided in two. The first part focuses on setting up the most lucrative match possible. This strategic orientation toward a future marriage is what guides Madame de Volanges and, at least initially, Cécile. But the future-oriented rhythm comes to an end when the couple is married. The act of marriage is a point of transition that marks the moment when futurity gives way to an "unbroken calm" that may be interpreted as either a sign of stable happiness or desperate boredom. It is Tourvel who, in a letter to the imposing Valmont, gives voice to the experience of married life:

> I am respected and cherished by a husband I love and respect, duty and pleasure combining in the same person. I am happy, that is right and proper [Je suis heureuse, je dois l'être]. If keener pleasures than these exist, I do not desire them. I do not wish to know them. Can there be a sweeter pleasure than to be at peace with oneself, to enjoy

days of unbroken calm, to fall asleep without anxiety and to wake without remorse? What you call happiness is but a tumult of the senses, a tempestuous sea of passions, a fearful spectacle even when it is viewed from the shore. So how can I confront these storms? How dare I embark upon a sea covered in the debris of thousands upon thousands of shipwrecks? And with whom? No, Monsieur, I shall stay on land. I cherish the bonds which tie me to it. Even if I could break them, I should not wish to. If I did not have them I should make haste to acquire them.

(121 [138])

Married life, and the alleged *marital happiness*, here denotes stability and security. Adventures are tumultuous and end in shipwreck, but duty leads to pleasure and finds its object in the husband. As critics of the marital institution would agree, marriage is a bond that ties individuals but whereas this bond is conceived as a threat to liberty by Cécile, Tourvel claims to find happiness in being sheltered from the storms of passion. Tourvel's position is a conservative one favoring the stability and containment of fixed relations over the freedom to act upon one's will. What marriage can offer is a smaller world, but it is tranquil and free from threats. Read against the grain, however, the erratic style of the letter reveals Tourvel's desperation. Trying to convince herself, she writes, "I am happy" but immediately adds "I have to be," which, as Winnett emphasizes, is "not the same thing."[35] Unwilling to embark upon the adventure of passion, the interjection "and with whom?" nonetheless reveals that her desire has already led her there. As such, Tourvel's letter is one of the many that has to be interpreted in the tension between its overt statement and its opposite stylistic gesture. Doing this, the desperate insistence with which she claims marital happiness becomes the telling sign of her actual unhappiness. Momentarily disregarding this important example of textual ambivalence, the quoted passage exemplifies the second half of the rhythm of arranged marriage sociality. After the strategic planning and anxious waiting of the first part comes a second calm yet happy part. But as Jean Pestré insisted in his *Encyclopédie* article "Happiness," and as the discrete interjections of Tourvel's letter indicate, a happiness that is not interrupted by pleasure from time to time is not true happiness but merely "a state of tranquility, a very sorry kind of happiness indeed!"[36]

The rhythm of arranged marriages is split in a first future-oriented phase dominated by strategic planning and a second phase characterized by the sad happiness of unchanging calm but the rhythm of libertinism is wholly focused on future conquests. Notice the future tense favored by Valmont in an early letter to Merteuil about his planned seduction of Tourvel:

I shall have [J'aurai] this woman. I shall take her [je l'enlèverai] away from the husband who defiles her. I shall dare [j'oserai] to ravish her even from the God she adores. How delicious to be both object and conqueror of her remorse! Far be it from me to destroy the prejudices which beset her! They will only add [ils ajouteront] to my happiness and my triumph.

(22 [27–28])

Valmont thrives in the knowledge that he *will* succeed, he *will* have it his way and this will to control the future is part of his enjoyment. From a temporal perspective there is a similarity between the first phase of arranged marriages and libertinism in that they both have to do with planning and controlling the future. Libertine happiness is not simply sexual pleasure. Valmont finds enjoyment in orchestrating people and future events. This wish to control the future can bring the libertines into conflict with the proponents of arranged marriages, which is what happens in Merteuil's reply to the letter quoted earlier from Madame de Volanges. Instead of criticizing the unfreedom of marriage, Merteuil takes the opportunity to praise the marital institution in a carefully crafted letter. Besides from highlighting the financial benefits of a lucrative engagement, and besides from echoing Madame de Volanges's own contention that arranged marriages are the result of mothers using their experience to helpfully guide an inexperienced daughter, Merteuil also offers an argument that obtains its legitimacy from the emotional reservoir of sympathy, happiness, and trust. Here, Merteuil writes about the newly wed strangers:

> What happens in such cases between two married people, assuming they behave correctly? Each studies the other; they observe how they behave to one another, seek and soon recognize what compromises they must make in their tastes and desires for mutual happiness. These small sacrifices are made painlessly because they are reciprocal and have been anticipated. Soon this gives rise to mutual benevolence. And habit, which strengthens all the inclinations that it does not destroy, brings about, little by little, that loving friendship, that tender trust which, together with respect, form, or so it seems to me, the true and solid basis of a happy marriage.
>
> (253)

Marrying out of love, Merteuil claims, has the disadvantage that the lovers think they know each other before they marry. Maybe they do but the lifelong commitment of marriage necessitates compromise to a degree which is wholly foreign from the brief love affair. The happy marriage is based on loving friendship, tender trust, and respect and these affects are produced in a dance of observation and slow pace experimentation. What Merteuil describes is a state of calm, similar to the ideals of Tourvel, but very different from any passionate love affair and that difference makes love a poor determinant for a happy marriage. How should these moralistic lines from the wicked pen of Merteuil be interpreted? They differ markedly from the libertine principles declared in Letter 81 and Merteuil is quick to inform Valmont, and hence the reader, that this Letter 104 was designed to strategically manipulate Madame de Volanges: "I go on such a lot about virtue and flatter her so much, she must be persuaded I am right" (260). Merteuil's long-term ambition is to have revenge on Gercourt for what she considers his past infidelity (13–14). To do this, she wants Gercourt married to Cécile and Cécile infested with libertine principles; principles she shall learn from Valmont who, in turn, is guided by Merteuil herself. Merteuil, in other words, is the master plotter and exactly as future oriented as Valmont. Her ambition to orchestrate the future at this point, however, brings libertinism and arranged marriages into a complex confrontation. Libertinism, in the form of Merteuil's advice, advances the project of an arranged marriage but only to prepare its later downfall from within. As Merteuil writes to Cécile, in what is both a genuine defense and an undermining of arranged marriages: Such an arrangement may in fact give women "more freedom of action" (257). To the wise libertine, an arranged marriage is just a construction, a game with rules, and once the libertine understands these rules, she may begin to exploit them for her own pleasure.

The rhythm of love is diametrically opposed to the planning and future orientation of arranged marriages and libertinism. As demonstrated, love in this novel is portrayed as a mystical force; it makes blind and it tangles up its powerless victims. Without fully realizing it himself, Valmont falls in love with Tourvel somewhere along the way of his attempted libertine seduction. The novel's utmost characterization of love and its temporality comes in Letter 125 in which Valmont boasts to Merteuil about his sexual success with Tourvel.

> It was with such naïve or sublime candour that she gave herself and her charms to me, and increased my happiness by sharing in it. The delight [l'ivresse] was complete and reciprocal; and for the first time my happiness lasted longer than the pleasure. I left her arms only in order to fall at her feet, and swear eternal love. And, to be absolutely truthful, I believed what I was saying [je pensais ce que je disais].
>
> (312 [351])

Valmont's experience in this case differs markedly from his seduction of Cécile and other women, something which makes Georges Poulet suggest that Valmont's love for Tourvel has the character of a "countercurrent" in the narrative.[37] Love certainly differs from libertinism in *Les Liaisons*, but it also has its own recurring logics and temporality. Thus,

Tourvel describes her love in a letter to Rosemonde and places an equal emphasis on the intoxication of love:

> Intoxicated [Enivrée] with the pleasure of seeing him, of listening to his words, of the sweet delight of feeling him near, of the greater happiness of being able to make him happy, I have lost all power and strength. [...] What is my life without him?
>
> (246 [276])

The importance of shared and reciprocal feelings in Valmont's letter sets love apart from the libertine's wish to manipulate and hunt down his or her victim. Love is an irrational affect and from a temporal perspective it is devoid of any future orientation, wholly concerned as it is with the moment. Here is no planning and no manipulation which seems to come as a surprise to Valmont himself when he writes, "je pensais ce que je disais;" a passage that should be taken to mean not only that he believes what he says but also that he says what he thinks. The libertines routinely lie about their opinions and about their motivations in order to manipulate people around them but this tendency to separate thought from speech for strategic purposes disappears in the meeting of Valmont and Tourvel because Valmont's strategic sense evaporates. Instead of a future waiting to be realized and controlled, he experiences the intoxication of a shared present.

Laclos revisited the distinction between a moment-oriented and a future-oriented life rhythm in his 1783 essay "Des femmes et de leur education." Some critics have found the two essays Laclos wrote on female education "deprived of life and originality" and have dismissed them as "applied rousseauism."[38] The essays do borrow heavily from Rousseau but in arguing that women are entitled to a useful education and in insisting that the unequal relationship between the sexes is entirely unjustified, the essays present feminist ideas that are wholly absent from the writings of the Genevan predecessor. The essays were left unpublished by Laclos for unknown reasons but they were both attempted answers to a question raised by the academy of Chalons-sur-Marne: How can the education of women best be improved? In trying to answer that question, Laclos went back to Rousseau's nature/society distinction because he there found the intellectual tools to condemn the inequality of the sexes of his contemporary society. His opposition of life in the state of nature and in the state of society adds a philosophical depth to his analysis of life rhythms, but it also testifies to the discursive and intellectual proximity between Laclos and the Declaration Debate participants. In the second chapter of his essay, Laclos writes,

> The natural woman is, like the natural man, a free and strong creature; free, in that she has the entire exercise of her faculties; strong, in that her faculties are equal to her needs. Is such a creature happy? Yes,

without a doubt, and if, according to our ideas, her happiness seems paradoxical, a more thoughtful examination soon allows us to recognize the truth of this. Men wanted to perfect everything, and they have corrupted everything; they burdened themselves with chains [il se sont chargés de chaînes] then complained of being overwhelmed by their weight; senseless and unjust, they abandoned the nature that made them happy, then they slandered it, accusing it of the ills that this abandonment caused them, which they themselves brought about.[39]

The quote reiterates the vocabulary of Rousseau. Not only is the man of society "burdened with chains," as was the case in the opening lines of the first chapter of *Du Contrat social*.[40] Laclos also, as Versini notices, parallels Rousseau's description of life in the state of nature; a state in which men lived "free, healthy, good, and happy."[41] The happiness of natural man is absolute and results from his physical activity and his ability to relax: When he is awake, he struggles to satisfy his immediate bodily needs, and as soon as food is found and consumed, he sleeps. In the social state, contrarily, man must constantly "see to [veille à] the execution of the social contract" and this state of constant alertness means that social man can never enjoy true repose.[42] Instead, the rhythm of social men and women is one of perpetual physical inactivity and mental hyperactivity; a state of being that causes an expansion of their temporal experience. Enjoyments and disappointments of the past as well as hopes and fears of things to come invade social man's experience of the moment and render him unable to simply *live* the present. Free from the will to perfect and control everything and free from constantly comparing past, present, and future feelings, natural men and women are happy and free to enjoy bodily sensations and to exercise their faculties. Theirs is a state of immediate being, of *natural happiness*. The presence of this valorized opposition between the presentist and futurist life rhythm invites us to consider if this same valorization is operative in the novel.

One critic has claimed that the essays express "the morals" and "the dynamic and positive conclusion" to *Les liaisons*.[43] Others have found Tourvel "the most natural person of the book" and consider her "intentionally close to the natural woman" of the essay.[44] The fact that Merteuil mourns the "chains" (179) of women in modern society while social man is characterized precisely by his self-imposed "chains" in the essay further adds to the parallel between novel and essay. And is not the characterization of social man as physically inactive and intellectually hyperactive also an apt description of the rhythm of the waiting and scheming libertine? Despite those significant parallels between essay and novel, I remain unpersuaded that *Les liaisons* is best understood as a defense of Tourvel and the love and natural life she incarnates in this interpretation.

The first reason for my skepticism has to do with the troublesome authenticity of love. After Tourvel has come to doubt the love of Valmont, the latter writes Tourvel and invokes "those loving feelings which made our hearts beat as one, this voluptuousness of the soul ever reborn and ever more deeply felt" (338). Valmont here picks up the novel's depiction of love as uncontrollable and communal but the authenticity of his feelings at this moment in the story is highly questionable and serves to expose the vulnerability of love as an ideal state of being. If love can be so easily faked, how can it form the basis of social life? This critical question becomes increasingly relevant after Valmont sends the infamous "pas ma faute" letter penned by Merteuil.[45] After this point of no return, Tourvel moves permanently into the convent of her youth and her condition is described as a "delirium [transport violent/délire]" (400; 357; 361 [355/402; 407]). Eventually, she dies of a broken heart which is of course tragic but also a reminder of the vulnerability of love and of the ease with which it can be corrupted. Love is no stable ideal alternative to arranged marriages and libertinism but itself a form of social interaction whose values and rhythm can be undercut by other competing social forms.

The second reason for my skepticism has to do with the status of the natural state in Laclos's essay. In his reading of Rousseau, Paul de Man drew attention to the deliberately artificial or fictive character of the Genevan's conception of the state of nature.[46] As argued in Chapter 1, and as emphasized by Susan Maslan, some deputies from the Declaration Debate used this fiction of the nature state to expose the "naturalized, social inequality" of Old Regime France.[47] In his discussion of Rousseau, Laclos points to the exact passage in which the Genevan emphasizes the "hypothetical" character of the nature state. In fact, he quotes it in a footnote:

> The Researches which can be undertaken concerning this Subject must not be taken for historical truths, but only for hypothetical and conditional reasonings better suited to clarify the Nature of things than to show their genuine origin.[48]

In Laclos, as well as in Rousseau, it is a challenge to strike the balance between acknowledging the ficticity of the state of nature and simultaneously insist upon its credibility. Laclos seeks this balance point in critical dialogue with two authoritative skeptics of the Rousseauian conceptualization of the state of nature: Comte de Buffon (1707–1788) and Voltaire. In addition to questioning the historical validity of Rousseau's depiction of the state of nature, both Buffon and Voltaire criticized what they regarded as the Genevan's wish to quit the benefits and struggles of society only to return to a pre-social state of *"apathetic sleep."*[49] In his refutation of the skeptics, Laclos avoids insisting upon the historical veracity of the state of nature – after all, he has himself confirmed its hypothetical quality. Instead he writes that neither Buffon nor Voltaire manages to prove that "the state we call 'the state of nature' does not exist" and he maintains that "it is impossible to prove that it has never existed."[50] By insisting upon its potential reality, while acknowledging its hypothetical nature, Laclos follows Rousseau – but for different ends – and uses the state of nature to demonstrate the historical contingency of inegalitarian gender relations. In other words, the natural state does not have the status of a realizable ideal in Laclos's essay. It is a hypothesis that serves the critical purpose of exposing a gendered version of what Maslan called "naturalized, social inequality."

Love and the natural state are not potentially realizable subjective and social ideals but unstable, hypothetical positions that function to expose the depravity of the social state as it is inhabited by libertines and Old Regime proponents of arranged marriages. By invoking the hopes of love and the sensual enjoyment of the present, the novel suggests a potential foundation for a less corrupt and less narcissistic form of social interaction. But because it is short-sighted and because it is so easily faked, love is too unstable to serve as a model for social interaction. It is constantly undercut by ambitious parents who seek to control the intergenerational transmission of power and wealth through advantageous marriages and by libertines who copy the signs of love in their individualistic pursuit of control and sexual pleasure. What love does do in the novel, however, is what the natural state does in the essay and in the philosophy of Rousseau. It exposes the falseness of libertines and of ambitious parents. It establishes a foundation from which the cynicism and individualistic idiosyncrasies of future-oriented rhythms can be displayed.

In what follows I continue the analysis of the three competing forms of social interaction but I shift my focus from rhythms to hierarchies. That shift allows me to explore the difference between libertinism and the proponents of arranged marriages in addition to the vulnerability of libertinism.

The Hierarchies of Social Forms

In *Forms* Levine explains that "*hierarchy* comes from the Greek *hieros*, meaning 'sacred,' and *arche*, meaning 'rule.'"[51] In the sixth century CE, it referred to "levels of angelic choruses, but it soon came to be applied to the governance of the Church, to describe its strictly ordered levels of authority and subordination."[52] Fast forwarding to present-day usage, she continues her definition: "hierarchies arrange bodies, things, and ideas according to levels of power or importance. Hierarchies rank – organizing experience into asymmetrical, discriminatory, often deeply unjust arrangements."[53] Hierarchical struggles can center on any number of issues but a crucial one in Laclos's work is the problem of gender inequality, a problem that gets complicated by its embeddedness in other hierarchical struggles. In his short first essay on women's education,

Laclos explicitly touched upon the hierarchy between the sexes and the problems it gave rise to. He begins by explaining that men cannot be expected to lead the transition to an egalitarian relationship between the sexes because it is not in their own best interest, and then continues:

> [L]earn that one does not emerge from slavery except through a great revolution. Is this revolution possible? That is for you alone to say, since it depends on your courage, in itself likely [C'est à vous seules à le dire puisqu'elle dépend de votre courage. Est-elle vraisemblable?]. I will say nothing about this question; but until it happens, and as long as men rule your fate, I shall be justified in saying, *and it will be easy for me to prove, that there is no means of improving the education of women.*[54]

Laclos considers equal access to education the premise for gender equality, and he argues that, in principle, women are fully entitled to any useful education. Such a change in educational policy cannot be realized through ordinary reform, though, because men are unlikely to accept the hierarchical degradation that gender equality would encompass for them. In her reading of Laclos's essays, Winnett criticizes this attitude and argues that Laclos opens up the possibility of greater gender equality only to immediately close it by emphasizing the practical impossibility of improving women's education.[55] My primary concern is not to judge whether Laclos's idea of a women-led revolution is progressive or not but to understand his analysis of the hierarchy between the sexes.[56] As he explains in his essays, the scheming and insincerity of women is an empirical fact but it is a fact grounded, not in biology but in the failure of the state to procure gender equality. If women want to pursue projects of their own they have to maneuver cleverly as they lack the hierarchical supremacy and the physical strength of men; a strength that allows men to pursue their ambitions by the use of force. Women, inversely, have to awaken man's desire because this allows them to indirectly control the actions of men. This opposition between men and women is played out in the novel through the different libertine strategies of Valmont and Merteuil.

Man's physical strength is signaled when Valmont, in a letter to Merteuil, describes how he managed to overpower the defenseless Cécile. His wording on this occasion is of particular interest.

> While you, handling the weapons of your sex so adeptly, were victorious by your subtlety, I restored to man his inalienable rights and subjugated her with my authority [rendant à l'homme ses droits imprescriptibles, je subjuguais par l'autorité]. Sure of seizing my prey [saisir ma proie] if I were able to reach her, I only needed a stratagem in order to approach her.
>
> (225 [253])

Elsewhere in the novel, the concept of rights is primarily used in descriptions of worldly manners as in the "right to expect" (60) a certain behavior in a specific situation or as the "right to complain of" (67) specific social mores. But by reintroducing the hunter-metaphor, and by contrasting physical strength with women's different kinds of weaponry, this passage gives another meaning to "rights." As signaled by the word *rendant* (restore; give back), man used to have a right to subjugate women and by the usage of his physical authority, Valmont is able to take back what he here considers his inalienable right and resume his sovereign position. What Valmont terms *his* inalienable right to sexual enjoyment is of course diametrically opposed to the "natural, inalienable, and sacred rights of man," which would be heralded by the deputies in the 1789 Declaration of Rights, but the choice of phrase signals the degree to which Laclos modeled the language of his novel on contemporary political discourse.[57] In the same letter, Valmont claims his right to possess Cécile as any other object: "I felt I was justified in claiming a few of those rights over a property that he [Danceny] only possessed because of my refusal and neglect" (224). In the hierarchy of libertine men and unsuspecting women, woman is a piece of property that man has a right to possess. Given the importance she ascribes to female liberty, it would seem logical for Merteuil to criticize the male violence of Valmont. Her position, however, is another. She has no respect for women unable to defend themselves against an unwanted seductive attack. Such unskilled women are nothing but "pleasure machine[s] [machines à plaisir]" (260 [291]).

The most programmatic description of female libertinism appears in Letter 81 where Merteuil describes her libertine "principles" in great detail and insists that they were not "discovered by chance, accepted uncritically or followed out of habit" (181). On the contrary Merteuil explains that "I have created them, and I can say that I am what I have created" (Ibid.). Her need to develop the libertine principles of strategic self-fashioning is a direct result of the inegalitarian hierarchy between men and women in society. "In this unequal contest [between the sexes]," Merteuil remarks, "we are lucky not to lose, and you are unlucky not to win." (179). Her libertine project is premised on her inability to act freely in society, an experience she describes with an analogy between marriage and slavery: "But if the unfortunate woman is the first to feel the weight of her chains, what risks she has to run in her attempts to escape or simply lighten them!" (179).[58] In striking the analogy between marriage and slavery, Laclos makes a critical comparison that recurs in the women's rights writings of the period.[59] Unlike Valmont, however, Merteuil does not have the possibility to use physical strength as a way to achieve freedom. Instead she does something else.

Merteuil's key to avoid subjection and to attain libertine pleasure is her ability to feign emotions and inspire them in others. Lies and manipulation are morally indefensible in the greater social sphere of the novel, but it is an integrated element of libertinism. Hence, as a reaction to Danceny's moral scruples at the prospect of lying to Madame de Volanges, Valmont coolly states,

> A typical man! We are all equally wicked in our plans, and whatever weakness we show in carrying them out we call probity [Voilà bien les hommes! tous également scélérats dans leurs projets, ce qu'ils mettent de faiblesse dans l'exécution, ils l'appellent probité].
>
> (141 [161])

The shift from third person to first person plural in the English translation misses the degree to which Valmont here considers himself and the libertines exempt from the typical weaknesses of ordinary men. The uncompromising will to push through a project is a given in the libertine philosophy and this means that manipulation, rather than being a moral wrong, becomes a necessary skill, particularly for women. In the account of her self-education, Merteuil describes how she battled with her own physiognomy:

> If I was feeling unhappy, I practiced adopting a look of serenity or even joy. I even went so far as to deliberately cause myself pain in order to make an attempt at the simultaneous expression of pleasure. I labored, with as much care and even more difficulty, to suppress the symptoms of an unexpected joy. And that is how I have been able to exercise over my physiognomy the power that you have on occasions found so astonishing. [...] From that moment on my thoughts were for my benefit and mine alone, and I only revealed to others what I found it useful to reveal.
>
> (181)

Emotions and thoughts are revealed in grimaces and minuscule bodily movements and anyone able to exercise control over visible symptoms of joy or regret is able to conceal inner feelings while observing the signs of the sentiments of others. In the attempt to realize a project, the libertine collects information through observation while adjusting all physical gestures to his or her designs. This allows the libertine to strike precisely at the right moment and at the right place. Manipulation of self and of others is an acquired skill learned through careful observation and even systematic reading:

> In novels I studied manners; in the philosophers, opinions, I even tried to find out from the strictest moralists what they demanded of us, to be certain of what it was possible to do, what it was best to think and how one must appear to be.
>
> (183–184)

This libertine rationality has inspired scholars to compare Laclos's libertinism to the ever questioning Enlightenment philosophy of René Descartes.[60] More appropriately, I think, the strategic self-fashioning could be seen as an inversion of the late eighteenth-century valorization of transparency in social and political matters.[61] Rousseau opened his *Confessions* with the claim that he here showed his fellow men "a man in all the integrity of nature" and as historians have shown, this kind of absolute transparency later became an ideal to the revolutionaries.[62] The success Merteuil gains through manipulation is an inversion of the ideal of transparency and a critical expansion on the Seneca epithet Laclos used in his first essay: "*There is no cure for evil once vice becomes habit.*"[63]

In her self-education Merteuil wages a hierarchical war against her own appearances and her success in that struggle allows her to wage another one against social norms and unsuspecting victims. But the most explicit declaration of war is the one Merteuil sends to Valmont in response to his insistence that she must again become his lover: "Very well, then. War!" she writes to great dramatic effect (369). The war between Valmont and Merteuil is not just a struggle for hierarchical supremacy between the two libertines but also a battle between two forms of social interaction, that is between love and libertinism. In unpacking this battle, it is necessary to return to the problem of textual ambivalence which was raised earlier in connection with Tourvel's alleged marital happiness. Love, in the novel, is described as a force that works in the shadows and unbeknownst to the subject in love but because of the novel's epistolary format, the reader's only access to the feelings of the characters is through either the potentially unknowing lover's own written words or the bystander whose credibility is also unsure. Laclos takes full advantage of the literary possibilities of this dilemma.

The interpretative dilemma of love is made explicit at the end of the novel when the feigned editor withholds a letter sent by Valmont to Tourvel after her retreat to the convent. In opposition to the reader, Madame de Volanges has read the letter and asks Madame de Rosemonde, "what do you think of the despair on the part of Monsieur de Valmont? First, are we to believe it, or does he just wish to deceive everybody till the bitter end?" (370). The feigned editor only adds to the problem when he writes, "Because nothing in the ensuing correspondence was found which could resolve this doubt, we have decided to suppress Monsieur de Valmont's letter" (Ibid.). In other words, the indecipherability of Valmont's love is a constitutive formal feature of the novel and it represents an important point: Love is opaque, and this opacity is the problem as seen from the perspective of libertines and matchmakers alike. Love, as the contemporary French philosopher Alain Badiou emphasizes, makes the world impossible to predict and this unpredictability explains why Merteuil writes of the "déraisonnement de l'amour" in an answer to Valmont about his interest in Tourvel.[64]

> *She must give herself,* you tell me. Ha! No doubt she must; so she will give herself, as the others have done, except that she will give herself with a bad grace. But so that she may end by giving herself, the proper thing to do is to take her at the outset. What a silly distinction – and typical of the illogicality of love [déraisonnement de l'amour]. Yes, love; for you are in love. Were I to call it by any other name, I should be deceiving you; I should be hiding your malady from you. So tell me then, my languorous lover, do you believe you have *raped* the women you have had? However much a woman wants to give herself, however eager she is to do it, she must still have a pretext; and is there a more convenient one than that which makes it seem she is yielding to force? I confess that, as far as I am concerned, one of the things which flatters me most is a vigorous and skillful attack, where everything happens in an ordered fashion, though rapidly.
>
> (28–29 [35])

This letter offers a model to the reader for approaching the interpretational problem of love. In a previous one, Valmont described how he wished to not simply possess Tourvel but wants her to give up herself to him (Letter 6). As he presents it, it is a greater libertine achievement to compel the virtuous Tourvel to seek him out actively than to simply take her using his "bold strategies" (23) as he did with Cécile. The favored nonviolent strategy would be a way of breaking down virtue from within, he argues. In interpreting Valmont's letter, however, Merteuil sees a contradiction between the stated ambition of Valmont and his actual endeavors. As was the case in Tourvel's letter on marital happiness, the style of Valmont's writing here reveals something which is not in his words. Valmont's reluctance to use the "bold" libertine strategies, claims Merteuil, proves his unacknowledged love for Tourvel. His distinction between taking a woman and allowing her to give up herself is "silly" and typical of the "illogicality of love." In fact, the libertine should never shy away from taking a woman by force, Merteuil insists, because force is something else entirely than rape. A vigorous attack only helps the woman to submit to the sexual pleasure that she wants yet feels she should abstain from for moral reasons. From the description of Valmont's forceful "attack" (226) on Cécile, it is clear that rape is a just name for one of Valmont's libertine seduction techniques but one that he deselects in the case of Tourvel. In meticulously justifying his avoidance of the use of force, Valmont, according to Merteuil, gives away his true feelings.

After Valmont has succeeded in seducing Tourvel, he repeatedly informs Merteuil that he is *not* in love. The most interesting of these not-in-love-letters, Number 125, exhibits all the contradictions between intention and unintended meanings generated by love. "I am surprised by the unfamiliar delight it gave me," Valmont dreamily states but continues to coldly characterize these thoughts as a "childish idea" (305). With Tourvel, "this astonishing woman," he has experienced "moments of weakness which resemble that unmanly passion" but, he insists, he has always been able to vanquish these passions and "adhere to my principles" (Ibid.). Even though he has momentarily "shared the passion and the delirium I created in her," the "passing illusion of love is nonetheless dispelled today" (Ibid.). And in the paragraph's last turn of the tables, he admits that the "fascination persists" and that he would like to give in to it if only the thought of doing that had not awakened "a certain anxiety" in him (Ibid.). For the first time the "happiness" of Valmont has "lasted longer than the pleasure" (312–313). The whole letter is a constant wavering between submission to the irrationality of love and a desperate insistence upon libertine control.

Merteuil responds in Letter 127 and she is furious. She immediately identifies Valmont's love but what she finds especially infuriating is his wish to collect an award he feels he now deserves. Early in the novel, Merteuil makes herself the "reward" for Valmont's successful seduction of Tourvel: "As soon as you have had your fair devotee, and can send me proof of that, come to me and I shall be yours" (45). Valmont now feels ready to collect on this promise and urges Merteuil to give up Danceny and focus on him. Merteuil considers this completely unacceptable because it would imply her hierarchical subjection to Valmont.

> Shall I sacrifice my inclination, and a new one at that, to devote my time to you? And in what manner? Waiting for my turn, like a submissive slave, for the sublime favours of *His Highness*. When, for example, you wish to distract yourself a moment from *this strange fascination* that *the adorable, heavenly* Madame de Tourvel has alone made you feel, or when you are afraid of compromising, with *the charming Cécile*, the superior idea you are so happy for her to have of you: then, descending to my level, you will come and seek out pleasures which are less exciting, of course, but of less consequence. And your precious favours, though passing rare, will be more than adequate to bring about my happiness!
>
> (316)

If the style of Valmont's writing reveals to Merteuil that he is a libertine in love, the form of her own suggests that she feels threatened by Valmont's letter. She mocks him by meticulously picking out phrases and quoting them back to him thus attempting to sarcastically expose his lack of self-insight. Michel Delon has argued that "the italicization transforms all writing into a palimpsest and renders all reading suspicious."[65] Here, the italicization works not primarily to give a double meaning to the text but rather to satirize Valmont's unacknowledged love. The quotations signal her anger but also reveal the opposition between Valmont's love and Merteuil's libertinism. The specific citations about the singular pleasures Valmont has experienced with Tourvel suggest feelings of jealousy; a jealousy, J. E. Fowler argues, that follows from Merteuil's suspicion that Valmont is more attracted to Tourvel than to her.[66] This may be true but besides from the personal conflict her fear also demonstrates that Valmont's love threatens her own libertine way of life. As she admitted herself, she likes to be seduced "in an ordered fashion [avec ordre]" (29 [35]) and with his irrational love Valmont is rapidly escaping her understanding of libertine order. Hence, the confrontation between Merteuil and Tourvel is not so much a personal question of jealousy – two women fighting over the same man – as a hierarchical confrontation between two opposite ways of social conduct. At play in the war between Merteuil and Valmont is a struggle for supremacy between love and libertinism; a struggle that ends unhappily with the death of Tourvel and Valmont and with the disfigurement and expulsion of Merteuil.

At the very end of the novel, after Merteuil's expulsion from the capital, we learn that Merteuil has not only been socially excluded, she has also been disfigured and ruined:

> The Marquis de –, who does not let slip any opportunity to say something spiteful, when he spoke about her yesterday said that 'her illness had turned her inside out and that presently her soul was in her face'. Unfortunately everyone thought the expression exact.
>
> Another event has added to her disgrace and wrongdoing. Her court case was decided the day before yesterday, and she lost it unanimously. Costs, damages, restitution of profits, everything has been awarded to the minors. So the small amount of her fortune which was not taken up by the proceedings has been absorbed, and more than absorbed, by the costs.
>
> (405)

What happens here? At least two things. First, the struggle Merteuil fought against her physiognomy during her self-education is lost. She strove to conceal her thoughts and feelings, to establish a hierarchy in which the inner motivation ruled over and controlled the outer expression. This hard fought inside/outside hierarchy now crumbles as her illness figuratively makes her soul visible. There is a sardonic perhaps providential element to this disfigurement. As if Merteuil's disease was the manifestation of God's just revenge for all her wrongdoing. But, and this is my second point about the passage, the revenge does not originate in God. Instead it brings together the justice of the penal system (the lost court case) and of the social world (there is a "marked display of public indignation" (402) when she enters the Comédie Italienne in Letter

173). Adding to these miseries is her disfigurement and her loss of an eye due to smallpox (405 [457]).[67] What the French revolutionaries sought to do with the Declaration of Rights was to bridge the gap between natural law and positive law, to instantiate legislation fit for both man and the citizen. It is tempting to interpret Merteuil's case of smallpox not as God's revenge but as nature's revenge. Her sickness is an outside, agent-less punishment that adds to the juridical verdict and the social shaming she experiences. As such, she loses not only in the hierarchical struggle she has fought against her physiognomy but also in the war she has waged against social norms. Coming out on top in this hierarchy of the novel's conclusion, it seems to me, is not exactly the traditional good manners of *le monde* but an authority that combines legal, social, and natural elements. To the degree that the novel reaches – and wants to reach – any moral conclusion, any right order, I suggest that this is where we find it. The right order of society is not found in any natural state or in the irrationality of love but in that unified authority of positive law, social law, and natural law that passes its harsh verdict on Merteuil on the novel's final pages.

* * *

Arranged marriages, libertinism, and love are three competing kinds of sociality and models of community. In *The Virtues of Abandon*, Charly Coleman distinguished between a culture of (Lockian) self-possession and (Rousseauian) self-abandonment.[68] In the culture of self-possession, the individual relates to his or her self as a kind of possession and this possessive self-relation forms the basis of interpersonal relations in the social field. This culture of self-possession, as Coleman shows, can take different forms but it reaches one culmination in the case of libertinism. When Valmont terms it his "right" to possess Cécile and when Merteuil opposes all kinds of "enslavement" and "subjection," both of them adhere to the culture of self-possession. From the perspective of political anthropology, this signals a confrontation between individual and community and clearly libertine personhood depends upon not being subjected to any kind of communitarian rules and obligations. Love, on the other hand, is aligned with the culture of self-abandonment in the sense that lovers lose their feeling of individuality and attain their identity from the small community of two that they belong to. They exist only as members of a community that is larger than themselves, which explains why Tourvel and Valmont seize to exist when their love becomes impossible. Arranged marriages are caught in the middle of this struggle between two extreme forms of personhood. Their proponents seek to establish a community capable of guiding the married couple and thereby take advantage of the communitarian culture of self-abandonment but they also wish to control (or possess) the created

Choderlos de Laclos's Liaisons dangereuses 153

communities and thereby position themselves above the community they seek to instantiate. Laclos's novel plays these contesting cultures of personhood out against each other and shows the fallibility of them all. Read politically, his juxtaposition of competing forms of sociality can thus be interpreted as a confrontation of those opposing political anthropologies, which the Declaration of Rights claims to unite in its linkage of collective happiness and individual rights.

My interpretation of *Les liaisons* sits uneasily with the dominating interpretations of the relationship between fictional literature and French revolutionary human rights. Lynn Hunt has argued that the importance of literature – in her case sentimental, epistolary novels – resides in its ability to produce empathy. By being transported into the minds of different fictional characters, readers learn to regard others as human beings, which, Hunt argues, is the basis for the development of human rights.[69] In his criticism of Hunt's position, Dan Edelstein emphasizes the importance of the political and social exclusion at work in the literature from this period. Readers are not taught to empathize uncritically but, more ambivalently, only to feel with sympathetic characters while rejecting ill-intentioned antagonists. "No one feels sorry for the villain," Edelstein writes in a pointed summation of his critique.[70] Finally, Susan Maslan has proposed to investigate the literary genealogy of the man/citizen-schism inherent in the title of the 1789 Declaration of Rights. In the early modern period, Maslan argues, humans and citizens were separated as the former belonged to the *oikos* and the latter to the *nomos*. The 1789 Declaration represents the wish to fuse the feeling human with the rational citizen, the document marks what Maslan sometimes calls "the dream of the feeling citizen."[71] None of these positions, valuable in each their right, can fully explain the relationship between Laclos's novel and the human rights thought of the period.

Even though it is an epistolary novel, *Les Liaisons* is no training ground in universal empathy. Most characters are presented as scheming and unwilling to disregard their own immediate desires. If the letters of the novel offer a "'stereoscopic' vision" of events,[72] stylistically adjusted to their different fictive authors as they are, they do not really invite the reader to sympathize or live with the various letter writers. In his correspondence with Madame Riccoboni, Laclos himself suggested that his novel functioned as a frightening reminder of moral depredation and argued that there could be an inversed form of morality in depicting immorality. "The merit, which I acknowledge, of mapping out *sentiments that one desires to imitate* does not, I believe, annul the usefulness of painting those sentiments one should defend oneself against."[73] Based on the moral outrage that his book produced, there is something to be said for this moral-through-immorality-interpretation but I consider it more accurate to say that the novel urges its reader to critically compare the diverse perspectives of the letters and reflect upon the opposite ambitions and strategic positionings of the characters. As such, the response to the novel, I argue, is more intellectual and reflective than emotionally engaging.

It also seems inadequate to suggest that Laclos's novel explores – or even exploits – the dynamics of political exclusion. The greatest villain of the novel, Merteuil, is being pushed out of Paris at the end but the novel presents convincing motivations for her conduct. Instead of presenting a moral critique of Merteuil, the novel explains how the dynamics of an inegalitarian society unfailingly produces immoral behavior. The problem is not Merteuil but the system that produces a Merteuil and that distinction means that the novel can teach us only little about *who*, according to the author, should be excluded from political membership. It can teach us a lot, however, about a social machinery that seems to be breaking down from within because it produces vice instead of virtue.

While I do not think that the ideas of Hunt and Edelstein can be productively extended to Laclos's novel, *Les Liaisons* does contain a fleeting interest in bridging the gap between human sensibility and rational citizenship. The final verdict on Merteuil is passed by an authority that combines the legitimacy of juridical, social, and natural law and could be said to represent an attempt to imagine a new source of legitimate authority. This alternative and legitimate source of authority is never fully developed but functions as a hypothetical image of political alterity.

In addition to the deliberately vague imaginary and visionary facets, *Les Liaisons* contains destructive and critical perspectives that accelerate what some historians have called the desacralization or desantification of symbols of authority.[74] The 1789 Declaration of Rights was caught between unfinishedness on the one hand and an alleged simplicity and sacrality on the other hand. There is here a tension between a complex set of social and political problems and an ambition to solve these issues in one sweeping movement. Mercier's *L'an 2440* and Chénier's *Fénelon* engage in this dilemma by proposing simple solutions to the complex problems of Old Regime France. The corruption, scandals, and inequality of French society can be washed away if only the principles of Mercier's philosophical prince or Chénier's heroic Fénelon figure are put into action. Laclos likewise intervenes in the dilemma but instead of proposing solutions, he highlights the problems and diagnoses the maladies of society. The *libelles* and the pornographic slander of the period, in Darnton's interpretation, desacralized monarchic authority by placing monarchs and particularly Marie-Antoinette in all kinds of compromising positions and contexts. Laclos adds to this body of literature in the sense that he lays bare the promiscuity, the uselessness, and the lack of transparency that dominated high aristocratic circles. His attack, however, was not directed at individuals but at the system that produced individual corruption. The politics of *Les liaisons* does not reside in the ambition to produce virtue or imagine social perfection but in the attempt to criticize vice at a systemic level and in the interpellation of a critical and reflective reader.

The social critique of *Les Liaisons* and the critical reflection it invites is a topical one set within the intellectual and discursive framework which parliamentary deputies would later re-invoke during the Declaration Debate. We see this in small scale when Merteuil subverts the revolutionary ideal of transparency and when Valmont reclaims his "imprescriptible right" (225 [253]) to sexually violate Cécile. These invocations of the period's political idiom are of an inversed, perverted nature but they demonstrate the degree to which Laclos modeled his depiction of social forms on contemporary politics. The most systematic attempt of his to think with those intellectual and discursive figures that would later dominate the Declaration Debate, however, is his intervention in the Rousseauian nature/society distinction. He makes this intervention in his second essay on the education of women but as I have demonstrated the temporal and hierarchical consequences of the nature/society distinction are very much operative in the novel. While *Les Liaisons* is political in its critical social diagnosis, it is related directly to the concerns of the Declaration Debate because it shared and built upon the intellectual and discursive framework used later by the parliamentary deputies. *Les Liaisons* scrutinized the tensions and contradictions of noble society in order to demonstrate *why* and *the degree to which* a reform of this class was necessary. In doing that, Laclos did his part in the collective effort to reimagine a new and happier France.

Notes

1 Throughout the chapter, I quote from Helen Constantine's English translation (Choderlos de Laclos, *Dangerous Liaisons*. London: Penguin Books, 2007) in the running text. When it is necessary I quote from the French original in [brackets]. French citations refer to the newest Pléiade edition of *Les Liaisons dangereuses* [Choderlos de Laclos, *Les Liaisons dangereuses*. Ed. Catriona Seth (Paris: Gallimard, 2011)]. As opposed to the older Pléiade editions edited by Marurice Allem (1932 and 1951) and Laurent Versioni (1979), Seth's version takes the revised 1787 edition of Laclos's novel as point of departure. There are only miniscule differences between this edition and the 1782 edition but one alteration is the insertion of a third extradiegetic preface, namely the "Avertissement du libraire" [5–6], that too probably written by Laclos himself.
2 The idea that the absolute monarchy was in "crisis" in the years preceding the revolution is much debated among historians. This topic is the focus of two recent anthologies: Thomas Kaiser and Dale K. Van Kley (eds.), *From Deficit to Deluge: The Origins of the French Revolution* (Stanford: Stanford University Press, 2011) and Julian Swann and Joël Félix (eds.), *The Crisis of the Absolute Monarchy: France from Old Regime to Revolution* (Oxford: Oxford University Press, 2013).

3 For a helpful overview see Colette Verger Michael's annotated bibliography: *Choderlos de Laclos: The Man, His Works, and His Critics. An Annotated Bibliography* (New York and London: Garland Publishing, Inc., 1982). Michael lists and comments on 446 texts about Laclos, books and articles alike. According to a MLA International Bibliography search conducted on 9 June 2016, 260 texts on Laclos have been published after the publication of Michael's book, bringing the total to a staggering, yet no doubt incomplete, 706 published texts (articles plus books) on Laclos.

4 Georges Poulet, *The Interior Distance*. Translated by Elliott Coleman (Baltimore: The Johns Hopkins Press, 1959), 45–65; Henri Coulet, "L'espace et le temps du libertinage dans Les Liaisons dangereuses" in *Laclos et le libertinage. 1782–1982 actes du colloque du bicentenaire des Liaisons dangereuses*. Preface by René Pomeau (Paris: Presses Universitaires de France, 1983), 177–191.

5 Tzvetan Todorov, "Choderlos de Laclos et la théorie du récit" in A. J. Greimas et al. (eds.), *Sign, Language, Culture* (The Hague and Pris: Mouton, 1970), 601–613.

6 Didier Masseau, "Le narrataire des 'Liaisons dangereuses'" in *Laclos et le libertinage*, 111–137; Janie Vanpée, "Dangerous Liaisons 2: The Riccoboni-Laclos Sequel" in *Eighteenth-Century Fiction*, Vol. 9, No. 1 (1996): 51–70.

7 Joan Dejean, *Literary Fortifications: Rousseau, Laclos, Sade* (Princeton: Princeton University Press, 1984), 191–263.

8 Jean-Luc Seylaz, *Les liaisons dangereuses et la création romanesque chez Laclos* (Genève and Paris: Librairie E. Droz and Librairie Minard, 1958), 11. In addition to Seylaz' study, other works within this tradition include: Jean Rousset, "Les lecteurs indiscrets" in *Laclos et le libertinage*, 89–97; Michel Delon: "Le discours italique dans *Les Liaisons dangereuses*" in *Laclos et le libertinage*, 137–151; David McCallam, "The Nature of Libertine Promises in Laclos's 'Les Liasons dangereuses'" in *The Modern Language Review*, Vol. 98, No. 4 (2003): 857–869.

9 Anne Marie Jaton, "Libertinage féminin. Libertinage dangereux" in *Laclos et le libertinage*, 151–163; Anne Deneys-Tunney, *Ecritures du corps. De Descartes à Laclos* (Paris: Presses Universitaires de France, 1992), 283–323.

10 Laurent Versini, *Le roman épistolaire* (Paris: Presses universitaires de France, 1979).

11 David McCallam, "Metrology: The Body as Measure in Les Liaisons dangereuses" in *Eighteenth-Century Fiction*, Vol. 27, No. 1 (2014): 83–104. For an analysis of the novel's description of furniture, see Peter Shoemaker, "The Furniture of Narrative in Crébillon's *Le sopha* and Laclos's *Les Liaisons dangereuses*" in *The Romanic Review*, Vol. 101, No. 4 (2010): 689–708.

12 Catriona Seth (ed.), *Laclos après Laclos* (Paris: Hermann, 2016).

13 Peter Brooks, *The Novel of Worldliness: Crébillon, Marivaux, Laclos, Stendhal* (Princeton: Princeton University Press, 1969), 172–219; Susan Winnett, *Terrible Sociality: The Text of Manners in Laclos, Goethe, and James*. (Stanford: Stanford University Press, 1993), 40–97.

14 When the 273 documents available from the period between 1770 and 1799 in the ARTFL-FRANTEXT database are listed according to the frequency with which they use the word *bonheur*, *Les Liaisons dangereuses* is number 23. In total *bonheur* is used 166 times in the novel. Cf. http://artfl-project.uchicago.edu/content/artfl-frantext [page last visited 13 May 2016].

15 I do not mean to imply that there are no political interpretations of *Les Liaisons dangereuses*. For an example, see, e.g., Jennifer Birkett, "Dangerous

Liaisons: Literary and Political Form in Choderlos de Laclos" in *Literature and History*, Vol. 8, No. 1 (1982): 82–94. Historicized interpretations of the novel's politics are, however, few in comparison with the enormous amount of formally oriented readings of Laclos.
16 Suzanne Desan, *The Family on Trial in Revolutionary France* (Berkeley: University of California Press, 2004), 3.
17 Desan, *The Family on Trial*, 7.
18 Brooks, *Novel of Worldliness*, 177.
19 Gerber, *Bastards*, 7.
20 Feher, "Introduction" in Michel Feher (ed.), *The Libertine Reader: Eroticism and Enlightenment*. New York: Zone Books, 1997, 17–18. Merteuil puts this naturalist philosophy into words when she derisively claims that women of feeling "imagine that the only source of pleasure is the man with whom they have sought it, and, like all truly superstitious people, accord to the priest the respect and the faith which is due to the Deity alone" (180).
21 Todorov, "Choderlos de Laclos," 604.
22 Knut Stene-Johansen, *Libertinske strategier 1620–1789: Cyrano, Don Juan, Casanova, Valmont, Sade* (Oslo: Spartacus Forlag, 1996), 31.
23 Feher, "Introduction," 11.
24 In his discussion of Casanova and Sade, McMahon makes no distinction between hedonism and libertinism but I believe the rational and systematic aspect of libertinism is worth emphasizing particularly in the case of Laclos. Cf. McMahon, *The Pursuit of Happiness*, 231–233.
25 For an analysis of the novel's military metaphor, see Dejean, *Literary Fortifications*, 191–263.
26 Poulet, *The Interior Distance*, 57. McCallam adds that the libertines are at once "êtres de projet" and "êtres de discours," cf. McCallam, "The Nature of Libertine Promises," 857.
27 Brooks, *Novel of Worldliness*, 177.
28 Madame de Lafayette, *The Princesse de Clèves* (London: Penguin Books, 2004).
29 Jean-Claude Perrot quoted from Carol Blum, *Strength in Numbers: Population, Reproduction, and Power in Eighteenth-Century France* (Baltimore and London: The Johns Hopkins University Press, 2002), 3.
30 Desan, *The Family on Trial*, 58–60.
31 She writes, "Literary critics, who excelled at spotting the difficult overlayings of multiple structures, who understood precisely how complex forms could be, seemed to be missing an opportunity to read social structures – politics – in the same alert, insightful way." Caroline Levine, *Forms: Whole, Rhythm, Hierarchy, Network*. (Princeton and Oxford: Princeton University Press, 2015), xi.
32 I am here thinking specifically of works associated with the Geneva School such as Georges Poulet, *The Metamorphoses of the Circle* (Baltimore: The Johns Hopkins Press, 1966) and Jean-Pierre Richard, *Proust et le monde sensible* (Paris: Seuil, 1990).
33 Deneys-Tunney, "Écritures du corps," 283–321. I like the gesture of Deneys-Tunney's analysis but I think she fails to distinguish between different value systems in the novel (here money vs. fetishized beauty) when she characterizes Merteuil's description of Cécile as a "financial transaction" quoting the passage "sixty thousand *livres*" as textual evidence (Deneys-Tunney, 287). Merteuil does invoke this figure in her reflection on what might have caused Gercourt to seek out Cécile, but the full quote

158   *Choderlos de Laclos's* Liaisons dangereuses

demonstrates that her point is actually not that Gercourt wants Cécile for monetary reasons:

> You know his ridiculous predilection for girls educated at convents and his even more ridiculous *penchant* for blondes. As a matter of fact, I wager that in spite of the sixty thousand *livres* the little Volanges girl will bring him, he would never have thought of marriage if her hair was dark or if she had not been to the convent.
>
> (14)

34 As a biographical aside, Laclos began the work on *Les liaisons* in 1778 at age thirty-six.
35 Winnett, *Terrible Sociality*, 62.
36 Jean Pestré, "Happiness" in *The Encyclopedia of Diderot & d'Alembert Collaborative Translation Project*. Trans. N. S. Hoyt and T. Cassirer. Ann Arbor: Michigan Publishing, University of Michigan Library, 2003. http://hdl.handle.net/2027/spo.did2222.0000.153 (accessed 21 December 2017).
37 Poulet, *The Interior Distance*, 62.
38 Laurent Versini, "Notice" in Laclos, *Œuvres complètes*. Ed. L. Versini (Paris: Gallimard, 1979), 1411. Versini continues and claims that Laclos was a "man of concretion [homme du concret]" who "lacked the gift of pursuing an abstract reflection" (Ibid., 1414). Georges Poulet is equally harsh in his judgment and finds the essays "entirely negligible" (Poulet, *The Interior Distance*, 56). Other critics have found the essays interesting, e.g., Anne Marie Jaton, "Libertinage féminin, libertinage dangereux," 156 and Henri Coulet, "Espace et temps du libertinage dans 'Les Liaisons dangereuses,'" 188–189 both in *Laclos et le libertinage*. Preface by R. Pomeau (Paris: Presses Universitaires de France, 1983).
39 Laclos, "On Women and their Education" in Feher (ed.), *The Libertine Reader*, 132.
40 "Man is born free, and everywhere he is in chains." Jean-Jacques Rousseau, *The Social Contract and Other Later Political Writings*. Ed. V. Gourevitch (Cambridge: Cambridge University Press, 2012), 41.
41 Jean-Jacques Rousseau, *Discourse on the Origin and the Foundations of Inequality among Men* in Jean-Jacques Rousseau, *The Discourses and Other Early Political Writings*. Trans. V. Gourevitch (Cambridge: Cambridge University Press, 1997), 167. This passage is an implicit answer to Thomas Hobbes who famously considered life in the state of nature "solitary, poor, nasty, brutish, and short." (Thomas Hobbes, *Leviathan*. Ed. N. Malcolm. (Oxford: Clarendon Press, 2012), Vol. 2, 192).
42 Laclos, "On Women and their Education" in Feher (ed.), *The Libertine Reader*, 157. [Laclos, "Des femmes et de leur éducation" in Laclos, *Œuvres complètes*, 423].
43 Georges Poisson, *Choderlos de Laclos ou l'obstination* (Paris: Bernard Grasset, 1985), 153
44 Laurent Versini, *Laclos et la tradition: Essai sur les sources et la technique des Liaisons dangereuses* (Paris: Librairie C. Klincksieck, 1968), 575. See also Stene-Johansen, *Libertinske strategier*, 192.
45 For an interesting formal reading of this letter, see Rousset, "Les lecteurs indiscrets," 94–95.
46 De Man, *Allegories of Reading*, 149; 155.
47 Maslan, "Nature and Society," 266.
48 Laclos, "On Women and Their Education" in Feher (ed.), *The Libertine Reader*, 132n.

49 Laclos, "On Women and their Education" in Feher (ed.), *The Libertine Reader*, 148.
50 Laclos, "On Women and their Education" in Feher (ed.), *The Libertine Reader*, 154.
51 Levine, *Forms*, 82.
52 Levine, *Forms*, 82.
53 Levine, *Forms*, 82.
54 Laclos, "Discourse on the Question Put Forth by the Academy of Chalons-sur-Marne" in Feher (ed.), *The Libertine Reader*, 131 [Laclos, "Discours sur la question" in Laclos, *Œuvres complètes*, 405].
55 "According to the essay, the particular social system in which *Les Liaisons dangereuses* plots the manifold versions of female demise is a particularly female convention, albeit one born of bitter necessity. With this stroke, Laclos both shows his sympathy for the plight of women and betrays them (inevitably) yet again." Winnett, *Terrible Sociality*, 75. Other critics have found Laclos's gender politics more progressive. Thus, Anne Marie Jaton writes, "Laclos gives no essentialist definition of woman neither in his novel nor in his essays but seems to always consider the woman, with her inferior physical strength and different psychological organization, the equal of man." Jaton, "Libertinage féminin," 156.
56 What I will say, however, is that Laclos calls attention to the gendered aspect of social contract theory. In other words, he does what Carol Pateman invites scholars to do in her classic *The Sexual Contract* (Cambridge: Polity Press, 1988).
57 *Déclaration des droits de l'homme et du citoyen* in Antoine de Baecque, Wolfgang Schmale, and Michel Vovelle, (eds.), *L'an 1 des droits de l'homme* (Paris: Presses du CNRS, 1988), 198.
58 Laclos reuses this analogy in his second essay when he writes, "Lacking strength, women could not defend and preserve their civil existence: companions in name, they soon became slaves in fact, and unhappy slaves; their fate could hardly have been better than that of the blacks of our colonies." (Laclos, "On Women and their Education" in Feher (ed.), *The Libertine Reader*, 155.)
59 See, e.g., Olympe de Gouges, *Les droits de la femme* in Olympe de Gouges, *Écrits politiques 1788–1791*. Edited by Olivier Blanc (Paris: Côté-femmes, 1993), 210. On the discursive linkage of marriage and slavery, see Karen Offen, "How (and Why) the Analogy of Marriage with Slavery Provided the Springboard for Women's Rights Demands in France, 1640–1848" in Kathryn Kish Sklar and James Brewer Stewart (eds.), *Women's Rights and Transatlantic Antislavery in the Era of Emancipations* (New Haven: Yale University Press, 2007), 57–81.
60 Deney-Tunney, *Écritures du corps*, 302–309.
61 The idea of transparency in French Enlightenment discourse was first explored by Jean Starobinski in his *Jean-Jacques Rousseau: La transparence et l'obstacle* (Paris: Gallimard, 1976 [1957]). For discussions of transparency in French revolutionary discourse, see, e.g., Lynn Hunt, *Politics, Culture, and Class in the French Revolution*. (Berkeley: University of California Press, 2004), 44–47 and Susan Maslan, *Revolutionary Acts: Theater, Democracy, and the French Revolution* (Baltimore: The Johns Hopkins University Press, 2005), chap. 3.
62 Jean-Jacques Rousseau, *The Confessions of Jean Jacques Rousseau* (London: Privately Printed for the Members of the Aldus Society, 1903). Online: www.gutenberg.org/files/3913/3913-h/3913-h.htm [page last visited 5 January 2018].

63 Seneca quoted from Laclos, "On the Education of Women" in Feher (ed.), *The Libertine Reader*, 129.
64 Alain Badiou, *In Praise of Love*. Trans. P. Bush. London: Serpent's Tail, 2012.
65 Delon, "Le discours italique" in *Laclos et le libertinage*, 147.
66 J. E. Fowler, "The Sense of an Ending: *Les Liaisons dangereuses* revisited" in *Neophilologus*, Vol. 91, No. 2 (2007), 197–213. Fowler argues that Merteuil denies Valmont his "reward" because she has realized that Valmont is attracted by the strength of Tourvel's resistance to his seduction attempts. Thus, she tries to surpass Tourvel's capacity for resistance by rejecting Valmont and thereby she comes to incarnate the ability that attracted the attention of Valmont in the first place.
67 In the French original, it says, "Elle en est revenue, il est vrai, mais affreusement défigurée; et elle y a particulièrement perdu un æil" (457) which in the English translation has (erroneously) become less dramatic: "[S]he is horribly disfigured. And in particular she has lost the sight of one eye" (405).
68 Charly Coleman, *The Virtues of Abandon: An Anti-Individualist History of the French Enlightenment* (Stanford: Stanford University Press, 2014), 1–17.
69 Lynn Hunt, *Inventing Human Rights: A History* (New York and London: W. W. Norton & Company, 2008), 35–70.
70 Dan Edelstein, "Enlightenment Rights Talk" in *The Journal of Modern History*, Vol. 86, No. 3 (2014). Quote from page 545.
71 Susan Maslan, "The Dream of the Feeling Citizen: Law and Emotion in Corneille and Montesquieu" in *SubStance*, Vol. 35, No. 1 (2006).
72 Todorov, "Choderlos de Laclos," 604.
73 Choderlos de Laclos, "Correspondance entre Madame Riccoboni et l'auteur des *Liaisons dangereuses*" in Choderlos de Laclos, *Les Liaisons dangereuses* (Paris: Gallimard, 2011), 478.
74 The "desacralization thesis" is presented in Robert Darnton, *The Literary Underground of the Old Regime*. (Cambridge and London: Harvard University Press, 1982), 33–35 and discussed more recently in Julian Swann, "Introduction: The Crisis of the Absolute Monarchy" in Julian Swann and Joël Félix (eds.), *The Crisis of the Absolute Monarchy: France from Old Regime to Revolution* (Oxford: Oxford University Press, 2013), 13–17.

Literature

Badiou, Alain: *In Praise of Love*. Trans. by Peter Bush. London: Serpent's Tail, 2012.

Baecque, Antoine de, Wolfgang Schmale, and Michel Vovelle (eds.): *L'an 1 des droits de l'homme*. Paris: Presses du CNRS, 1988.

Birkett, Jennifer: "Dangerous Liaisons: Literary and Political Form in Choderlos de Laclos." *Literature and History*, Vol. 8, No. 1 (1982): 82–94.

Blum, Carol: *Strength in Numbers: Population, Reproduction, and Power in Eighteenth-Century France*. Baltimore and London: The Johns Hopkins University Press, 2002.

Brooks, Peter: *The Novel of Worldliness: Crébillon, Marivaux, Laclos, Stendhal*. Princeton: Princeton University Press, 1969.

Coleman, Charly: *The Virtues of Abandon: An Anti-Individualist History of the French Enlightenment*. Stanford: Stanford University Press, 2014.

Coulet, Henri: "L'espace et le temps du libertinage dans Les Liaisons dangereuses" in *Laclos et le libertinage. 1782–1982 actes du colloque du bicentenaire des Liaisons dangereuses*. Preface by R. Pomeau. Paris: Presses Universitaires de France, 1983.

Darnton, Robert: *The Literary Underground of the Old Regime*. Cambridge and London: Harvard University Press, 1982.

Dejean, Joan: *Literary Fortifications: Rousseau, Laclos, Sade*. Princeton: Princeton University Press, 1984.

Delon, Michel: "Le discours italique dans *Les Liaisons dangereuses*" in *Laclos et le libertinage. 1782–1982 actes du colloque du bicentenaire des Liaisons dangereuses*. Preface by R. Pomeau. Paris: Presses Universitaires de France, 1983.

Deneys-Tunney, Anne: *Ecritures du corps. De Descartes à Laclos*. Paris: Presses Universitaires de France, 1992.

Desan, Suzanne: *The Family on Trial in Revolutionary France*. Berkeley: University of California Press, 2004.

Edelstein, Dan: "Enlightenment Rights Talk." *The Journal of Modern History*, Vol. 86, No. 3 (2014): 530–565.

Feher, Michael: "Introduction" in Michel Feher (ed.), *The Libertine Reader: Eroticism and Enlightenment*. New York: Zone Books, 1997.

Fowler, J. E.: "The Sense of an Ending: *Les Liaisons dangereuses* Revisited." *Neophilologus* Vol. 91, No. 2 (2007): 197–213.

Gerber, Matthew: *Bastards: Politics, Family, and Law in Early Modern France*. Oxford: Oxford University Press, 2012.

Gouges, Olympe de: "Les droits de la femme" in Olympe de Gouges, *Écrits politiques 1788–1791*. Ed. by Olivier Blanc. Paris: Côté-femmes, 1993.

Hobbes, Thomas: *Leviathan*. Ed. by Noel Malcolm. Oxford: Clarendon Press, 2012.

Hunt, Lynn: *Inventing Human Rights: A History*. New York and London: W. W. Norton & Company, 2008.

Hunt, Lynn: *Politics, Culture, and Class in the French Revolution*. Berkeley: University of California Press, 2004.

Jaton, Anne Marie: "Libertinage féminin. Libertinage dangereux" in *Laclos et le libertinage. 1782–1982 actes du colloque du bicentenaire des Liaisons dangereuses*. Preface by R. Pomeau. Paris: Presses Universitaires de France, 1983.

Kaiser, Thomas & Dale K. Van Kley (eds.): *From Deficit to Deluge: The Origins of the French Revolution*. Stanford: Stanford University Press, 2011

Laclos, Choderlos de: *Œuvres complètes*. Ed. by L. Versini. Paris: Gallimard, 1979.

Laclos, Choderlos de: "On the Education of Women" in Michel Feher (ed.), *The Libertine Reader: Eroticism and Enlightenment in Eighteenth-Century France*. New York: Zone Books, 1997.

Laclos, Choderlos de: *Dangerous Liaisons*. Trans. by H. Constantine. London: Penguin Books, 2007.

Laclos, Choderlos de: *Les Liaisons dangereuses*. Ed. by C. Seth. Paris: Gallimard, 2011.

Lafayette, Madame de: *The Princesse de Clèves*. London: Penguin Books, 2004.

Levine, Caroline: *Forms: Whole, Rhythm, Hierarchy, Network*. Princeton and Oxford: Princeton University Press, 2015.

Man, Paul de: *Allegories of Reading: Figural Language in Rousseau, Nietzsche, Rilke, and Proust*. New Haven and London: Yale University Press, 1979.

162   *Choderlos de Laclos's* Liaisons dangereuses

Maslan, Susan: "Nature and Society in Revolutionary Rights Debates" in Sophia A. McClennen and Alexandra Schultheis Moore (eds.), *The Routledge Companion to Literature and Human Rights*. London and New York: Routledge, 2016.

Maslan, Susan: *Revolutionary Acts: Theater, Democracy, and the French Revolution*. Baltimore: The Johns Hopkins University Press, 2005.

Maslan, Susan: "The Dream of the Feeling Citizen: Law and Emotion in Corneille and Montesquieu." *SubStance*, Vol. 35, No. 1 (2006): 69–84.

Masseau, Didier: "Le narrataire des 'Liaisons dangereuses'" in *Laclos et le libertinage. 1782–1982 actes du colloque du bicentenaire des Liaisons dangereuses*. Preface by R. Pomeau. Paris: Presses Universitaires de France, 1983.

McCallam, David: "Metrology: The Body as Measure in Les Liaisons dangereuses." *Eighteenth-Century Fiction*, Vol. 27, No. 1, (2014): 83–104.

McCallam, David: "The Nature of Libertine Promises in Laclos's 'Les Liasons dangereuses'." *The Modern Language Review*, Vol. 98, No. 4 (2003): 857–869.

McMahon, Darrin M.: *The Pursuit of Happiness: A History from the Greeks to the Present*. London: Penguin Books, 2007.

Michael, Colette Verger: *Choderlos de Laclos: The Man, His Works, and His Critics. An Annotated Bibliography*. New York and London: Garland Publishing, Inc., 1982.

Offen, Karen: "How (and Why) the Analogy of Marriage with Slavery Provided the Springboard for Women's Rights Demands in France, 1640–1848" in K. K. Sklar and J. B. Stewart (eds.), *Women's Rights and Transatlantic Antislavery in the Era of Emancipations*. New Haven: Yale University Press, 2007.

Pateman, Carol: *The Sexual Contract*. Cambridge: Polity Press, 1988.

Pestré, Jean: "Happiness" in Diderot, Denis and Jean le Rond d'Alembert (eds.), *The Encyclopedia of Diderot & d'Alembert Collaborative Translation Project*. Ann Arbor: Michigan Publishing, University of Michigan Library, 2017. Web. http://hdl.handle.net/2027/spo.did2222.0003.409.

Poisson, Georges: *Choderlos de Laclos ou l'obstination*. Paris: Bernard Grasset, 1985.

Poulet, Georges: *The Interior Distance*. Trans. by E. Coleman. Baltimore: The Johns Hopkins Press, 1959.

Poulet, Georges: *The Metamorphoses of the Circle*. Baltimore: The Johns Hopkins Press, 1966.

Richard, Jean-Pierre: *Proust et le monde sensible*. Paris: Seuil, 1990.

Rousseau, Jean-Jacques: *The Confessions of Jean Jacques Rousseau*. London: Privately Printed for the Members of the Aldus Society, 1903. Available online: www.gutenberg.org/files/3913/3913-h/3913-h.htm [page last visited 5 January 2018].

Rousseau, Jean-Jacques: *The Discourses and Other Early Political Writings*. Ed. by V. Gourevitch. Cambridge: Cambridge University Press, 1997.

Rousseau, Jean-Jacques: *The Social Contract and Other Later Political Writings*. Ed. by V. Gourevitch. Cambridge: Cambridge University Press, 2012.

Rousset, Jean: "Les lecteurs indiscrets" in *Laclos et le libertinage. 1782–1982 actes du colloque du bicentenaire des Liaisons dangereuses*. Preface by R. Pomeau. Paris: Presses Universitaires de France, 1983.

Seth, Catriona (ed.): *Laclos après Laclos*. Paris: Hermann, 2016.

Seylaz, Jean-Luc: *Les liaisons dangereuses et la création romanesque chez Laclos*. Genève and Paris: Librairie E. Droz and Librairie Minard, 1958.

Shoemaker, Peter: "The Furniture of Narrative in Crébillon's *Le sopha* and Laclos's *Les Liaisons dangereuses*." The Romanic Review, Vol. 101, No 4, (2010): 689–708.

Starobinski, Jean: *Jean-Jacques Rousseau: La transparence et l'obstacle*. Paris: Gallimard, 1976.

Stene-Johansen, Knut: *Libertinske strategier 1620–1789: Cyrano, Don Juan, Casanova, Valmont, Sade*. Oslo: Spartacus Forlag, 1996.

Swann, Julian and Joël Félix (eds.): *The Crisis of the Absolute Monarchy: France from Old Regime to Revolution*. Oxford: Oxford University Press, 2013.

Todorov, Tzvetan: "Choderlos de Laclos et la théorie du récit" in A. J. Greimas et al. (eds.), *Sign, Language, Culture*. The Hague and Pris: Mouton, 1970.

Vanpée, Janie: "Dangerous Liaisons 2: The Riccoboni-Laclos Sequel." in *Eighteenth-Century Fiction*, Vol. 9, No. 1 (1996): 51–70.

Versini, Laurent: *Laclos et la tradition: Essai sur les sources et la technique des Liaisons dangereuses*. Paris: Librairie C. Klincksieck, 1968.

Versini, Laurent: *Le roman épistolaire*. Paris: Presses universitaires de France, 1979.

Versini, Laurent: "Notice" in Choderlos de Laclos, *Œuvres complètes*. Ed. by Laurent Versini. Paris: Gallimard, 1979.

Winnett, Susan: *Terrible Sociality: The Text of Manners in Laclos, Goethe, and James*. Stanford: Stanford University Press, 1993.

5 The Regeneration of the State in Marie-Joseph Chénier's *Fénelon ou les religieuses de Cambrai*

A century before the French revolution, a young virtuous woman of unknown origin is raised in a convent. As she leaves childhood behind her, she is asked to pronounce her vows and permanently become a nun. Lately, however, she has felt "a new sentiment" and has begun questioning the alleged happiness of convent life.[1] As it turns out, she is the victim of a horrible plot. Prior to her birth, the young woman's mother was thrown into an underground dungeon below a monastery. The mother was a member of the high nobility and had committed the crime of falling in love with a man of less prestigious kin; something which was unacceptable to her father. Fifteen years later, in the hours preceding the undesirable religious ceremony, the young novice manages to locate the underground prison cell, establish a relationship with what turns out to be her hitherto unknown mother, find the city's archbishop, and persuade him to free her and her mother from the tentacles of the convent abbess. As he arrives on the scene, the archbishop sorts out the complicated plot, frees the victims, *and* unites the happy family by officially marrying the young woman's mother and long-lost father.

To modern readers, Marie-Joseph Chénier's *Fénelon ou les religieuses de Cambrai* (1793) seems foreign and outdated. The emotional hyper-intensity, the one-dimensional characters, and the unlikely plot alienate it from modern literary canons and conventions of taste. And yet, after its 1793 premiere at Théâtre de la République, a theater that seated up to 2,000 spectators, it ran a staggering 141 times and helped accelerate the success of the convent narrative, a popular subgenre of revolutionary theater.[2] Without including *Fénelon*, literary historian Audrey Viguier lists nine plays with this setting, two of those being *Le couvent, ou les vœux forcés* (1790, 42 runs) by Olympe de Gouges and *Les victimes cloîtrées* (1791, 109 runs) by Jacques-Marie Boutet de Monvel.[3] How should we understand these plays and their immense success? They exhibit none of the compositional complexity or the ironical destabilization of meaning that has made Laclos's *Les Liaisons dangereuses* a permanent member of literary canons. Instead, they developed what became the melodramatic genre conventions and explicitly encouraged certain forms of behavior while sharply condemning others.[4] As Chénier

The Regeneration of the State in Marie-Joseph Chénier's 165

wrote, it was his ambition to "perfect the social mores" and form "new men for the new laws" through the usage of theater.[5] Relying on sharp dichotomies of good and evil, happiness and death, these plays intervened in the ongoing discussion of what it meant to be a good citizen of the new France.

Years before Lynn Hunt made the argument that sentimental epistolary novels taught their readers lessons of sympathy, scholars of sentimental literature insisted that eighteenth-century lachrymose writing was politically or socially engaged.[6] Peter Brooks argued that melodrama strove to locate and express those "basic ethical and psychic truths" that were overturned with the turmoil of the revolution.[7] "We may legitimately claim," he writes, "that melodrama becomes the principal mode for uncovering, demonstrating, and making operative the essential moral universe in a post-sacred era."[8] Brooks focuses on the early nineteenth-century melodrama, and even though Chénier's peculiar definition of tragedy has affinities with the genre of melodrama, *Fénelon* lacks the melodies that co-define that genre.[9] In *Sentimental Narrative and the Social Order in France*, David Denby intervenes in the discussion of sentimentalism's desacralized universe but from the perspective of narrative fiction. He accepts Brooks's definition of melodrama but suggests that sentimentalism "belongs firmly on the optimistic and triumphant slope of the Enlightenment project."[10] He continues:

> [I]t most certainly operates within the problematic of a desacralized universe, but as a bearer of the message of secularization rather than an expression of fears concerning the unidimensionality of such a world. [...] Morality exists, virtue is not an empty notion, but these categories do not need the guarantee of a traditionally conceived principle of transcendence: they exist as immanent forces in human society.[11]

In Denby's interpretation, literary sentimentalism belongs in that desacralized world described by Brooks, but unlike the melodrama, sentimentalism needs no villain and has no problem with the post-sacredness of the era. A great benefit of Denby's thesis is that it challenges the idea of a fundamental gap between reason and sentiment of this period. As the diversity of, say, Rousseau's or Diderot's writings shows, individual authors had no problem appreciating and producing both philosophical and emotive texts. The social objective of sentimentalism, Denby claims, is aligned with the Enlightenment project because it insists upon the natural existence of virtue by heaping one touching example of this upon another. Importantly, however, and this is in opposition to Denby's definition of sentimentalism, *Fénelon* does operate with a "threat posed to virtue by a strongly personified villain, or principle of villainy."[12]

Most recently, Cecilia Feilla has revisited the debate about the politics of sentimentalism but from the perspective of French revolutionary theater. Inspired by Susan Maslan and others, Feilla criticizes the assumption that revolutionary drama primarily consisted of political tragedies and notes that the most popular plays of the era were sentimental *drames*. This prompts her to suggest that

> the Revolutionary decade is characterized less by the infiltration of the political into all areas of public and private life, as has been the common wisdom, than by the externalization of private affective forms and conventions into public discourse and performance.[13]

Along similar lines, Maslan argues that proponents of the sentimental drama believed that in bringing the private realm to the stage, they helped create models of familial responsibility. By doing that, they furthered the cause of "happiness," and "private happiness, in turn, contributed to making a happier community, one less at risk from the excesses and disorder to which unhappy families can give rise."[14] This, Maslan emphasizes, was the argument of the proponents of sentimental drama, but often enough, the politically charged audiences reacted in highly unpredictable ways.

As this chapter progresses, I shall have occasion to specify how my reading relates to the aforementioned interpretations (among others), but here, I would like to offer a brief general explanation of my understanding of the relationship between Chénier's sentimental play and the politics of the period. I take my cue from Rabaut de Saint-Etienne, who during the Declaration Debate argued that the task of the deputies was to "regenerate" France.[15] In the Declaration Debate, to "regenerate" meant to constitute the National Assembly as a legislative body, and it meant to reconstitute France as a collective entity. In *Fénelon*, regeneration means renegotiating the rules of political exclusion and inclusion. It means participating in the struggle to define the requirements for political membership, but it also means sharply condemning the Old Regime practice of institutionalized religion and family formation. In *The Politics of Privilege*, Gail Bossenga argues that the French revolution failed to inaugurate a society of absolute freedom and equality but succeeded in shifting the contours of social conflict. While Old Regime activists had fought against the injustice of privileges, revolutionaries and their successors struggled to define citizenship in ways that made them and their fellows full members of the nation-state.[16] Chénier's play intervenes in the discussion about a new and happier France at the exact moment when the logics of political conflict shifted, and the tensions of this shift have influenced the play's dichotomous depiction of virtue and corruption.

Cecilia Feilla explicitly addresses the problem of political membership in French revolutionary theater. She claims that sentimental drama allowed "diverse groups who were excluded from direct political participation – such as women, the poor, children, the elderly, and foreigners, among others – the possibility of imagining a new social and political order that included them."[17] I agree to the extent that *Fénelon* makes a case for the social inclusion of children born outside of wedlock. It is an important point of my analysis that Chénier embeds the "large" question of state politics and the "small" question of family formation within one another.[18] The play, however, also sharply condemns anyone unable to accept natural children as members of the body politic. In Chénier's play, regeneration amounts to reforming society's inclusion *and* exclusion mechanisms. When he states that his task as a playwright is to form "new men for the new laws" by using theater's particular "kind of scene," he suggests that politics comes first, and that theater functions as an ideological dissemination machine.[19] I prefer to think of revolutionary politics and theater not as "virtually indistinguishable" but as two different kinds of institutions that at times were made to pursue parallel ambitions.[20] Seen in this perspective, *Fénelon* is an attempt to create a happy onstage community and to invite spectators to participate herein. But as are all communities, that of *Fénelon* is based on a certain set of rules and norms, and members are included or excluded according to their ability to perform and agree with these norms. The politics of *Fénelon* resides in its wish to regenerate the political community by altering the rules of inclusion and exclusion, and in its invitation to the spectators to accept the suggested communitarian rules and norms.

I begin with an analysis of the world of the nunnery and continue by considering questions of humanness, political agency, and the aesthetics of the tableau. My overall ambition is to present the workings and implications of the happy community presented onstage.

Convent Life and Paternal Inflexibility

Chénier's play opens with an exhibition of a social world gone astray. The small world of the Cambrai convent should be a peaceful sequestered space for religious benevolence but is actually a prison whose false promises hide the truth of moral depravity and inhumanity. Unlike the convent plays of Monvel and Gouges, staged first in 1790 and 1791, *Fénelon* is a historical play set in the time of the Old Regime. This difference, as I will show, was significant to contemporary critics, but it is important to note that Chénier uses the space of the convent very much like his contemporary colleagues. To all of them, the nunnery is a model place. The convent is a physically delimited place of gothic horror, but its seclusion only serves to make visible and amplify moral and social logics considered general of the larger society. The authors also share the ambition to use the physical presence of the convent as an integrated element in the narratives' psychological and social investigations. The dungeons, cells, walls, and aisles of *Fénelon* are much more than background to the drama. Particularly in the staged version of the play – but also in the lines of the characters – the locality is part of the character and plot development.

Fénelon is set in the "interior of a women's convent," in "the Archbishop's palace," and in "an underground cell" (266). In the first act, the convent is described as an "asylum" (1.2), and from the outset, this place attains great emotional and symbolic ambiance. The term asylum signals physical distance from the world and promises a degree of sheltered protection. The protective connotations of the place remain present when the nunnery is synecdochically described with a reference to "these peaceful walls" (1.1), but walls also carry the potential meaning of imprisonment and enclosure. Those negative implications are developed when Amélie refers to the "space of darkness" (1.1) and the "coffin" (1.1) from which she hears voices. The convent space thus flutters symbolically between protective seclusion and burial, but the gloomy metaphors become increasingly dominant and culminate when Isaura says, "[A]ll I see around me is a grave" (1.4) and when Amélie says, "This horrible place bears down on my senses. / These arcs, this basement, this silence, these shadows, / everything gives a gloomy diminution that goes to the bottom of the heart." (2.3).

The increasingly unhappy connotations of the convent space are the result of the "new sentiment" (1.1) that has taken hold of Amélie in the outset of the play. In an early exchange with Isaura, Amélie says,

> I have changed despite myself; can you punish me for that?
> I have seen the enchanting error dispel before me:
> Instead of the happiness that has been unceasingly painted to me,
> My eyes have perceived nothing but an immense future
> Without hope, alas! and without memory.
> There is then my destiny! The peace of this asylum
> Eternalize the time that runs motionless. [Éternise le temps qui s'écoule immobile]
>
> (1.2)

Amélie used to believe in the idyllic narrative of convent happiness that was constantly suggested to her. When she confirms her vows, the abbess tells her, "happiness will begin" (1.2); life as a nun, she is told, is a "supreme happiness" (1.1) that will soon start. But this happiness narrative – or, to use the visual metaphor of the quote, this painting of happiness – has begun to appear untrue. A painting is here a false reproduction of reality; it is an enchanting error that now dissolves as when the sun clears away the fog. Chénier develops this metaphor of a veiled/unveiled perception of the world throughout the play. Thus, Fénelon regrets that his compatriot "misconceives and fears the truth" (3.2); truth is at one point "unveiled

The Regeneration of the State in Marie-Joseph Chénier's   169

[dévoilé]" (4.3); and toward the end, the characters finally "wake up [réveil]" (5.2), "see again [revoir]" (5.2; 5.4), and are "reborn" (5.4). The convent, in other words, places a real *and* figural veil before the eyes of the characters, and only when this veil is removed can the convent be seen as the grave that it actually is.[21]

In his novelistic version of the convent narrative, the posthumously published *La Religieuse* (1796), Denis Diderot is every bit as critical of the convent as Chénier. Diderot, to an even greater degree than Chénier, emphasizes that the convent produces a set of practices and affects:

> Man is born to live in society. Separate him, isolate him, and his way of thinking will become incoherent, his character will change, a thousand foolish fancies will spring up in his heart, bizarre ideas will take root in his mind like brambles in the wilderness. Put a man in a forest and he will become wild; put him in a cloister, where the idea of coercion joins forces with that of servitude, and it is even worse.[22]

The Nun is an institution novel, probably written in 1760, and it provocatively argues that the convent turns ordinary people perverse because it places them in a perversely regulated space. Chénier is less interested in attacking the convent as a form of institutionalized religion, and Gauthier Ambrus even claims that Chénier used the convent and its religious fanatics only as a metaphor of revolutionary fanaticism.[23] It would be nonsensical to criticize monastic vows onstage in January 1793, Ambrus argues, because their intangibility was abolished by law on 13 February 1790. But as a journalist wrote in December 1791, the Chapelier Law, which momentarily abolished theater censorship, ignited an incredible fascination with convents among Parisian playwrights:

> Barely was the liberty of the press and of the theater declared alongside the political liberty before the monks and the nuns became one of the premier objects taken on by the crowd of writers. [...] All the theaters represented convents from the moment when the vows were forbidden and our poets attacked the convent railings as soon as the laws made it possible.[24]

Clearly, convents were dramatic settings that attracted writers, but the legal changes also prompted authors to develop a different take on the institution. Ambrus, I think, goes too far in downgrading the importance of religious fanaticism, but he does right to call attention to the fact that Chénier does more than simply criticize the convent institution in the way Diderot had done to great effect. Instead, Chénier strikes a parallel between the small world of the convent and larger societal patterns, hereby making the convent a condensed emblem of Old Regime practices.

The parallel between the convent and the outside world is apparent in the play's depiction of villainy. Villainy in this play entails a combination of the ultra-traditionalist values of the church and those of society. Thus, when the forbidden love story of Héloïse and D'Elmance is brought to light, the father of Héloïse is consequently described as an Old Regime conservative unable to accept any uncontrolled social mobility in marriages. When he learns of his daughter's love interest, his angry reaction is grounded in pride and unfulfilled expectations: "In his daughter he saw the dying out of a famous name; / The pride made him angry: my pains and my consistency / could not vanquish the resistance of this pride" (2.3). D'Elmance later tells Fénelon that he asked this "ambitious father" of "famous blood" (3.2) for the daughter's hand in marriage but was met with a refusal based on the father's insistence upon "a name equal to his own" (3.2). This uncompromising behavior causes Héloïse to describe her father as "inflexible" and as a "cruel tyrant" (2.3). These adjectives, Jean-Claude Bonnet has argued, were highly pejorative in this period, and the *pater familias* they describe is under heavy fire from an only seemingly soft and friendly paternal counter-figure:

> The new image of the father, more familial and calm, is destined to not only supplant an ancient tyrannical – 'gothic,' as they said back then – form of paternity. It is also used in a militant project. In his domestic simplicity and stripped of all other attributes, the private father acquires a surplus of symbolic interest because he comes to represent nature: before her the distinctions and privileges of a society of order crumble and this allows a view of a more homogeneous and more egalitarian world. Claims upon a universalist ethic and demand to change to a new order of things are made through the figure of the father.[25]

Writers such as Rousseau, Diderot, Rétif de la Bretonne, and Madame de Staël all contributed, Bonnet writes, to the development of a new domestically oriented father figure. In the depiction of Héloïse's father, Chénier draws upon the image of the gothic and tyrannical paternalist, and hereby creates a villain that combines elements from Old Regime religion, aristocracy, and paternal inflexibility. The mixed origin of this villainous character again testifies to the intertwinement of high politics and family patterns in the period. The radical changes in state politics, Suzanne Desan emphasizes, influenced the everyday organization of families and were, in turn, motivated by new family patterns.[26] Authors of late eighteenth-century French fiction – and Chénier is a prime example of this – repeatedly built upon this dialectic of a small family world and a larger political world in their attempts to engage with politics through literature.

In addition to its criticism of inflexible paternalism, *Fénelon* attacks the Old Regime stigmatization of natural children. The drama of the play revolves around the figure of the bastard and of its potential inclusion in the nuclear family and the social body. After Héloïse gives birth to an illegitimate child, she is thrown into the underground convent prison cell, the child (Amélie) is raised in the convent, and the father gives up his career to find out what happened to his young family. In his intervention in the debate about natural children, Chénier draws upon the period's fascination with populationism, a set of ideas summed up by Carol Blum with an old monarchical axiom: "The greatness of kings is measured by the number of their subjects."[27] Before I return to Chénier's play I want to make a historical detour and explain how the natural child became a cause for political struggle in this period.

In combination with the commonly held, yet mistaken, belief that France was losing population in the eighteenth century, to equate the number of subjects with the strength of a nation was a potentially subversive cocktail. It facilitated critical questions and uncommon proposals. Populationist texts, Blum writes,

> urge such programs as the reduction or even interdiction of celibacy, the legalization of divorce, the introduction of polygamy, and the elimination of a whole variety of ecclesiastical and legal sexual taboos, even those against violence and incest. Thus a purportedly objective referent, the numerical representation of the nation's population, became the vehicle for a wide-ranging critique of the most intimate details of the citizens' lives as well as a powerful weapon in the Enlightenment's battles against the monarchy and the Church.[28]

These populationist ideas were easy to appropriate in discussions about the legitimacy of natural children and they were well-suited to create the characteristic dialectic between state and family politics. When politicians accepted basic populationist arguments they were prone to consider illegitimate children a societal resource rather than a threat to stability:

> The distinction [between legitimate and illegitimate children] worried many delegates, as did the increasing number of neglected, fatherless children who in principle should have been treasured as the nation's demographic asset but were in fact living on the streets in misery.[29]

Louis XIV himself, Matthew Gerber writes, had argued that foundlings could "become soldiers and serve in our troops" or become "inhabitants of the colonies that we are establishing for the commercial good of our realm."[30] In other words, thinking about subjects as a useful resource was an important step in the process of destigmatizing the natural child and as Figure 5.1 illustrates, the idea of being reproductively useful to

Figure 5.1 L'Erreur et la folie nous avoit jetté dans des cloîtres, mais la raison nous rend au monde: [estampe] / [non identifié]. (Paris: [s.n.], 1790). Bibliothèque nationale de France.

the world simultaneously challenged the traditionally held ideas about celibacy and convent life.

Olympe de Gouges, first-generation feminist and author of the convent play *Le couvent, ou les vœux forcés* (1790), went further in her defense of the natural child than did Chénier. In 1791 she introduced natural right theory into the debates about family politics. More precisely, she rewrote the entire *Déclaration des droits de l'homme et du citoyen* from a women's right perspective and famously called it *Déclaration des droits de la femme et de la citoyenne*. Much has been written about Gouges's Declaration of Rights but I want to call attention to her version of Article 11 in which she explicitly addresses the question of natural children.[31] I quote first the original article, focused on freedom of speech and print, and then Gouges's version:

> XI. The free communication of thoughts and opinions is one of the most precious of the rights of man. Every citizen may therefore speak, write and print freely, if he accepts his own responsibility for any abuse of this liberty in the cases set by the law.[32]
> XI. The free communication of thoughts and opinions is one of the most precious rights of woman, because that liberty ensures the legitimacy of children with respect to their fathers. Therefore,

without a barbarous prejudice forcing her to disguise the truth, every female Citizen may freely say, 'I am the mother of a child who belongs to you,' although she must answer for the abuses of this liberty in cases set by the Law.[33]

In his analysis of the differences between the two versions, John Cole primarily comments on the aspects of the original that are absent from Gouges's article: "the issues of public speaking, writing, and publishing."[34] He explains this absence with a reference to Gouges's "revulsion from irresponsible journalists who encouraged bloodshed," Jean-Paul Marat being "the worst."[35] More important than those omissions, I think, is Gouges's intervention in the ongoing debates about inheritance law and family politics. She repeatedly invokes natural children in her writings and the radical nature of her proposition that women should have the right to freely appoint the fathers of their illegitimate children deserves attention.[36] Her version of Article 11 uses equal rights principles to argue better conditions for unwed mothers at a time when illegitimate children were still considered to be a potential threat to social stability. Bastards destabilized the nuclear family and raised inconvenient questions about inheritance rights but populationist and equal rights ideas made it increasingly difficult to argue for the continued political exclusion of natural children.

With his play, Chénier intervenes in those ongoing discussions about natural children. The villains are clerics and members of the high nobility and their inability to understand and respect natural love and natural family relations is the decisive trait of their villainy. Feilla is right to claim that the sentimental drama externalizes domestic issues but *Fénelon* carefully attaches the question of family relations to the problem of state organization and effectively makes family and state organization two sides of the same coin. Villainy is hence the simultaneous inability to accept bastards as members of the domestic family and as valuable resources for the state. Before returning to the question of villainy, I want to analyze the play's conception of virtue. Inspired by parallel discussions in the theory of sentimental literature and human rights philosophy, I shall address the question of virtue as a question of humanness.

The Problem of Humanness

Both Lynn Hunt and David Denby propose social interpretations of sentimental literature. Despite my admiration of their work, I think they underestimate the importance of villainy or evil in the sentimental genre of writing and this has implications for their understanding of the human rights discourse of the period.[37] Chénier's play operates with a "personified villain, or principle of villainy" and this fact calls for an adjusted understanding of sentimentality.[38] Focusing on the different topic of sentimentality in the eighteenth-century colonial discourse, Lynn Festa helpfully suggests that sentimental writing is concerned with deciding who or what qualifies as human:

> Whereas sympathy alludes to the mobility of emotion between different individuals, and sensibility describes individuals' susceptibility to particular kinds and degrees of feeling, sentimentality as a crafted literary form moves to locate that emotion, to assign it to particular persons, thereby designating who possesses affect and who elicits it. [...] Sentimentality, in other words, is bound up with the interests of empire, not only because sentimental texts describe and elicit emotion, but also because they *locate* it. By governing the circulation of feeling among subjects and objects, sentimentality helps to define who will be acknowledged as human.[39]

As a specific literary form, sentimentality distinguishes between the subjects and objects of sympathy and, I would add in accordance with Festa's work, between those who have and those who lack the ability to sympathize with suffering. This conception of the sentimental writing resonates well with *Fénelon* and its stark opposition between those able and those unable to accept the inclusion of natural children in the *chose public*. Festa's work also links the sentimental style with the question of the human or more precisely with the question of who qualifies as a human being. Humanness has received much attention in recent human rights philosophy because, in the words of Sharon Sliwinski, "to be human, these [declarations of rights] resoundingly declare, is to be free and equal in dignity and rights."[40] Humanness serves as a qualifier for rights and the linkage between the two has made it necessary to analyze historically shifting conceptions of what it means to belong wholly and fully to the "community called humanity."[41] Humanness may seem an abstract, ahistorical concern but – and this is part of what Balibar hints at with his concept of "political anthropology"[42] – eighteenth-century observers themselves linked humanness with the question of political rights. Thus, French revolutionary politician, philosopher, and mathematician Marquis de Condorcet (1743–1794) unhesitatingly used the humanness/rights-connection to defend the political rights of everyone despite their religion, color, and sex:

> The rights of man stem exclusively from the fact that they are sentient beings, capable of acquiring moral ideas and of reasoning upon them. Since women have the same qualities, they necessarily also have the same rights. Either no member of the human race has any true rights, or else they all have the same ones; and anyone who votes against the rights of another, whatever his religion, colour or sex, automatically forfeits his own.[43]

The quote exhibits an irrefutable logic but it also clouds the magnitude of practical problems Condorcet here proposes to solve. Is it really an ahistorical "fact" that man is a "sentient being, capable of acquiring moral ideas and of reasoning upon them"? If rights necessarily follow from such a definition of man, why have they historically most often belonged to "particular people – freeborn English men, for example"– and what could be done to change that unequal distribution of rights?[44] Scholars, and none more forcefully than Hannah Arendt, have addressed these problems of the practical institutionalization of the inherent rights of man from various perspectives but here I want to break off the theoretical detour and return to Chénier and more precisely to the question of humanness in his play.[45] If the theoretical detour holds the message that sentimental literature deals with politics, it also highlights an analytical and anthropological question that needs to be answered from one individual case to another: How does the sentimental text delimit the human and to what political effect?

The problem of humanness and of the ability to recognize humanness initially manifests itself as a sensory concern in *Fénelon*. From the very first scene, Amélie has heard a distant "cry from a feeble creature" (1.1). As the play progresses it becomes clear that it is Amélie's unknown mother who mourns her fate in the underground cell but from the outset the cry is just a faraway sound that overwhelms Amélie: "This plaintive voice, those slow and funeral-like sounds, / even more heart-rending in the darkness, / have assailed my frozen senses [mes sens glacés] with a dreary terror" (1.1). The non-linguistic cry assails the *frozen* senses of Amélie, Chénier writes in yet another variety of his favored veiled/unveiled figure. In his philosophy of the origins of human knowledge, Étienne Bonnot de Condillac (1714–1780) proposed that communication and sympathy rose together. In some speculative pre-communicative past, a suffering individual had no means of expressing his need but could only move his body and utter frustrated cries. The witness to these frustrated sounds and movements began to interpret them as need and felt a spontaneous wish to relieve the suffering of the victim. "The act of imagination," writes Denby about Condillac, "which attributes meaning also reacts sympathetically, indeed the sympathetic reaction is prior to any formulation of sense, and both processes take as their point prelinguistic communication."[46] Communication hence arises as a response to the perceived suffering of another and Denby's greater argument is that the sentimental text reproduces this configuration: "[A]n aesthetic feature (the foregrounding of non-linguistic forms of communication) parallels and supports the moralizing philosophical project of establishing and celebrating sentiment as the basis of social solidarity."[47]

Denby's idea and his invocation of Condillac match well with Amélie's auricular perception of the distant cries. She hears the non-linguistic, heart-rending sounds and intuitively interprets them as just cries for help. As such, her sympathy arises as an immediate consequence of her ability to hear the cry and interpret it as a call for help. And yet her registration and interpretation of the cry is not sufficiently strong as a sign of her sympathy. She needs to descend to the convent dungeon and *see* the suffering victim. Equally important, I think, the audience needs to see the suffering individual and Amélie's act of sympathy. In *The Surprising Effects of Sympathy*, David Marshall discusses the aesthetics of the abbé Du Bos (1670–1742) who makes much of the difference between seeing and hearing. Sight, according to Du Bos, is stronger than sound and better able to awaken sympathy in man:

> The cries of a wounded man whom we do not see do not affect us (even if we are aware of the subject who makes him bring forth the cries we hear) in the same way as the sight of his blood and his wound would affect us […] sight has more power over the soul than the other senses have… the eye is nearer to the soul than is the ear.[48]

This hierarchy of the senses is noticeable in Chénier's favored veiled/unveiled metaphor but also in the first encounter between mother and daughter.

When Amélie first finds her mother Héloïse in the underground prison cell, both are unaware of their kinship, and yet both of them immediately feel compassion for the other and demonstrate it in the play's characteristic hyperbole fashion:

HÉLOÏSE

Oh! Whoever you may be, please come closer to me:
But your eyes halt upon mine in silence!
Your compassionate tears run in abundance!
I see clearly that you feel pity for my pains.

AMÉLIE

You attract me, tell me of your unhappiness.
Do not be afraid: Pour into my touched soul
All the bitter sorrows of your withered soul:
They are already mine; I want to share them, [Ils sont déjà les miens; je veux les partager,]
And my caressing cares will relieve them. [Et mes soins caressants pourront les soulager.]

(2.3)

The important rhyme *partager/soulager* expresses the fundamental belief that to share pain is to ease it. Suffering is shared or distributed out when it is deplored by someone else. The tears of the quote demonstrate an intensity of feeling but the intensity of Héloïse's suffering is actually relieved by Amélie's tears. The first thing to notice about the quoted passage, then, is that the virtuous characters of the play have the willingness and the capacity to share feelings and thereby lessen suffering by taking upon themselves parts of the pain of others. The second thing is that the process of sharing and easing feelings begins with the silent meeting of the eyes and a non-linguistic reaction to this meeting in the form of running tears. The two characters, who are strangers at this point, are drawn toward each other first because Amélie is moved by the distant cry of Héloïse and then because Héloïse is moved by the compassion she sees in the wet eyes of Amélie. The passage, finally, invites the audience to partake in this display of shared feelings. The apostrophic "Oh!" is followed up with the deliberately imprecise deixis "whoever you are [qui que vous soyez]." The effect of that impersonal address is to signal that anyone, including members of the audience, has the ability to feel with anyone. The requirement for sympathy is not personal acquaintance but simply the recognition of suffering.

But if sympathy is presented as a universal capacity, family lineage powerfully enforces the emotional ties of sympathetic affective networks. Thus, when Héloïse and her daughter recognize each other after fifteen years of involuntary separation, the mother's comment is

> Come, so I can embrace both the daughter and the father;
> Oh my goodness, my treasure! Come, it is me, it is your mother,
> Who in this moment leaves the pit of demise,
> Who sees you, who hears you, who is reborn in your arms.
>
> (2.3)

These lines again emphasize the importance of sensory recognition (see, hear, touch) but they also testify to the specific power of family love and of the ability of family members to intuitively recognize one another. Old Regime clerics and the inflexible father separated mother and child shortly after Amélie's birth, but the familial tie allows the characters' immediate access to an affective connection which cannot be faked and which extends even to the absent father, D'Elmance. In the next scene, when Isaura asks Amélie how she can positively *know* that the prisoner is in fact her mother, Amélie simply answers, "It is my mother, I tell you, I can be in no doubt about it" (2.4). The father, D'Elmance, feels the same kind of spontaneous affection and unconscious recognition the first time he sees Amélie. Without knowing that she is his daughter, the sight of her awakens the painful past: "I seem to re-see her that I have lost; / It was this innocence, this artless grace: / An object so touching awakens my pain" (3.3).[49]

The intuitiveness of familial recognition calls for two opposing interpretations. On the one hand, it highlights the degree to which family love is predicated on emotional ties rather than institutional or paternal acceptance. This interpretation follows Denby's secularist understanding of sentimental literature because it renders superfluous the religious sanctification of marriage. Family love exists as an immanent force between human beings and has no need of traditional or transcendent institutionalization. On the other hand, and more in line with Festa's critical reading of sentimentalism, the family relationship between Amélie and Héloïse calls into question the universality of sympathy. The family bond enforces the compassion felt by the characters and strengthens the emotional network that exists between these particular individuals. In other words, the sympathy felt with family members is stronger than the one felt with strangers. This might be an uncontroversial point of view but if the play and the genre posits the existence of a naturally existing, universal sympathy, and this is Denby's general argument, and if it invites the audience to share this belief, it is paradoxical that it falls back on family lineage in its exemplification of the allegedly universal ability to feel sympathy.

I shall return to the aforementioned interpretational dilemma but I want to address another question first. By the end of the second act, the play has already presented its audience with its conception of villainy and its proposal to replace it with a greater respect for intuitive and familial sympathy. After this exposition, what can the last three acts be but a repetition of these positions? Repetition, in fact, serves an important purpose in the tableau aesthetics of the play, but so does the figure of Fénelon, who is the prime mover of the play's plot and who raises the problem of political agency.

Political Agency: From Unhappiness to Happiness

In presenting quite detailed visions of both unhappiness and happiness, *Fénelon* sets up a dichotomy that is typical of this period's politically engaged literature. In *L'an 2440* Mercier made an absolute temporal divide between triumphant descriptions of future happiness and harsh condemnations of his present-day unhappiness. In *Les Liaisons dangereuses* Laclos dissected those high nobility mores that produced unhappiness and only offered fleeting visions of a happier form of social community. Unlike his two predecessors, Chénier uses the unhappiness/happiness dichotomy as elements of plot construction.[50] In *The Structure of the Artistic Text*, Jurij Lotman defines plot as the movement from one semantic field to another, as the transition from one sphere of values to another.[51] *L'an 2440* has no plot according to this definition because the semantic fields of present unhappiness and future happiness are simply placed next to each other. When one of the future guides of the novel explains that the transition from unhappiness to happiness just happened through the miraculous workings of a philosophical prince, Mercier (deliberately) shies away from the creation of literary plot. *Fénelon*, on the other hand, is a plotted narrative that centers on the transition from convent unhappiness to familial happiness.

By raising this transitory question in the plotting of the play, Chénier must necessarily handle the problem of political agency. Who or what has the capacity to move the play and its characters from one semantic field to another? Who or what can bring happiness about? The answer is Fénelon.

François de Salignac de la Mothe-Fénelon (1651–1715) became the archbishop of Cambrai in 1696 and acted as royal tutor between 1689 and 1697. During his years as a tutor, he wrote his most famous work, *Les Aventures de Télémaque* (1699), and used it in his education of the Duke of Burgundy who during his childhood was second in line for the French throne. In his 1793 foreword to *Fénelon*, Chénier explains that his piece was motivated by his rereading of *Télémaque* and his

> desire to represent on stage its immortal author; to communicate, to converse so to speak, with this sweet soul and to begin sketching the model of unstained virtue at the exact time when I drew up the virtue of pure patriotism and of republican energy.[52]

Chénier also explains that he based the narrative of *Fénelon* on the actual experiences of Esprit Fléchier (1632–1710), late seventeenth-century bishop of Nîmes, who had rescued a woman imprisoned in a convent. D'Alembert, co-editor of the *Encyclopédie*, presented an *éloge* to Fléchier to the French Academy in 1778 and thereby made this anecdote famous, something which prompted Charles de Pougens to write a fictionalized account of it shortly before Chénier did the same.[53] In substituting Fléchier with Fénelon, Chénier distanced his narrative from the historical precedent with the aim of creating an onstage model of virtue. In his preface, he praised Fénelon exorbitantly: "his name alone inspires a soft veneration, a respectful will to do good; the simplicity of his soul, the superiority of his spirit, this persuasive and touching eloquence that his virtues inspire" etc.[54] Fénelon according to Chénier was a larger than life hero.

Sympathies and idols, however, shifted rapidly during the revolutionary decade and this made it potentially dangerous to use a historical figure such as Fénelon as a heroic example of moral virtue. Even though Rousseau among others greatly admired Fénelon, the latter came to be associated with political moderation during the revolution.[55] Charles Pigault-Lebrun brought the protagonist of Fénelon's didactic novel to the Parisian stage in his colonial play *Le Blanc et le noir* (1795) shortly *after* the fall of Robespierre. In this play, Télémaque struggled to learn revolutionary moderation; a timely lesson, one could say, a year after the Directory had assumed power and made moderation, rather than revolutionary zeal, the ideal virtue.[56] But in 1793 the moderation of Fénelon was politically suspicious. Thus, Jean-Charles Laveaux, editor of the Jacobin *Journal de la Montagne*, wrote that *Fénelon* "presents the most subtle poison." "Fénelon," he continued, "might have had virtues, he no doubt had some, but Fénelon was a courtesan!"[57] To complete the image of the minefield of revolutionary ideology, the conservative critic Julien Louis Geoffroy questioned if an avowed revolutionary such as Chénier was worthy of praising a figure like Fénelon. "I confess," Geoffroy said in an 1802 course on dramatical literature,

> that I would have more confidence in the moralist who preaches sweetness, humanity, and tolerance to me if he hadn't terrified the nation with a public homage to the most execrable monster to have ever dishonored human nature. Is he who has suggested an altar for Marat worthy of being the interpreter of Fénelon?[58]

Chénier, in other words, entered a heated and rapidly shifting ideological landscape when he presented Fénelon as a hero onstage.

To appreciate the controversy surrounding Chénier's Fénelon figure it is fruitful to compare him with the heroic character, M. de Francheville, from Jacques-Marie Boutet de Monvel's equally successful convent play *Les Victimes cloîtrées* (1791). M. de Francheville has a narrative function parallel to that of Chénier's Fénelon but instead of being an archbishop, he is an elected mayor. Monvel, who was known primarily as an actor and who actually played the role of Fénelon in Chénier's play, goes to great lengths to describe the power and legitimacy vested in elected officials. Before the revolution, M. de Francheville held a high position at court but he was never satisfied with this prestigious rank because it was not "merited."[59] It was merely, Francheville says, the compensation of actions done by his ancestors. He finds a different enjoyment in the position of mayor because his revolutionary "co-citizens" have shown him the "honor" of placing their "esteem and hopes" in him.[60] Such revolutionary ideas are unfathomable to his sarcastic and counterrevolutionary sister, Mme de St. Alban, and the opposing views of the two clash in the following dialogue:

MME DE ST. ALBAN

What pettiness! In truth, I don't recognize you anymore. These votes to which you owe your newfound dignity came from people whose esteem is truly a highly flattering tribute.

M. DE FRANCHEVILLE

They are good citizens, men.

MME DE ST. ALBAN

Ah! Here we have the great argument of philosophy! Men! Your equals, right? Your fellows. [Vos égaux, n'est-ce pas? vos semblables.]

M. DE FRANCHEVILLE

Yes, my fellows; yes, my equals.[61]

M. de Francheville feels personal and professional satisfaction only when the recognition from others resonates with his own feeling of having deserved it. In Monvel's play, holding a public office is emblematic of virtuous behavior recognized and appreciated by others. The citizenry recognizes the humanity of certain individuals and rewards them for it by electing them and this idea of a merit-based election makes the mayor an interesting variety of the man-citizen. This figure, in the words of Susan Maslan, is capable of combining "the claims of humanity and the claims of citizenship," he is the feeling man of the *oikos* and the political speaker of the *polis*.[62] As demonstrated in Chapter 1, the man-citizen is the ideal double subject whose existence is posited in the title of the Declaration of Rights. In *Les Victimes cloîtrées* the citizenry is made up of such double subjects and the executive power or political agency of M. de Francheville resides in his having been elected by his fellows. The man-citizen is the original source of authority but he hands over a degree of political power to a representative of his choice who through that process acquires legitimate agency.

The legitimacy of Fénelon's agency is never questioned but it originates from a different source of authority than that of Monvel's mayor. Fénelon's agency derives from a combination of Chénier's controversial interpretation of Fénelon's extratextual reputation and of the intratextual actions of the Fénelon character. I have discussed the shifting ideological implications of Fénelon earlier, but in the play, his virtue consists in (i) his ability to recognize and willingness to ease suffering and (ii) his insistence upon the public good. Both of these character traits reraise the questions of humanness and of the equal access to political membership.

Fénelon exemplifies the virtue of recognizing pain when he meets Amélie and learns of her mother's suffering. In reaction to the story, he says,

> My heart hears her cries and I run to her;
> This is my first duty: to serve humanity; [C'est mon premier devoir: servons l'humanité;]
> Afterwards, we show grace to the Divinity Après, nous rendrons grâce à la Divinité].
>
> (3.4)

Again, suffering expresses itself as a non-linguistic cry and to be virtuous is to be able to hear and act upon this cry. In this passage too, Chénier takes advantage of the rhymed couplets, this time to establish a relationship between *l'humanité* and *la Divinité*. Drawing upon Denby's argument that the sentimental text is a secular text this rhyme can be interpreted as an attempt to locate a natural human capacity for sympathy that has no need for any religiously sanctioned obligation to serve humankind. In his praise of Fénelon, D'Elmance explicitly associates the archbishop's virtue with the ability to change unhappiness into happiness: "Virtue is in itself everywhere respectable; / You double its empire by making it amiable. / Fénelon, I am tired of my unhappiness; / Offer me consolation with your happiness" (3.2). The consolation and amiable virtue of Fénelon here establishes the possibility of a transition from unhappiness to happiness.

The emphasis upon public good, the second reason why Fénelon's agency is legitimate, shines through in his celebration of utility. Common utility was an integrated element of Sieyès's political philosophy and of his attack upon the useless nobility. His ideal of social usefulness even found its way into the Declaration Debate in which it was made clear that Frenchmen would demonstrate their civic spirit and gain social distinction by their ability to be useful.[63] In the first dialogue between Fénelon and D'Elmance, the archbishop wonders why his childhood friend, D'Elmance, who was "born to do great work" (3.2), seems to wander aimlessly around, not using his talents. As he himself underscores, one of Fénelon's principles is to be useful: "I want to cultivate pleasure with amiability, / and useful work fills my spare time [Je veux de l'amitié cultiver les plaisirs, / Et d'utiles travaux rempliront mes loisirs]" (3.2). Just as the nobility, the institutionalized church was vulnerable to a critique founded on the notion of social utility because monks and nuns, even though they did attend to much poor relief, were considered to be withdrawn from the common social world. Héloïse strongly objects to this uselessness of convent life in her countervision of a happy future. In this monologue, she hopes...

HÉLOÏSE

That the religion, which you [the abbess] dishonor,
Finally close and destroy these abominable cells;
That liberty reigns at the foot of the sanctuary;
That never a mortal, feeble, or frightened person,
Will ever preach before God the nonsensical sermon
To be useless to this world in which God has placed him!

(4.3)

As in other convent narratives and as in the populationist theory, the emphasis on usefulness is here used to attack the unfree and unproductive convent life.[64] As Figures 5.2 and 5.3 demonstrate, the importance of common utility is repeated in much revolutionary imagery. The images underscore the importance of the productive and worldly activities of Third Estate women. Whereas the utility of d'Elmance consisted in him being "born to do great work" (3.2), the breast-fed child of Figure 5.3 illustrates the populationist content of female utility. Despite these striking gender differences, to be useful to the world is in both instances the positive ideal that substantiates the criticism of *Le grand abus* of institutionalized religion and noble uselessness.

The Regeneration of the State in Marie-Joseph Chénier's   183

Figure 5.2 Le Grand abus: [estampe] / [Villeneuve]. (Paris: chez Villeneuve, 1790). Bibliothèque nationale de France.

What Fénelon can do is actually no different from what the other sympathetic characters of the play do. He recognizes the non-linguistic cry of the suffering and he responds to the call. He stands out from the rest of the characters, however, because he is in a position to execute his principles. In general terms, he deplores the fact that "We have forgotten nature and her laws; / the cries of prejudice have silenced her voice" (3.2). Like Amélie, Héloïse, and D'Elmance, Fénelon hears the voice of nature but unlike the other sympathetic characters, he can make an impact on the basis of his sensory experience. As was the case with the seemingly universal network of sympathetic characters, there is an interpretational dilemma here, which Laveaux in part unearthed in his critical review of the play. Why is it necessary to use a larger than life hero – and a courtesan at that! – as the example of a person capable of acting on the universal experience of unjust suffering? The voice of nature is difficult

Figure 5.3 La Bonne justice: [estampe] / [Villeneuve]. (Paris: chez Villeneuve, 1790). Bibliothèque nationale de France.

to hear but multiple characters manage to do so, and yet only Fénelon can free Héloïse and reunite the natural family. The message of that dilemma seems to be that anyone is in principle capable of hearing and accepting the laws of nature but the executive power to police these laws reside with the special few. On some level, this is what Laveaux, based on his Jacobin belief in the power of the people, responded to: The laws might apply equally to everyone, but some are better suited than others to police the universal law.

Before concluding the analysis, I want to zoom in on the happy ending of the play. Happy in the sense that the sympathetic characters are reunited but happy, also, in the sense that the villains are conveniently excluded from the happy community.

The *Tableau Vivant*: The Politics of the Happy Ending

The carefully set up final tableau of *Fénelon* depicts the happy reunion of father, mother, and child. Amélie and Héloïse were actually reunited already in the second act and d'Elmance learned most of the truth of his daughter and her mother in the second scene of act five. But Fénelon deliberately postpones the final family reunion because, as he says, Héloïse needs time to accustom herself to her sudden "happiness" (5.2). In order not to over-agitate her, Fénelon plans to tell her of d'Elmance's presence and then afterward call upon him to let the two involuntarily separated lovers reunite. While d'Elmance hides in a next-door room, Fénelon answers the many questions of Héloïse in a suspenseful dialogue when she arrives on the scene. "Does anyone know where [d'Elmance] draws his breath these days?" "He has established himself," Fénelon answers, "on these parts." (5.2). "Has he entered a new marriage?" "His hand has been given to no one this entire time." Gradually, Héloïse realizes that d'Elmance still loves her, even though he was told that she was dead, and that he is close by. "When will he come again to see his most tender wife?" Fénelon: "In this very moment of our talk, he can already hear you" (5.2), at which point d'Elmance steps forth and exclaims "Héloïse!" Present in the scene, besides from Fénelon and the lovers, are Isaura and Amélie. The latter cries out "my father!" in response to Héloïse's call "my husband!" and d'Elmance completes the round of familial recognition with the outcry "Oh my daughter!" (5.2).

This sentimental reunion is an emotionally hyper-charged stoppage of narrative progression that largely conforms with the *tableau vivant* as it was theorized by Denis Diderot and multiple later commentators. In *Entretiens sur le fils naturel*, Diderot has his character Dorval distinguish between the *tableau* and the *coup de théâtre*:

> An unforeseen incident which takes place in the action and abruptly changes the situation of the characters is a *coup de théâtre*. An arrangement of these characters on stage, so natural and so true that, faithfully rendered by a painter, it would please me on a canvas, is a tableau.[65]

In the final scene of *Fénelon* the characters are carefully placed next to each other and their mutual recognition is a physical as well as an emotional "arrangement" of characters. The tableau, Diderot writes, shall be dominant in the "domestic tragedy"; a new "intermediate genre" that, and this resonates well with Chénier's poetological reflections, lies "between tragedy and comedy" and is yet to be developed.[66] The new bourgeois dramatic genre, Diderot – or more precisely: Dorval – continues, will "have a different kind of action, a different tone, and a sublimity all its own."[67] For Diderot, the new genre of domestic tragedy is a possibility to reapproach theater to virtue and the naturalness of lived life.[68] Louis-Sébastien Mercier wrote along similar lines in his influential *Du théâtre, ou nouvel essai sur l'art dramatique* (1773) and he did so in a language that explicitly related the tableau to questions of truth, usefulness, and morals:

> Theater [le spectacle] is a lie; the task is to approach it to the greatest truth. Theater is a tableau; the task is to make this tableau useful. That is: to bring it within the reach of the largest number possible so the presented image can tie humanity [les hommes] together through the victorious sentiments of compassion and pity. Hence, it is not enough for the soul to be occupied or even moved. It must be tied to the good. The moral goal, without being hidden or overly obvious, must seize the heart and forcefully establish itself there.[69]

In 1796, more than twenty years after the publication of the quoted theatrical considerations, Mercier would sharply condemn paintings and painters. A painting, he insisted, is the "idiot sister of poetry," "a childish production of the human mind, a continually impotent enterprise that is in most cases laughably intrepid."[70] In his 1773 theatrical reflections, however, Mercier supports Diderot's idea of the painterly tableau. It is important for Mercier that theater should be useful and the tableau aesthetics promotes theater's ability to exercise human "sensibility" and to move "the rich faculties we have received from nature."[71] If these faculties are left dormant, they die out which is why Mercier proposes that theater should strive to "awaken them" and make them "tender, sensible, and compassionate."[72] This sensuous connection between art and morals recurs in Mercier's aesthetics but he might in fact simply be reiterating an idea put forth by Diderot in his "Praise of Richardson" (1762). "Richardson," Diderot wrote,

> sows in our hearts the seeds of virtues which at first remain still and inactive: their presence is hidden until the moment comes for them to stir and come to life. Then they develop and we feel ourselves driven towards what is good with an enthusiasm we did not know was in us.[73]

But how more specifically does Chénier's tableau of familial reunion follow up upon this sensationalist idea about the moral usefulness of the tableau? It is after all one thing to posit a theoretical connection between moral enlightenment and the tableau and another to produce it aesthetically. I am convinced that the tableau has a political function in the sense that it, somewhat similar to Mercier's usage of the communitarian "we," creates a community or an "arrangement of characters" and invites spectators to partake in this community. As theater

The Regeneration of the State in Marie-Joseph Chénier's   187

historians Jeffrey Ravel and Susan Maslan have shown, the *parterres* of French revolutionary theaters were vibrant and politically charged spaces.[74] Chénier's tableau seeks to activate the audience and to include its members in a truthful, yet staged, kind of community. But as all communities, that of *Fénelon* is founded on a set of norms, and persons are included or excluded from membership on the basis of their ability to accept and live by those norms. The politics of the tableau resides in its creation of and in its invitation to join the community operated by this particular inclusion/exclusion mechanism. Let me begin by addressing what critics agree is a crucial element in the aesthetics of the tableau: repetition.[75]

In *Fénelon*, the final scene repeats numerous elements that have already been put forth throughout the play: First, it shows the spectators that mother, father, and child, despite years of separation, can *immediately* recognize each other and identify themselves with the emotionality of loving family members. This immediacy echoes the first encounter of mother and daughter and, following Denby's Enlightenment reading of sentimentality, we can interpret this iteration as yet another confirmation of the worldly existence of natural sympathy. Second, the final tableau reiterates *the fact* of the family bond even though narrative encounters and explanations in the dialogue have already made the familial ties of the protagonists abundantly clear. As such, the tableau allows the spectator not simply to comprehend the fact of family but rather to *see* family recognition at work in what amounts to a scene of initiation. According to Marshall's reading of Du Bos's aesthetics, this visual aspect of recognition is significant because it maximizes the spectator's feeling of sympathy. Third, the final tableau contains yet another variety of Chénier's favored veiled/unveiled metaphor. D'Elmance is absent from Héloïse's field of vision until Fénelon has cleared away her mistaken beliefs about d'Elmance and visual presence here again goes hand in hand with intellectual realization.

In his critical essay on Diderot's theory of drama, Marxist critic Peter Szondi perceptively addresses Diderot's dichotomous understanding of reality and false appearance on the stage. His analysis does not entirely conform with Chénier's usage of the tableau, nor does it sufficiently appreciate the political significance of virtue and family formation in late eighteenth-century France, but Szondi's analysis does shed light on the repeatedly invoked veiled/unveiled metaphor and brings forth some of the political content of Chénier's tableau. The *coup de théâtre*, according to Szondi, is aligned with an aristocratic type of social behavior. Its sudden shifts of fate differs markedly from a bourgeois way of life, which Szondi under the inspiration of Max Weber finds "notable for its careful weighing of decisions, aversion to speculation, and a conception of work as a constant occupation."[76] Part of the appeal of the beautiful tableau, then, resides in its difference from the aristocratic real world of the Old

Regime. Szondi goes on to complicate this distinction of the real world and theatrical appearance:

> The world of beautiful – or, more accurately, of virtuous – appearance is not, however, merely one in which men would like to live. It is also, and this is Diderot's essential point, the true world, for it shows how man truly is, namely good. The spectator, fleeing from wicked reality into the theater, is thus able to reconcile himself with the world, since on the stage that reality is volatized into a mere appearance, with aesthetic appearance being asserted as the true reality.[77]

In *Fénelon* the veiled conception of reality is one in which characters are blinded by the influence of pride and religious prejudice whereas unveiled characters see through falsity and immediately recognize kinship and friendship. As a variety of this metaphor, Fénelon prepares the final tableau by clearing away Héloïse's various misunderstandings about d'Elmance. As she reaches full clarity, d'Elmance steps forth and truth meets virtue in their encounter. The tableau thus contains that paradoxical truth claim, which Szondi emphasizes. The spectator is invited to enjoy the truth and virtue of the family reunion but it is a staged, fictive truth and as Chénier himself acknowledges in his preface, his narrative departs significantly from historical truth. The twist in Szondi's reading of Diderot, however, is that the staged tableau contains a higher truth than the wicked reality outside of theater. Denby too emphasizes the higher truth of the tableau. The tableau, he writes, is "a form of synecdoche" because it displays an emotionally charged situation, which is a part of or an example of a larger truth (*pars pro toto*) about the worldly existence of virtue.[78] For Szondi the tableau and its celebration of truth and virtue is a flight from reality:

> In Diderot's France, the France of the *ancien régime* [...], virtue was something private, with which the citizen could console himself as he sought refuge from the intrigues and wickedness of society within the security of his four walls, or in other words, as he fled from the world of the *coup de théâtre* into that of the *tableau*.[79]

For Szondi the tableau is an opportunity for the spectator to flee the real world of wicked politics and take refuge in a bourgeois sphere of private domesticity. Szondi, however, fails to see the political implications of family formation in this period and he, wrongly to my mind, argues that virtue is a private matter in Diderot's time.[80] In the tradition of republican political thought, virtue was a political concept and even though the significance of republicanism increased during the revolution, Dan Edelstein has demonstrated its presence in earlier Enlightenment thought.[81] While I disagree with Szondi's exclusive linkage of virtue and the private sphere, I like his analysis of the paradoxical truth claim of the tableau and of his idea that the tableau invites the spectator to partake in its world. Denby goes a step further in this communitarian interpretation of the tableau as he argues that its politics reside in the ability to create a "community of like minds drawn together by their common reaction to a common scene."[82] In Chénier, the community is made up of everyone who shares the virtuous sentiments displayed onstage, and this includes fictional characters as well as members of the audience.

Literary historian Jay Caplan has argued that the tableau represents a loss, which "is meant to be made good by the beholder, who must supply the loss by supplementing or standing in for the missing family member."[83] Caplan's analysis revolves around an unhappy family with one or more members absent and it hence differs from the happy family reunion of *Fénelon* but his general idea that the tableau invites the participation of the spectator fits well with *Fénelon*. In fact, we may even say that the play establishes a bond between certain onstage characters and the audience and then uses the final tableau to strengthen and expand that bond. Unlike the audience, Héloïse is unaware of d'Elmance's presence and, again unlike the audience, d'Elmance and Amélie have yet to fully realize their kinship. As such, the final unveiling scene repeats truths that spectators know already and the tableau marks the moment when the protagonists learn the truth and gain access to the community of the knowing. The tableau is a scene of initiation, a scene in which characters learn a higher truth, but the audience have been initiated before the onstage characters and is hence invited to relive the moment of truth and to enjoy the initiation of new community members. The tableau is a celebration of natural familial virtue and spectators are invited to partake in the celebration but as members who have already been initiated in the virtuous onstage community.

Not everyone, however, is invited to join the celebrations. The politics of the tableau resides in its creation of a community and communities are established with the help of an inclusion/exclusion mechanism. The final scene of *Fénelon* is one of reconciliation and happiness but the villains of the play are conveniently removed from the stage. Chénier does not reflect explicitly on the function of the villain in his play but Monvel's parallel play, *Les Victimes cloîtrées* (1791), concludes with a reflection on this precise issue. I quote from the final monologue given by M. de Francheville and afterward return to Chénier's tragedy.

> Come, my friends, let us all run to the feet of the alter and thank God who has reunited us, this God of the good who finally lets us purify His culture from the shameful abuses that degrade it. This God who, to better signal His justice, sometimes allows the vicious a day's triumph but who never tolerates that we confuse the good man [l'homme de bien], the model of virtue, object of our respect, and the glory of religion, with the skeleton who betrays religion without ever being able to really debase it.[84]

Within the logics of *Les Victimes cloîtrées*, this monologue serves as a response to the theodicy raised by Dorval earlier in the play.[85] Dorval's illegitimate love interest has (also) been imprisoned in a convent dungeon, and when he finds out, that knowledge prompts him to contrast the power and goodness of God with his unhappy situation: "Crime... and an eternal justice!... Crime... and an almighty God!"[86] Regarded as a philosophical solution to the theodicy, the riddle of evil in a world controlled by an all-powerful God, Francheville's claim that God occasionally allows evil a small victory to better signal the superior force of justice could, any philosopher would probably agree, be better developed. But understood as a description of the role of evil in the melodramatic plot structure it is perfectly accurate and in accordance with Peter Brooks's analysis of the narrative scheme of early nineteenth-century melodramas.[87] Importantly, villains are characterized with the descriptive terms "vicious [méchants]" and "skeleton." What Monvel's recurring descriptive terms, "tiger," "monster," "skeleton," and "barbarian," have in common is the rejection of the villain's humanity.[88] The metaphors of the uncivilized barbarian, the aggressive tiger, the dead skeleton, and the inhuman monster establish a discursive pattern whose function is to relegate villains to a realm of non-civilization and inhumanity. This rhetoric of political exclusion was, as demonstrated in Chapter 1, operative too in the natural rights philosophy of Diderot, in the *Marseillaise,* and in Robespierre's 1793 proposed Declaration of Rights.

Chénier too adopts the discourse of inhuman villains. It is true that the play ends on a forgiving note with Héloïse saying "D'Elmance, I no longer have the strength to hate. / My heart is tired of torments, fatigued with vengeance, / Ready for tenderness, for gratitude" (5.5). This forgiving tone suggests that depravity is bad but essentially excusable and, hence, acceptable among humans. Prior to this scene, however, descriptive phrases such as "inhuman" (1.4; 2.3; 4.3; 4.4), "monster" (2.3; 4.3; 5.5), and "barbarian" (4.3) have figured as prominently as in Monvel.[89] Forgiveness could have been a way of reintroducing the formerly dehumanized characters into the human realm and in fact, this is what happens in the case of Héloïse's father when Héloïse says, "I pardon all his actions because he has repented [Je lui pardonne tout, puisqu'il s'est repenti]" (5.4). As indicated by the word *puisque*, however, repentance is necessary for forgiveness to occur. The abbess, who shows no sign of remorse, simply disappears from the play before the last act, and the joyful family reunion of the ending ignores her existence. Thus, rather than being a solved problem, inhumanity ends up being simply disregarded or excluded from the happy family celebrations.

* * *

The Regeneration of the State in Marie-Joseph Chénier's   191

It was Chénier's explicit ambition to create "new men for the new laws."[90] Chénier believed that theatrical performances could appeal to their spectators and produce virtue in a singular way. "[The philosopher] teaches how to be good, [the dramatic poet] inspires the desire to be so; one talks about virtue, the other puts it into action, and makes it amiable and easy."[91] I interpret this ambition of Chénier's as an attempt to regenerate France through theater. As the quote illustrates, the regenerative efforts work through morality or, more precisely, through virtue.

In Lynn Hunt's interpretation of sentimental literature, epistolary novels taught readers to empathize with strangers and their distant sufferings. Before the mid-eighteenth century, she suggests, Frenchmen would feel empathy with neighbors, friends, and family but in order for universal human rights to become credible, people first had to appreciate the autonomy of others.[92] The psychological depictions of strangers in sentimental epistolary novels, taught readers this lesson. There is a certain affinity between Hunt's interpretation and the aspirations of Chénier's theater. He hoped that spectators would recognize the miseries of his unhappy protagonists and acquire the capability characteristic of his virtuous characters, that is the ability to recognize and ease the pain of others. But as my analysis has shown, family members are especially prone to sympathize with one another and only the heroic Fénelon has the power and agency to react effectively upon his sympathies. These limitations to the universality and effectivity of sympathy suggest that not all are equally capable of feeling with others. "No one feels sorry for the villain," Edelstein writes, and he suggests, parallel to Festa's critical interpretation of sentimentalism, that the human rights discourse might be less universal that we usually think.[93]

The limited extension or the non-universalism of the sentimental discourse is characteristic of *Fénelon* and the happy community the play presents. Continuing the political interpretation, another distinguishing feature of the play is its idealization of common utility. Members of the happy community are expected to be useful to their co-citizens, a virtue Fénelon incarnates. In the Declaration Debate and in the distinction between active and passive citizenship, common utility was a two-edged sword. On the one hand, Sieyès used it to attack the inactive, useless nobility but to the distress of Robespierre, Sieyès and others also used the distinction to exclude the poor from full political membership with a reference to their insufficient talents and lacking fiscal contributions. In Chénier's play, common utility serves primarily to expose the procreative and professional inactivity of Old Regime clerics. Along with the tendency to exclude villains (or make them disappear), the emphasis on common utility does, however, signal the degree to which Chénier's happy community is a selective one, controlled by a particular inclusion/exclusion mechanism. He takes seriously the productive aspect of *making* new men for the new laws as he proposes a specific sentimental and utility-oriented form of subjectivity. Speaking with Coleman, these communitarian values set the tone for the form of personhood of the new men.[94]

The presentation of Chénier's selective community attains much of its effectiveness from the play's tableau aesthetics. Mercier, in his futuristic novel, tried to build a communitarian bond with his readers through the development of a prophetic voice and the prefatory usage of a "we" that positioned the reader alongside the values of the prophet. But if readers were interpellated as members of a communitarian "we" in Mercier, Laclos urged his readers to critically reflect upon the scheming and opacity of his high nobility protagonists. The stereoscopic vision of *Les Liaisons dangereuses*, I think, activates the intellect of its reader to a degree which is foreign from Chénier's ambition to "*unnoticeably* form new men for the new laws [former *insensiblement* des hommes nouveaux pour les lois nouvelles (*my emphasis*)]."[95] Chénier instead sought to position his spectator as a member who had already accepted and been initiated in the play's happy community. The community proposed by Chénier, and the norms that guided it, were, however, controversial when the play was staged in 1793. This controversy testifies to the fact that even after the 1789 Declaration of Rights, it remained a real challenge to imagine a new and happy France. Like the 1793 and 1795 alternative rights declarations, Chénier's play thus displays the open-endedness of the problems that assembly deputies hoped they had solved once and for all in 1789.

Notes

1 Marie-Joseph Chénier, *Fénelon ou les religieuses de Cambrai* in Marie-Joseph Chénier, *Théâtre*. Eds. G. Ambrus and F. Jacob. (Paris: Flammarion, 2002), Act 1, Scene 1. This chapter's further references to *Fénelon* are in the running text.
2 Size of the theater is taken from Gauthier Ambrus, "Voix politiques dans les tragédies révolutionnaires de Marie-Joseph Chénier." [*Littératures*, Vol. 62 (2010)], 141n1. Number of runs are from Emmet Kennedy, Marie-Laurence Netter, James P. McGregor, and Mark V. Olsen, *Theatre, Opera, and Audiences in Revolutionary Paris*. (Westport, CT and London: Greenwood Press, 1996), 125.
3 Numbers taken from Kennedy, *Theatre, Opera, and Audiences*, 168; 118. The seven other plays on Viguier's list are Joseph Fiévée: *Les rigeurs du cloître* (1790, 71 perf.); Pierre Laujon: *Le couvent, ou les fruits du caractère et de l'éducation* (1790, 28 perf.); anonyme: *Les fourberies monacales* (1790, not listed in Kennedy, *Theatre, Opera, and Audiences*); Claude de Flins: *Le mari directeur, ou le déménagement du couvent* (1791, 6 perf.); Louis-Benoît Picard: *Les visitandiennes* (1792, 286 perf.); Charles-Antoine Pigault-Le-Brun: *Les dragons et les Bénédictines* (1793, 143 perf.); Jean-François Corsange: *Le dernier couvent de France ou l'hospice* (1796, 99 perf.). Audrey Viguier, "L'abbé Gouttes et le curé du *Couvent ou les vœux forcés* d'Olympe de Gouges (1790)." *The French Review*, Vol. 85, No. 6 (2012): 1114.
4 For the genre of melodrama, particularly in its nineteenth century form, see Peter Brooks, *The Melodramatic Imagination: Balzac, Henry James,*

Melodrama, and the Mode of Excess. (New Haven, CT and London: Yale University Press, [1976] 1995), esp. 24–56 and Christopher Prendergast, *Balzac: Fiction and Melodrama* (New York: Holmes and Meier Publishers, Inc., 1978).
5 Chénier, "Discours préliminaire (1793)" in Chénier, *Théâtre*, 253.
6 Lynn Hunt, *Inventing Human Rights: A History.* (New York and London: W. W. Norton & Company, 2008).
7 Brooks, *The Melodramatic*, 15.
8 Brooks, *The Melodramatic Imagination*, 15.
9 See Paul-Édouard Levayer for a reading that defines Chénier's play as a melodrama.
10 David J. Denby, *Sentimental Narrative and the Social Order in France, 1760–1820.* (Cambridge: Cambridge University Press, 1994), 87.
11 Denby, *Sentimental Narrative*, 87.
12 Denby, *Sentimental Narrative*, 87.
13 Cecilia Feilla, *The Sentimental Theater of the French Revolution* (Surrey: Ashgate, 2013), 15.
14 Susan Maslan, *Revolutionary Acts: Theater, Democracy, and the French Revolution.* (Baltimore, MD: The Johns Hopkins University Press, 2005), 185.
15 18 August 1789, Rabaut de Saint-Etienne in *AP* VIII, 452/*L'an 1*, 138.
16 Gail Bossenga, *The Politics of Privilege: Old Regime and Revolution in Lille* (Cambridge: Cambridge University Press, 1991).
17 Feilla, *The Sentimental Theater of the French Revolution*, 16.
18 In the large corpus of historical literature on eighteenth century French family politics I have found much inspiration in the following works: Jean Delumeau and Daniel Roche (eds.), *Histoire des pères et de la paternité.* (Paris: Larousse, 1990); Suzanne Desan, *The Family on Trial in Revolutionary France* (Berkeley, Los Angeles, London: University of California Press, 2004); Suzanne Desan and Jeffrey Merrick (eds.), *Family, Gender, and Law in Early Modern France* (University Park, PA: The Pennsylvania State University Press, 2009); Matthew Gerber, *Bastards: Politics, Family, and Law in Early Modern France* (Oxford: Oxford University Press, 2012).
19 Chénier, "Discours préliminaire (1793)" in Chénier, *Théâtre*, 253.
20 For the claim that theater and politics were virtually indistinguishable, see Paul Friedland, *Political Actors: Representative Bodies & Theatricality in the Age of the French Revolution.* (Ithaca, NY and London: Cornell University Press, 2003), 196. My position is similar to that of Susan Maslan, who writes: "Precisely because neither the politics nor the theater of the Revolution was determined by the other, their relationship is critical. The relationship between revolutionary politics and theater was not simply one between two discourses; instead, as investigating theater and politics together reveals, there were manifold relations among linguistic, social, artistic, intellectual, and political discourses and practices that were themselves unstable." (Maslan, *Revolutionary Acts*, 3).
21 Monvel's play *Les Victimes cloîtrés* likewise presents the convent space as a paradoxical space, e.g., by calling attention to the name of the convent prison cell: "Vade in pace [go in peace]." (Monvel, *Les Victimes cloîtrés*, 93).
22 Denis Diderot, *The Nun*. Trans. Russell Goulbourne. (Oxford: Oxford University Press, 2008), 104–105.
23 Ambrus, "Voix politiques," 152–153.

24 *Mercure de la France* (24 December. 1791); qtd. in Edmond Estève, *Études de littérature préromantique* (Paris: Librarie ancienne Honoré Champion, 1923), 85–86 and Feilla, *The Sentimental Theater*, 52n141.
25 Jean-Claude Bonnet, "De la famille à la patrie" in J. Delumeau and D. Roche, eds, *Histoire des pères et de la paternité*. (Paris: Larousse, 2000), 259
26 Desan, *The Family on Trial in Revolutionary France*, 3.
27 Carol Blum, *Strength in Numbers: Population, Reproduction, and Power in Eighteenth-Century France*. (Baltimore, MD and London: The Johns Hopkins University Press, 2002), 8.
28 Blum, *Strength in Numbers*, ix.
29 Blum, *Strength in Numbers*, 154. See also Desan, *The Family on Trial*, e.g., 55 for a discussion of natural children and populationist argumentation.
30 Gerber, *Bastards*, 133.
31 For literature on Gouges, see, e.g., Joan Wallach Scott, *Only Paradoxes to Offer: French Feminists and the Rights of Man*. (Cambridge and London: Harvard University Press, 1996), 19–57; Sophie Mousset, *Women's Rights and the French Revolution: A Biography of Olympe de Gouges*. Translated by Joy Poirel. (New Brunswick and London: Transaction Publishers, 2007); Lisa Beckstrand, *Deviant Women of the French Revolution and the Rise of Feminism*. (Madison and Teaneck, NJ: Fairleigh Dickinson University Press, 2009), esp. 74–122.
32 *Déclaration des droits de l'homme et du citoyen* in Baecque et al. (eds.), *L'an 1*, 199. English translation in Hunt, *Inventing Human Rights*, 222.
33 Olympe de Gouges, *Écrits politiques 1788–1791, tome 1*. Edited by Olivier Blanc. (Paris: côté-femmes éditions, 1993), 208. English translation in John Cole, *Between the Queen and the Cabby: Olympe de Gouges's Rights of Woman*. (Montreal and Kingston, NY: McGill-Queen's University Press, 2011), 33. Translation slightly modified.
34 Cole, *Between the Queen and the Cabby*, 129.
35 Cole, *Between the Queen and the Cabby*, 130.
36 Biographically, Gouges apparently considered herself to be the illegitimate child of the archbishop Jean Georges Lefranc de Pompignan. In her works, I have come across the illegitimate child in *Zamore et Mirza* (1788) – which is the original title of the play *L'esclavage des noirs* – and in the epistolary novel *Mémoire de Madame de Valmont* (1788), in the pamphlet *Séance Royale. Motion de Mgr le duc d'Orléans, ou Les songes patriotiques* (1789) and in *Les droits de la femme* (1791).
37 Cf. Dan Edelstein, "Enlightenment Rights Talk." *The Journal of Modern History*, Vol. 86, No. 3 (2014): 545–546.
38 Denby, *Sentimental Narrative*, 87.
39 Lynn Festa, *Sentimental Figures of Empire in Eighteenth-Century Britain and France*. (Baltimore, MD: The Johns Hopkins University Press, 2006), 3.
40 Sharon Sliwinski, "The Aesthetics of Human Rights" in *Culture, Theory & Critique*, Vol. 50, No. 1 (2009): 18.
41 Sliwinski, "The Aesthetics of Human Rights," 17.
42 Étienne Balibar, *Equaliberty: Political Essays*. Translated by James Ingram. (Durham and London: Duke University Press, 2014), 79.
43 Marquis de Condorcet, "On the Emancipation of Women: On Giving Women the Right of Citizenship" in S. Lukes and N. Urbinati (eds.), *Political Writings*. Cambridge: Cambridge University Press, 2012), 156–157.
44 Hunt, *Inventing Human Rights*, 21–22.
45 Hannah Arendt, *The Origins of Totalitarianism*. (San Diego, New York, and London: Harcourt, Inc., 1973), 11–54. Other important examples are

The Regeneration of the State in Marie-Joseph Chénier's   195

Karl Marx, "Zur Judenfrage" in Karl Marx and Friedrich Engels, *Werke* band 1. (Berlin: Dietz Verlag, 1976), 347–377; Giorgio Agamben, *Homo Sacer: Sovereign Power and Bare Life*. Translated by Daniel Heller-Roazen. (Stanford, CA: Stanford University Press, 1998), 126–136; and Jacques Rancière, "Who Is the Subject of the Rights of Man?" in *The South Atlantic Quarterly* 103, no. 2/3 (2004), 297–310.
46 Denby, *Sentimental Narrative*, 85–86.
47 Denby, *Sentimental Narrative*, 86.
48 David Marshall, *The Surprising Effects of Sympathy: Marivaux, Diderot, Rousseau, and Mary Shelley*. (Chicago, IL and London: The University of Chicago Press, 1988), 18.
49 Gouges's convent play contains a similar belief in the spontaneous recognition of long-lost family members. When Julie is reunited with her mother, who has also been imprisoned, she says, "You, my mother! Oh my heart had told me so in advance." (Gouges, *Le Couvent, ou les vœux forcés*, 3.14).
50 Ambrus and Jacob rightly argue that the play places much emphasis on dialogue and *tableaux* but they go too far, I think, in down-toning the importance of narrative plot: "the piece distinguishes itself by its particular usage of the pathetic where the part of the action is greatly reduced: the dramatic effect depends much more on dialogues and tableaux." (Ambrus and Jacob, "Introduction" in Chénier, *Théâtre*, 34.
51 Jurij Lotman, *The Structure of the Artistic Text*. Trans. R. Vroon. (Michigan: Ann Arbor, 1977), 231–239.
52 Chénier, "Discours préliminaire (1793)" in Chénier, *Théâtre*, 247.
53 Adolphe Liéby, *Étude sur le théâtre de Marie-Joseph Chénier*. (Paris: Société française d'imprimerie et de librairie, 1902), 99–103.
54 Chénier, "Discours préliminaire (1793)," 247.
55 It might be worth inserting here, that Fénelon's idea of an ideal state, as expressed in *Les aventures de Télémaque*, can be both republican and monarchical, cf. Dan Edelstein, *The Terror of Natural Rights: Republicanism, the Cult of Nature, & the French Revolution* (Chicago, IL and London: The University of Chicago Press, 2010), 61–62. For the relationship between Rousseau and Fénelon, see, e.g., Judith N. Shklar, *Men & Citizens: A Study of Rousseau's Social Theory*. (Cambridge: Cambridge University Press, 1985), 4–8.
56 For a reading of this play, see my article "What are Robespierre and Télémaque Doing in Saint-Domingue? Humanness, Revolutionary Legitimacy, and Political Order in Charles Pigault-Lebrun's *Le blanc et le noir* (1795)" in *Orbis Litterarum* vol. 73, No. 2 (2018): 186–212.
57 Laveaux, *Journal de la Montagne* (6 séptembre 1793); qtd. in Feilla, *The Sentimental Theater*, 54. See Ambrus, "Voix politiques," 154 for other examples of Jacobin condemnations of Chénier in September and October of 1793.
58 Julien Louis Geoffroy, "Fénélon" in *Cours de littérature dramatique* (24 frimaire an 11) (Paris: Pierre Blachard, 1825), tome iv: 121–122.
59 Monvel, *Les Victimes*, 2.3.
60 Monvel, *Les Victimes*, 2.3.
61 Monvel, *Les Victimes*, 2.3.
62 Susan Maslan, "The Anti-Human: Man and Citizen before the Declaration of the Rights of Man and of the Citizen" in *The South Atlantic Quarterly* Vol. 103, No. 2/3 (2004): 372.
63 Emmanuel Joseph Sieyès, "*What Is the Third Estate?*" In Emmanuel Joseph Sieyès, *Political Writings*. Ed. M. Sonenscher. (Indianapolis, IN and Cambridge: Hackett Publishing Company, Inc., 2003), 96n3. See also my article

"The inequality of common utility: active/passive citizenship in French revolutionary human rights" in K.-M. Simonsen and J. R. Kjærgård (eds.), *Discursive Framings of Human Rights: Negotiating agency and victimhood* (Abingdon and New York: Birkbeck Law Press, 2017), 43–59.

64 Thus, Diderot in his version of this populationist argument has the character Manouri write,

> To make a vow of poverty is to swear to be an idler and a thief. To make a vow of chastity is to swear to God constantly to break the wisest and most important of his laws. To make a vow of obedience is to renounce man's inalienable prerogative: freedom. If you keep these vows, you are a criminal; if you do not keep them, you are guilty of perjury before God. To live the cloistered life, you have to be either a fanatic or a hypocrite.
>
> (Diderot, *The Nun*, 75)

65 Denis Diderot, "Conversations on *The Natural Son*" in Denis Diderot, *Selected Writings on Art and Literature*. (London: Penguin Books, 1994), 12.
66 Diderot, "Conversations" in Diderot, *Selected Writings*, 56.
67 Diderot, "Conversations" in Diderot, *Selected Writings*, 56.
68 As discussed in Chapter 2, the question of theater's relation to natural life was at the center of Diderot's discussion with Madame Riccoboni.
69 Louis-Sébastien Mercier, *Du théâtre, ou nouvel essai sur l'art dramatique* in Louis-Sébastien Mercier, *Mon bonnet de nuit suivi de Du théâtre*. Ed. Jean-Claude Bonnet. (Paris: Mercure de France, 1999), 1141.
70 The comments stem from a speech Mercier gave before the Council of Five Hundred in December 1796. Qtd. from Joanna Stalnaker, *The Unfinished Enlightenment: Description in the Age of the Encyclopedia*. (Ithaca, NY and London: Cornell University Press, 2010), 153.
71 Mercier, *Du théâtre* in Mercier, *Mon bonnet de nuit*, 1147.
72 Mercier, *Du théâtre* in Mercier, *Mon bonnet de nuit*, 1147.
73 Denis Diderot, "In Praise of Richardson" in Diderot, *Selected Writings*, 83.
74 Jeffrey Ravel, *The Contested Parterre: Public Theater and French Political Culture, 1680–1791*. (Ithaca, NY and London: Cornell University Press, 1999), esp. 191–224; Maslan, *Revolutionary Acts*, esp. 25–74.
75 Cf. Jay Caplan, *Framed Narratives: Diderot's Genealogy of the Beholder*. (Manchester: Manchester University Press, 1985), 19–20; Denby, *Sentimental Narrative*, 77–78; Feilla, *The Sentimental Theater*, 75.
76 Szondi, "*Tableau* and *Coup de Théâtre*: On the Social Psychology of Diderot's Bourgeois Tragedy" in Peter Szondi, *On Textual Understanding and Other Essays* (Manchester: Manchester University Press, 1986), 121.
77 Szondi, "*Tableau* and *Coup de Théâtre*" in Szondi, *On Textual Understanding*, 125.
78 Denby, *Sentimental Narrative*, 77.
79 Szondi, "*Tableau* and *Coup de Théâtre*" in Szondi, *On Textual Understanding*, 128.
80 I here agree with Feilla whose study seeks to demonstrate "the way sentimental and civic notions of virtue blended onstage, presenting not just complementary but sometimes competing and contradictory prescriptions for virtuous citizenship and virtuous government." (Feilla, *The Sentimental Theater*, 16).
81 Edelstein, *The Terror of Natural Rights*, 45–127.
82 Denby, *Sentimental Narrative*, 80.
83 Caplan, *Framed Narratives*, 20.

84 Jacques-Marie Boutet de Monvel, *Les Victimes cloîtrées*. Edited by Sophie Marchand (London: Modern Humanities Research Association, 2011.), Act IV, Scene 7. For an analysis of *Les Victimes cloîtrées* and its relation to the gothic novel and the early nineteenth century melodrama see Levayer, "Le 'noir' au théâtre," 88–96.
85 On the theodicy, see Susan Neiman, *Evil in Modern Thought: An Alternative History of Philosophy*. With a new preface by the author. (Princeton, NJ and Oxford: Princeton University Press, 2004).
86 Monvel, *Les Victimes*, Act IV, Scene 5.
87 Cf. Brooks, *The Melodramatic Imagination*, esp. 24–56.
88 Monvel, *Les Victimes*: "tigre" (3.9); "monstre" (3.9; 3.11); "scélérat" (3.11; 4.7); and "barbares" (3.11).
89 The same metaphors recur in Olympe de Gouges's convent play, *Le couvent, ou les vœux forcés*: "inhumain" (2.1; 2.7); "tigre" (2.1); "barbare" (2.2).
90 Chénier, "Discours préliminaire (1793)" in Chénier, *Théâtre*, 253.
91 Chénier, "Discours préliminaire (1793)" in Chénier, *Théâtre*, 253.
92 Hunt, *Inventing Human Rights*, 26–35.
93 Edelstein, "Enlightenment Rights Talk," 545.
94 Charly Coleman, *The Virtues of Abandon: An Anti-Individualist History of the French Enlightenment*. (Stanford, CA: Stanford University Press, 2014), 1–17.
95 Chénier, "Discours préliminaire (1793)" in Chénier, *Théâtre*, 253.

Literature

Agamben, Giorgio: *Homo Sacer: Sovereign Power and Bare Life*. Trans. by Daniel Heller-Roazen. Stanford, CA: Stanford University Press, 1998.

Ambrus, Gauthier: "Voix politiques dans les tragedies révolutionnaires de Marie-Joseph Chénier." *Littératures*, Vol. 62 (2010): 141–157.

Archives parlementaires de 1787 à 1860. Paris: Librairie administrative de P. Dupont, 1862-.

Arendt, Hannah: *The Origins of Totalitarianism*. San Diego, New York, and London: Harcourt, Inc., 1973.

Baecque, Antoine de, Wolfgang Schmale, and Michel Vovelle (eds.): *L'an 1 des droits de l'homme*. Paris: Presses du CNRS, 1988.

Balibar, Étienne: *Equaliberty: Political Essays*. Trans. by James Ingram. Durham, NC and London: Duke University Press, 2014.

Beckstrand, Lisa: *Deviant Women of the French Revolution and the Rise of Feminism*. Madison and Teaneck, NJ: Fairleigh Dickinson University Press, 2009.

Blum, Carol: *Strength in Numbers: Population, Reproduction, and Power in Eighteenth-Century France*. Baltimore, MD and London: The Johns Hopkins University Press, 2002.

Bonnet, Jean-Claude: "De la famille à la patrie" in J. Delumeau and D. Roche (eds.), *Histoire des pères et de la paternité*. Paris: Larousse, 2000.

Bossenga, Gail: *The Politics of Privilege: Old Regime and Revolution in Lille*. Cambridge: Cambridge University Press, 1991.

Brooks, Peter: *The Melodramatic Imagination: Balzac, Henry James, Melodrama, and the Mode of Excess*. New Haven, CT and London: Yale University Press, 1995.

Caplan, Jay: *Framed Narratives: Diderot's Genealogy of the Beholder*. Manchester: Manchester University Press, 1985.
Chénier, Marie-Joseph: *Théâtre*. Edited by G. Ambrus and F. Jacob. Paris: Flammarion, 2002.
Cole, John: *Between the Queen and the Cabby: Olympe de Gouges's Rights of Woman*. Montreal and Kingston, NY: McGill-Queen's University Press, 2011.
Coleman, Charly: *The Virtues of Abandon: An Anti-Individualist History of the French Enlightenment*. Stanford, CA: Stanford University Press, 2014.
Condorcet, Marquis de: "On the Emancipation of Women: On Giving Women the Right of Citizenship" in S. Lukes and N. Urbinati (eds.), *Political Writings*. Cambridge: Cambridge University Press, 2012.
Delumeau, Jean and Daniel Roche (eds.): *Histoire des pères et de la paternité*. Paris: Larousse, 1990.
Denby, David J.: *Sentimental Narrative and the Social Order in France, 1760–1820*. Cambridge: Cambridge University Press, 1994.
Desan, Suzanne: *The Family on Trial in Revolutionary France*. Berkeley, Los Angeles, London: University of California Press, 2004.
Desan, Suzanne and Jeffrey Merrick (eds.): *Family, Gender, and Law in Early Modern France*. University Park, PA: The Pennsylvania State University Press, 2009.
Diderot, Denis: *Selected Writings on Art and Literature*. Trans. by G. Bremner. London: Penguin Books, 1994.
Diderot, Denis: *The Nun*. Trans. by R. Goulbourne. Oxford: Oxford University Press, 2008.
Edelstein, Dan: "Enlightenment Rights Talk." *The Journal of Modern History*, Vol. 86, No. 3 (2014): 530–565.
Edelstein, Dan: *The Terror of Natural Rights: Republicanism, the Cult of Nature, & the French Revolution*. Chicago, IL and London: The University of Chicago Press, 2010.
Estève, Edmond: *Études de littérature préromantique*. Paris: Librarie ancienne Honoré Champion, 1923.
Feilla, Cecilia: *The Sentimental Theater of the French Revolution*. Surrey: Ashgate, 2013.
Festa, Lynn: *Sentimental Figures of Empire in Eighteenth-Century Britain and France*. Baltimore, NY: The Johns Hopkins University Press, 2006.
Friedland, Paul: *Political Actors: Representative Bodies & Theatricality in the Age of the French Revolution*. Ithaca, NY and London: Cornell University Press, 2003.
Geoffroy, Julien Louis: "Fénélon" in *Cours de littérature dramatique*. Vol. IV (24 frimaire an 11). Paris: Pierre Blachard, 1825.
Gerber, Matthew: *Bastards: Politics, Family, and Law in Early Modern France*. Oxford: Oxford University Press, 2012.
Gouges, Olympe de: *Zamore et Mirza; ou l'heureux naufrage*. Paris: [n.p.], 1788.
Gouges, Olympe de: *Écrits politiques 1788–1791, tome 1*. Ed. O. Blanc. Paris: Côté-femmes éditions, 1993.
Gouges, Olympe de: *L'esclavage des noirs, ou l'heureux naufrage*. Paris: [n.p.], 1792a.
Gouges, Olympe de: *Le Couvent, ou les vœux forcés*. Paris: [n.p.], 1792b.

Hunt, Lynn: *Inventing Human Rights: A History*. New York and London: W. W. Norton & Company, 2008.
Kennedy, Emmet, Marie-Laurence Netter, James P. McGregor, and Mark V. Olsen: *Theatre, Opera, and Audiences in Revolutionary Paris*. Westport, CT and London: Greenwood Press, 1996.
Kjærgård, Jonas Ross: "The inequality of common utility: active/passive citizenship in French revolutionary human rights" in K.-M. Simonsen and J. R. Kjærgård (eds.), *Discursive Framings of Human Rights: Negotiating agency and victimhood*. Abingdon and New York: Birkbeck Law Press, 2017: 43–59.
Kjærgård, Jonas Ross: "What are Robespierre and Télémaque Doing in Saint-Domingue? Humanness, Revolutionary Legitimacy, and Political Order in Charles Pigault-Lebrun's *Le blanc et le noir* (1795)." *Orbis Litterarum* vol. 73, No. 2 (2018): 186–212.
Levayer, Paul-Édouard: "Le 'noir' au théâtre, des Victimes cloîtrées au mélodrame." *Europe*, Vol. 62, No. 659 (1984): 88–96.
Liéby, Adolphe: *Étude sur le théâtre de Marie-Joseph Chénier*. Paris: Société française d'imprimerie et de librairie, 1902.
Lotman, Jurij: *The Structure of the Artistic Text*. Trans. by R. Vroon. Michigan: Ann Arbor, 1977.
Marshall, David: *The Surprising Effects of Sympathy: Marivaux, Diderot, Rousseau, and Mary Shelley*. Chicago, IL and London: The University of Chicago Press, 1988.
Marx, Karl: "Zur Judenfrage" in Karl Marx and Friedrich Engels (eds.), *Werke*. Vol. 1. Berlin: Dietz Verlag, 1976.
Maslan, Susan: *Revolutionary Acts: Theater, Democracy, and the French Revolution*. Baltimore, MD: The Johns Hopkins University Press, 2005.
Maslan, Susan: "The Anti-Human: Man and Citizen before the Declaration of the Rights of Man and of the Citizen." *The South Atlantic Quarterly*, Vol. 103, No. 2/3 (2004): 357–374.
Mercier, Louis-Sébastien: "Du théâtre, ou nouvel essai sur l'art dramatique" in Louis-Sébastien Mercier (ed.), *Mon bonnet de nuit suivi de Du théâtre*. Ed. J.-C. Bonnet. Paris: Mercure de France, 1999.
Monvel, Jacques-Marie Boutet de: *Les Victimes cloîtrées*. Ed. S. Marchand. London: Modern Humanities Research Association, 2011.
Mousset, Sophie: *Women's Rights and the French Revolution: A Biography of Olympe de Gouges*. Trans. by Joy Poirel. New Brunswick and London: Transaction Publishers, 2007.
Neiman, Susan: *Evil in Modern Thought: An Alternative History of Philosophy*. With a new preface by the author. Princeton, NJ and Oxford: Princeton University Press, 2004.
Prendergast, Christopher: *Balzac: Fiction and Melodrama*. New York: Holmes and Meier Publishers, Inc., 1978.
Rancière, Jacques: "Who Is the Subject of the Rights of Man?" *The South Atlantic Quarterly*, Vol. 103, No. 2/3 (2004): 297–310.
Ravel, Jeffrey: *The Contested Parterre: Public Theater and French Political Culture, 1680–1791*. Ithaca, NY and London: Cornell University Press, 1999.
Scott, Joan Wallach: *Only Paradoxes to Offer: French Feminists and the Rights of Man*. Cambridge and London: Harvard University Press, 1996.

Shklar, Judith N.: *Men & Citizens: A Study of Rousseau's Social Theory*. Cambridge: Cambridge University Press, 1985.

Sieyès, Emmanuel Joseph: "*What Is the Third Estate?*" in Emmanuel Joseph Sieyès: *Political Writings*. Edited by M. Sonenscher. Indianapolis, IN and Cambridge: Hackett Publishing Company, Inc., 2003.

Sliwinski, Sharon: "The Aesthetics of Human Rights." *Culture, Theory & Critique*, Vol. 50, No. 1 (2009): 23–39.

Szondi, Peter: *On Textual Understanding and Other Essays*. Trans. H. Mendelsohn. Manchester: Manchester University Press, 1986.

Viguier, Audrey: "L'abbé Gouttes et le curé du *Couvent ou les vœux forcés* d'Olympe de Gouges (1790)." *The French Review*, Vol. 85, No. 6 (2012): 1113–1122.

Conclusion

To work on the French revolution presents the challenge of trying to understand what people thought they were doing when they were living through the events of what historians have since come to regard as the birthplace of the modern world.[1] If the epochal shift from early modernity to modernity is defined politically by the transition from absolutism to representative democracy, nowhere is this change brought about more dramatically and more influentially than in revolutionary France. The combination of Enlightenment ideas, the necessity of structural change in the state apparatus, and the great international attention makes the French revolution stand out as a singular and world historical event. But did the revolutionaries themselves know that? And if they in fact believed they were in the process of writing world history, what could they have taken this to mean? What did it mean for them to imagine a new France? In my attempt to answer those questions, I have turned to the fictional literature of the late eighteenth century.

Authors of fiction partook in the public discussion of the political future of France. They intervened in and co-established the social imaginary within which revolutionary politicians would later work when they struggled to agree on the Declaration of the Rights of Man and of the Citizen (1789). I am not the first to posit an important relationship between fictional literature and the human rights of the period. Lynn Hunt has suggested that epistolary novels taught readers to feel empathy with strangers, something that was important for the idea of universal human rights to become thinkable and even self-evident.[2] Susan Maslan has investigated the literary genealogy of the man-citizen schism characteristic of the Declaration of Rights, and she argues that literature's affinity with the imagination made the peculiar double subject thinkable or "real."[3] My ambition has been to reinvestigate the relationship between literature and human rights from the different perspective of two historical premises: the singular *role of the author* in the period and the *unfinishedness of the Declaration of Rights*.

The social function of literature and the role of the author changed in France in the last third of the eighteenth century, and the new role of the author is important for the *kind* of political interventions that could be made through literature. The Enlightenment movement lost most of its key figures between 1778 and 1785, and thereby also much of its critical edge and inventive spirit. It had become a closed elitist circle, and a new generation of writers felt excluded from it, both culturally and financially. In addition to the push away from the literary *monde*, there was a pull toward politics. Politics in this period increasingly became a popular activity, and authors of fiction tried to contribute with emotionally engaging, recognizable, and imaginative visions of social alterity. The result was a diverse literary scene and, particularly during the revolutionary decade, a very vibrant theatrical scene. The simultaneous pull toward politics and push away from the literary *monde* sparked the ambition to develop a new literature and set the sociological premises for the development of the author-politician figure.

The second premise of this study is that the Declaration of Rights and its combination of individual rights and collective happiness was a poignant yet highly ambiguous political document. After much debate, the National Assembly deputies decided that the Declaration of Rights should preface the unwritten Constitution, which would again set the tone for all further positive legislation. This legislative composition made the deputies highly aware of the political implications of semantics and miniature linguistic nuances because the wording of the 1789 Declaration articles would influence all future legislation. This exponential logic of the legislative process put enormous pressure on the deputies during the Declaration Debate, and the result was a comprise text, which the deputies themselves considered unfinished when it was ratified. The unfinishedness and compromise character of the 1789 Declaration involved a number of unsolved questions, which legislators would have to reconsider in their 1793 and 1795 declaration debates. Despite the ongoing discussions and unsolved questions of the Declaration of Rights, the document also followed another, seemingly opposite, trajectory. From its ratification, the Declaration of Rights was disseminated widely through school catechisms, popular publications, and revolutionary imagery. The result of these two opposite trajectories was a highly authoritative, almost sacred document whose legislative content was continuously debated and changed through the revolutionary decade.

My interpretation of the Declaration Debate focused in particular on three dilemmas: nature and society, rights and duties, and political exclusion. I have reintroduced these dilemmas in the analytical chapters, but I would like to conclude by revisiting them from the perspective of the work of Mercier, Laclos, and Chénier. I argue that each of these dilemmas entails different and competing forms of political anthropology, by which I mean different ways of balancing the relationship between individual and society, and different kinds of subjectivity more or less defined by a set of communitarian values.

When the National Assembly deputies appealed to natural rights, natural law, or the natural order, their concept of nature had historical, philosophical, and political connotations. Historically, the American Founding Fathers had set an important example with their 1776 Declaration of Independence, and like other Europeans, the French deputies thought of America as an uncorrupted and newfound *natural* country. Philosophically, the deputies were well aware of Rousseau's social critique, and without necessarily adopting the totality of his philosophy, they did use his vocabulary and, like him, contrasted a hypothetical idea about the natural order with the inequalities of their own social order. In combination with the reference to the American example, this juxtaposition of nature and society had profound political consequences. Conservatives devised a "realist" critique of the natural order because they considered it inopportune to allow visions of political alterity into the Declaration Debate. As John Adams had realized on the other side of the Atlantic, rights discussions had a tendency to escalate once radically different ways of organizing society entered the debate. Whenever someone posited the existence of natural universal equality all kinds of claims could be made and soon, as he wrote, "[t]here will be no end to it."[4]

Mercier did not look to a speculative past or across the Atlantic to find his alternative to the existing social order. Instead, he created a vision of future perfection and used that "dream, if ever there was one," as the critical alternative to the miseries of his present. It says much about his scorn of things past and of his belief in human progress that he looked to the future for social perfection but structurally, he performed a gesture similar to that of the Assembly deputies. He used an imaginary vision of perfection to exhibit the imperfections of his own day. Laclos in his essayistic writings cited precisely the passages about the hypothetical character of the natural order from Rousseau's *Second Discourse*. In his essays, Laclos, unlike Rousseau, used the hypothesis of the natural order to argue that women had the right to an education and to an equal relation with men. In *Les Liaisons dangereuses*, the equality and happiness of the natural state has subsided and given place to an exposure of the scheming and opacity of the libertines and other members of the high aristocracy. Unlike Mercier, Laclos offered no sustained vision of perfection but invited his reader to critically reflect on the mores of his day. Chénier, finally, posited an affinity between sensual recognition and sympathetic response. He described a social space in which corruption and unenlightened prejudice had silenced the voice of nature and made some unable to follow their natural inclination and respond to suffering. With that social diagnosis as his point of departure, he set out to demonstrate the existence of natural virtue and to describe an affective network of virtuous characters capable of recognizing the signs of suffering and willing to act upon them.

During the Declaration Debate, deputies discussed whether they should supplement the list of rights with a list of duties. When the Directory assumed power and rewrote the Declaration of Rights, they in fact made a Declaration of the Rights and Duties of Man and of the Citizen (1795). In 1789, however, the deputies abandoned the idea – and this I think is important – not because they were opposed to the idea of the citizens having duties but because they believed the duties were implicit in the notion of citizenship. To belong wholly and fully to the political body, citizens, to the distress of Robespierre, had to fulfill a number of explicit requirements but more generally, they had to prove their common utility. The only explicit mention of duties in the Declaration of Rights is in the preface but a close reading of the document reveals that Frenchmen (and they *were* all men) should meet a set of criteria to qualify as active citizens. This means that the inalienable rights of the 1789 Declaration in actuality came with a set of expectations that were defined by the political elite.

Mercier made no attempt to hide that he preferred for women to remain at home instead of intervening in the politics of the public sphere. His gender politics resembles that of most eighteenth-century writers, but they deserve emphasis in their own right *and* as an example of the requirements Mercier believed people had to fulfill to qualify as members of the perfect future society. Mercier's vision is communitarian and he expects the members of the ideal society to contribute voluntarily to the fiscal coffers and to share the appreciation of particular forms of clothing and belief. In *Les Liaisons dangereuses* the libertines struggle to free themselves from the duties of a set of Old Regime social elite expectations. Instead of honoring the marriages arranged by socially superior parents, the libertines attempt to maneuver freely in a highly regulated social space and the result is a confrontation of different kinds of social norms and forms of interaction. Through the heroic figure of Fénelon, Chénier emphasized the necessity of serving not only God but also humanity. Actually, Fénelon cherishes social usefulness and in addition to its religious prejudices, the unproductive and hence useless life of the convent institution is what the play critically puts on display.

The question of outright political exclusion was present in the natural rights philosophy of Denis Diderot but it acquired particular relevance in the years of the execution of the king and in Robespierre's draft Declaration of Rights from 1793. The active/passive distinction drew a line between full and partial members of the body politic and thereby entailed what I have called *internal political exclusion*. The *external political exclusion* of Diderot and Robespierre, contrarily, implied a line drawn between members and non-members of the political body. Because this line was often drawn rhetorically with the usage of dehumanizing metaphors, there is here an important similarity between the natural rights philosophy and the genre of sentimental writing. This excluding and dehumanizing element of the natural rights philosophy is downplayed in Hunt's more celebratory analysis of the 1789 human rights. It is emphasized in different ways, however, in the work of both Dan Edelstein and Lynn Festa.[5]

In *L'an 2440*, most enemies of society have simply misconceived the truths and shared values of the community and a group of virtuous citizens will pay them a visit to put them right. In rare examples, more drastic means are necessary, however. God's all-seeing eye will then haunt and punish the sinner not just through one life but through a cycle of multiple reincarnations. In less dramatic cases, criminals finally realize their wrongs and signal to their co-citizens that they deserve to be punished by death. In Laclos's novel, exclusion is part of the social reality and libertines who fall into disfavor risk being exposed as libertines and excluded from their social environments. Most dramatically, the sins of Merteuil become public knowledge at the end of the novel, and she faces social, juridical, and natural punishment as she is forced to flee Paris, loses a court case, and becomes disfigured from disease. Throughout *Fénelon*, Chénier develops a dehumanizing chain of metaphors – skeleton, tiger, monster – to characterize the sinners who oppose the virtuous protagonists. The villains, as in the example of the inflexible father, can be forgiven for their sins if they repent but if they refuse to apologize, they simply disappear. They can either accept the communitarian values or disappear from sight.

To understand the diverse ways literature contributed to the political task of reimagining a happy France, I have chosen to focus on few but very different works of literature. They differ in genre, in style, in medium, in quality, and in fame. From the perspective of literary studies, I think it is crucial to avoid getting stuck in never ending rereadings of a few hundred canonical titles because those works cannot be expected to be representative of the history of literature. On the contrary, the canonical works are those that stand out because of their quality, their strangeness, or the originality of their ideas. Statistically, they are anomalies and anomalies are important to understand but to grasp their specificity, we need to not only develop ever more sophisticated theoretical perspectives but also, and more importantly, know much more about the 99% from which the canonical works depart. We need to study the masterpieces alongside what Margaret Cohen has called "the great unread."[6]

The different types of literature have intervened in the political discussion about the future of France but in diverse ways. By juxtaposing dissimilar limited perspectives on a shared fictional reality, Laclos uses the epistolary format to force his reader to compare and reflect on the actions and self-presentations of his characters. Instead of empathizing with the figures of the narrative, we as readers are challenged to think about the characters' strategies and the incompatibility of the Old Regime intersubjective forms of sociality that they adhere to. In different ways, Mercier and Chénier tried to create a communitarian bond with their readers and spectators, enjoining them to share a set of beliefs. Mercier advanced a communitarian "we" and built upon it throughout his prophetic narrative and Chénier interpellated his spectator as a member of the onstage affective network of the virtuous characters. While the texts invite different audience and reader responses, they also have different ways of intervening in the dichotomy of an unhappy past and a happy future. While Laclos only offers a slight glimpse of an ideal ordering of society, he is ruthless in his exposure of the unsustainability of the Old Regime forms of sociality and subjectivity. Unlike Laclos, Chénier and Mercier present detailed visions of communitarian virtues and social forms that they feel will lead France toward a happy future.

Some authors worked to tear down the old and others to propose something new but they shared the wish to intervene in politics and reimagine society through literature.

Notes

1 Examples are the four-volume anthology published on the occasion of the bicentenary Keith Michael Baker, Colin Lucas, François Furet, and Mona Ozouf, eds., *The French Revolution and the Creation of Modern Political Culture I–IV* (Oxford: Pergamon Press, 1987–1994) and Christopher A. Bayly, *The Birth of the Modern World 1780–1914* (USA: Blackwell Publishing, 2004).
2 Lynn Hunt, *Inventing Human Rights: A History* (New York and London: W. W. Norton & Company, 2008).
3 Susan Maslan, "The Anti-Human: Man and Citizen before the Declaration of the Rights of Man and of the Citizen" in *The South Atlantic Quarterly*, Vol. 103, No. 2/3, 2004, 363. See also Susan Maslan, "The Dream of the Feeling Citizen: Law and Emotion in Corneille and Montesquieu" in *SubStance*, Vol. 35, No. 1 (2006): 69–84; Susan Maslan, "'Gotta Serve Somebody': Service; Autonomy; Society" in *Comparative Literature Studies*, Vol. 46, No. 1 (2009): 45–75; and Susan Maslan, "Nature and Society in Revolutionary Rights Debates" in Sophia A. McClennen, and Alexandra S. Moore. (eds.), *The Routledge Companion to Literature and Human Rights* (London and New York: Routledge, 2016).
4 John Adams, qtd. from *Hunt, Inventing Human Rights*, 147.
5 Lynn Festa, *Sentimental Figures of Empire in Eighteenth-Century Britain and France* (Baltimore, MD: The Johns Hopkins University Press, 2006); Dan Edelstein, "Enlightenment Rights Talk" in *The Journal of Modern History*, Vol. 86, No. 3 (2014): 530–565.
6 Margaret Cohen, *The Sentimental Education of the Novel* (Princeton: Princeton University Press, 1999), 3–26.

Literature

Baker, Keith Michael, Colin Lucas, François Furet, and Mona Ozouf, (eds.): *The French Revolution and the Creation of Modern Political Culture I–IV*. Oxford: Pergamon Press, 1987–1994.

Bayly, Christopher A.: *The Birth of the Modern World 1780–1914*. Malden, MA: Blackwell Publishing, 2004.

Cohen, Margaret: *The Sentimental Education of the Novel*. Princeton: Princeton University Press, 1999.

Edelstein, Dan: "Enlightenment Rights Talk." *The Journal of Modern History*, Vol. 86, No. 3 (2014): 530–565.

Festa, Lynn: *Sentimental Figures of Empire in Eighteenth-Century Britain and France*. Baltimore, MD: The Johns Hopkins University Press, 2006.

Hunt, Lynn: *Inventing Human Rights: A History*. New York and London: W. W. Norton & Company, 2008.

Maslan, Susan: "The Anti-Human: Man and Citizen before the Declaration of the Rights of Man and of the Citizen." *The South Atlantic Quarterly*, Vol. 103, No. 2/3 (2004): 357–374.

Maslan, Susan: "The Dream of the Feeling Citizen: Law and Emotion in Corneille and Montesquieu." *SubStance*, Vol. 35, No. 1 (2006): 69–84.

Maslan, Susan: "'Gotta Serve Somebody': Service; Autonomy; Society." *Comparative Literature Studies*, Vol. 46, No. 1 (2009): 45–75.

Maslan, Susan: "Nature and Society in Revolutionary Rights Debates" in Sophia A. McClennen and Alexandra S. Moore (eds.), *The Routledge Companion to Literature and Human Rights*. London and New York: Routledge, 2016.

Index

Abensour, Miguel 96, 120n17
absolutism 1–2
"A City in Words: Louis-Sébastien Mercier's *Tableau de Paris*" (Popkin) 83n22, 83n29
A Critical Dictionary of the French Revolution (Furet and Ozouf) 124n70
Active/passive citizenship 24, 38–42, 48n86, 48n90, 104, 114–115, 191, 195n63, 204
Adams, John 206n4
Adorno, Theodor 120n20, 136
"The Aesthetics of Human Rights" (Sliwinski) 194n40
Agamben, Giorgio 194n45
Ahmed, Sara 9, 18n39–18n40
Allegories of Reading: Figural Language in Rousseau, Nietzsche, Rilke, and Proust (de Man) 47n52
alternative visions of society 32, 99; *see also* utopianism
Althusser, Louis 125n92
America 25, 32, 110; as example to French revolutionaries 27, 29–30, 203; Founding Fathers 25
The Ancien Régime and the French Revolution (Tocqueville) 82n7, 82n9
An 2440, rêve s'il en fût jamais, L' (Mercier) 14–15, 59, 64–5, 82n14, 83n26, 93–129, 135, 154, 178, 205; *see also* Mercier, Louis-Sébastien
An Essay on Privileges (Sieyès) 48n81; *see also* Sieyès, Emmanuel Joseph
Annales patriotiques 60
anthropology 30–1, 175; philosophical anthropology: 24, 33; political anthropology 10–14, 38, 58, 108, 118, 152–3, 174, 202
"The Anti-Human: Man and Citizen before the Declaration of the Rights of Man and of the Citizen" (Maslan) 19n50, 84n47, 88n125, 125n87, 195n62, 206n3
Anti-Seneca or the Sovereign Good (la Mettrie) 8, 18n35
Arago, M. F. 48n84
Arendt, Hannah 175, 194n45
"A Response to Jonathan Israel" (Edelstein) 46n26, 46n34, 47n76
A Rhetoric of Bourgeois Revolution: The Abbé Sieyès and What Is the Third Estate? (Sewell) 48n79, 76, 82n11, 88n113–88n114
Aristotle 63, 79
arranged marriages 132–5, 137–40, 143–4, 152
arrêts de règlement 107
Ars Poetica (Horace) 71, 86n74, 86n80; *see also* Horace and Horatian concepts
ARTFL-FRANTEXT database 156n14
Articles: Six 35–8, 41; Ten 105; Eleven 172; Twelve 36; Thirteen 34; *see also* Declaration Debate; *Déclaration des droits de l'homme et du citoyen*
author-legislator, literature (Chénier) 72–89
author-politician, figure of 5, 14, 55–9, 65–66, 68, 70, 73, 81, 202
Autobiography of Du Pont de Nemours, The (Du Pont) 82n8
autonomy 38–9
Aventures de Télémaque, Les (Fénelon) 9, 97, 120n23, 179, 195n55
"Avertissement du libraire" (Laclos) 155n1

Baczko, Bronislaw 94–6, 98, 120n5, 120n11, 120n16–120n18, 120n21, 120n25–120n26, 121n31, 122n48

210 *Index*

Badiou, Alain 148, 160n64
Baecque, Antoine de 22, 45n6, 45n16, 45n19, 45n22, 46n30, 46n46, 82n11
Baker, Keith Michael 17n24, 45n8–45n9, 45n12, 47n72, 80–1, 82n13, 88n128, 89n129, 120n27, 122n52–122n53, 206n1
Balibar, Étienne 1, 10–13, 16n4, 18n41, 18n43, 18n52–18n53, 19n46–19n49, 38, 40, 48n83, 104, 118, 122n45, 125n88, 174, 194n42
Balzac: Fiction and Melodrama (Prendergast) 192n4
Banlieues uprisings 39
Bastards: Politics, Family, and Law in Early Modern France (Gerber) 157n19, 193n18, 194n30
Bastille, storming of 2
The Bastille: A History of a Symbol of Despotism and Freedom (Lüsebrink and Reichardt) 16n8
Bayly, Christopher A. 206n1
Beckett, Samuel 7
Beckstrand, Lisa 194n31
Béclard, Léon 83n25
Becoming a Revolutionary: The Deputies of the French National Assembly and the Emergence of a Revolutionary Culture (1789–1790) (Tackett) 45n19, 46n28
Before the Deluge: Public Debt, Inequality, and the Intellectual Origins of the French Revolution (Sonenscher) 45n18, 82n10, 123n61
Begriffsgeschichte 7
belles lettres 62, 64
Bertrand Barère 87n104–87n105
Between the Queen and the Cabby: Olympe de Gouges's Rights of Woman (Cole) 194n33
Bien, David D. 122n60
"*bilan d'états de conscience*" 18n36
"The Birthplace of the Revolution: Public Space and Political Community in the Palais-Royal of Louis-Phillippe-Joseph D'Orléans, 1781–1789" (McMahon) 85n58, 85n66
Blanc et le noir, Le (Gouges) 179
Blanc, Olivier 159n59, 194n33
Blum, Carol 15, 157n29, 171, 194n27–194n29

body metaphor 106–7
Bonaparte, Napoleon 22, 66
Bonheur *see* happiness
Bonnay, M. le marquis de 28, 46n30
Bonnet, Jean-Claude 84n33, 84n35, 84n48, 120n8–120n9, 121n36, 121n41, 125n84, 170, 194n25, 196n69
Bonney, Richard 124n70
Bosher, John 122n51, 123n69
Bossenga, Gail 43–4, 45n18, 49n103, 109, 123n61, 124n70, 166, 193n16
Bouche, M. 17n16, 45n9
Bourdieu, Pierre 17n20, 82n4
"bourgeois spirit" 109, 116, 130, 185
Boursault-Malherbe, Jean-François 83n16
Bretonne, Restif de la 88n121, 170
Brissot, Jacques Pierre 59
Brooks, Peter 130, 132, 156n13, 157n18, 157n27, 165, 190, 192n4, 193n7–193n8, 197n87
Bruno, Giordano 133
Brutus (Voltaire) 75
Buckley, Matthew S. 83n17
Buffon, Comte de 143

Cahiers des doléances (Lists of grievances) 26, 33–4, 68, 110
Caïus Gracchus (Chénier) 73, 75–6
Calonne, Charles-Alexandre de 110, 123n65, 123n68
Calvin, Jean 133
Cambridge School 6, 14
Candide and Other Stories (Voltaire) 97–8, 120n24
capitation tax 111
Caplan, Jay 189, 196n75, 196n83
Carra, Jean-Louis 60
Censorship 6, 59, 85n71; of opinion 105; of theater 73–75, 169; freedom of the press 74, 93–4, 119n2
Chalons-sur-Marne academy 141
"Champ intellectuel et projet créateur" 17n20, 82n4
Chapelier Law 74, 87n99, 169
Charles, Shelly 120n8
Charles IX (Chénier) 72–3, 77, 86n89
Chartier, Roger 80, 88n127, 101, 121n40
Cheney, Paul 62, 82n10, 84n38
Chénier, Marie-Joseph 5, 6, 9, 14–6, 54–7, 62–3, 66, 68, 95, 117, 135,

154, 202–6; biography and views on theatre 72–81; *Fénelon ou les religieuses de Cambrai* 164–197; political life of 73–4
children 39, 167, 170–2; natural children 16, 70–1, 167, 170–2
"Choderlos de Laclos et la théorie du récit" (Todorov) 156n5, 157n21, 160n72
Choderlos de Laclos ou l'obstination (Poisson) 84n51–84n52, 85n54, 85n61–85n62, 85n65, 158n43
Cicé, M. Champion de 45n25
cinquantième tax 111
citizenship dilemmas 10–13, 165–6; agent-citizen 12–13; enmity and passive citizenship 38–43; membership importance 43–4; nature and society 29–32; rights and duties 32–8
Citizens to Lords: A Social History of Western Political Thought from Antiquity to the Middle Ages (Meiksins Wood) 17n25
"Citizen Subject" (Balibar) 16n4
civic payments 114; *see also* taxation
Clarissa (Richardson) 85n70
Clément, Jean-Marie Bernard 88n122
Clermont-Lodève, M. de 33, 35, 47n63
Clermont-Tonnerre, Comte de 46n38
Clootz, Anacharsis 39
code of history 55–60
Cohen, Margaret 206n6
Cole, John 194n33–194n35
Coleman, Charly 13, 18n56–18n59, 38, 58, 108, 112, 122n56, 124n73, 125n88, 152, 160n68, 192, 197n94
Collège des Quatre-Nations 59
Comédie-Française 72–74, 87n106
comédie genre 75
Comédie-Italienne 74, 151
Comité de cinq, Le (The Committee of Five) 4, 28
Comité de distribution du travail sur la Constitution 26
Comité d'instruction publique 73
Comité du Salut public 75
Committee of Five 4, 28
community: members, line between 42; onstage 167, 189–90; usefulness 191

Compte rendu au Roi (Necker) 85n57, 110, 123n65, 123n67
Condillac, Étienne Bonnot de 5, 175
Condorcet, Antoine-Nicolas Caritat de (Marquis de) 15, 17n14, 39, 48n84, 56, 59, 82n11, 98–100, 104, 121n28–121n30, 121n44, 122n48, 174–5, 194n43
The Confessions of Jean Jacques Rousseau (Rousseau) 148, 159n62
"*conscience d'exister*" 18n36
Considérations sur les intérêst du tiers-état adressés au peuple des provinces par un propriétaire foncier (Rabaut de Saint-Etienne) 56, 82n13
Constitution 1, 3, 10, 25–9, 40–1, 48n88, 76–7, 114, 202
Constitutional committee 45n25
The Contested Parterre: Public Theater and French Political Culture, 1680–1791 (Ravel) 87n97, 87n106, 88n118, 196n74
Contraband: Louis Mandrin and the Making of a Global Underground (Kwass) 16n8, 123n61
convent life 167–73
Cordorcet: From Natural Philosophy to Social Mathematics (Baker) 98, 120n27
corpus mysticum 58
"Correspondance entre Madame Riccoboni et l'auteur des *Liaisons dangereuses*" (Riccoboni and Laclos) 86n73, 86n75–86n76, 86n82–6n84, 86n86–6n87, 160n73
Correspondance secrète, politique et littéraire 85n71
corvée tax 111
Coulet, Henri 156n4, 158n38
Council of Five Hundred 196n70
counterrevolution 1, 27, 42, 180
coup de théâtre 185, 187–8, 196n79
Cours de littérature dramatique (Geoffroy) 195n58
Couthon, Georges 75, 87n101–87n103
Couvent, ou les vœux forces, Le (Gouges) 164, 172, 195n49, 197n89
cradle metaphor 73–4
Crénière, Jean-Baptiste 4, 17n17, 45n15

The Crisis of the Absolute Monarchy: France from Old Regime to Revolution (Swann and Felix) 155n2, 160n74
The Cultural Origins of the French Revolution (Chartier) 88n127, 121n40
culte des droits de l'homme, Le (Zuber) 24, 45n14, 45n22
Cupis, M. 59, 83n23

D'Alembert, Jean le Rond 5, 8, 179
Dangerous Liaisons, see *Liaisons dangereuses, Les*
"Dangerous Liaisons: Literary and Political Form in Choderlos de Laclos" (Birkett) 156n15
"Dangerous Liaisons 2: The Ricciboni-Laclos Sequel" (Vanpée) 156n6
Darnaudat, Louis-Jean-Henry 27, 46n27
Darnton, Georges 73, 86n90
Darnton, Robert 5–6, 14, 17n21–17n23, 57, 83n15, 83n26–83n27, 93–4, 100–1, 119n1, 119n3, 120n6–120n7, 120n21, 121n35, 121n38, 122n49, 125n82, 154, 160n74
David, Jacques-Louis 73
Declaration Debate 22–53, 58, 77, 82n11, 104, 119, 131, 141, 143, 155, 166, 182; enmity and passive citizenship 38–43; nature and society 29–32; rights and duties 32–8
Déclaration des droits de l'homme et du citoyen (Declaration of the Rights of Man and Citizen) 3–5, 10–13, 22–53, 58, 74, 95, 109–10, 117, 123n63, 124n50, 135, 146, 152–4, 181, 190; article six 35–8, 41; article ten 105; article eleven 172; article twelve 36; article thirteen 34
Declaration of Rights/Déclaration des droits: Traduite de l'Anglois, avec l'original à coté (Condorcet) 48n84
DeJean, Joan 156n7
"De la famille à la patrie" (Bonnet) 194n25
De la liberté du théâtre en France (Chénier) 72, 74, 87n98, 88n115

De la littérature et des littérateurs suivi d'un nouvel examen de la tragédie française (Mercier) 63, 84n45–84n46, 84n50
De L'Allemagne (Staël) 124n80
Delandine, Antoine-François 32, 42, 46n41, 47n56, 95, 120n12
De la poésie dramatique (Diderot) 86n79
Delon, Michel 150, 156n8, 160n65
Delumeau, J. 193n18, 194n25
de Man, Paul 31–2, 46n51, 47n52, 143, 158n46
Demeunier, M. 120n11
Democratic Enlightenment: Philosophy, Revolution, and Human Rights 1750–1790 (Israel) 17n18, 44n3
Denby, David J. 87n110, 165, 173, 175, 177–8, 181, 187, 189, 193n10–193n12, 194n38, 195n46–195n47, 196n75, 196n78, 196n82
Deneys-Tunney, Anne 137, 156n9, 157n33, 159n60
Dénonciation des inquisiteurs de la pensée (Chénier) 72
Desacralization, desanctification 154, 160n74
Desan, Suzanne 15, 131, 157n16–157n17, 157n30, 170, 193n18, 194n26
Descartes, René 148
"Des femmes et de leur éducation" (Laclos) 141, 158n42
Desmoulines, Camille 159
despotism 103
Deviant Women of the French Revolution and the Rise of Feminism (Beckstrand) 194n31
Devoir (Droit nat. Relig. nat. Morale.) (*Encyclopédie*) 33, 47n64
d'Holbach, Baron 93
Dialectic of Enlightenment: Philosophical Fragments (Adorno and Horkheimer) 120n20
Diderot, Denis 5, 8, 42–3, 49n101, 57, 60, 71, 78, 81n81, 86n72, 86n77–86n80, 88n120, 107, 121n42, 122n55, 165, 169–70, 185–8, 190, 193n22, 196n64–196n68, 196n73
direct taxes 111
Discourse on the Origin and the Foundations of Inequality among

Index 213

Men (Rousseau) 30–1, 46n49–6n50, 158n41, 203
"Discourse on the Question Put Forth by the Academy of Chalons sur Marne" (Laclos) 159n54
Discours préliminaire (Chénier) 17n19, 60, 76, 87n93, 87n111–87n112, 88n116, 88n122–88n123, 89n130, 193n5, 193n19, 195n52, 195n54, 197n90–197n91, 197n95
Discours prononcé de l'ordre du roi et en sa présence par M. De Calonne, contrôleur général des finances, dans l'Assemblée des notables, tenue à Versailles, le 22 février 1787 (Calonne) 123n65, 123n68
Discursive Framings of Human Rights: Negotiating Agency and Victimhood (Simonsen and Kjærgård) 48n86, 121n34, 195n63
dispossession culture 13, 108; *see also* Coleman, Charly
distribution of rights 44
"distribution of the sensible" (Rancière) 31
Dits et écrits II. 1976–1988 (Foucault) 18n42, 125n88
dixième tax 111
Dobie, Madeleine 46n40
Dorigny, Marcel 84n37
Douzinas, Costas 44n4
Doyle, William 107, 122n52, 122n59
"Draft Declaration of the Rights of Man and of the Citizen" (Robespierre) 49n95–49n96, 49n98
drame genre 16, 60, 75, 87n107
dream of a happy future: background 93–6; duty of patriotism 108–19; taxation 108–19; temporality, utopian thought 96–102; *see also* happiness
"The Dream of the Feeling Citizen: Law and Emotion in Corneille and Montesquieu" (Maslan) 19n51, 160n71, 206n3
droits de la femme, Les (Gouges) 159n59, 172–173, 194n33, 194n36
Droit naturel, (Morale.) (Diderot) 42–43, 49n101
Du Bos (abbé) 176, 187
Duc d'Orléans 57, 66–8
Du Contrat social (Rousseau) 19n54, 35–36, 47n69–47n70, 49n93, 104–105, 122n46–122n47, 142, 158n40
dulce et utile 66–72, 77
Duperré, Marie-Soulange 66
Du Pont de Nemours, Pierre Samuel 62, 82n8, 84n38–84n40, 120n12
Duport, M. 47n61
Du Théâtre, ou nouvel essai sur l'art dramatique (Mercier) 60, 64, 100, 118, 196n69, 196n71–196n72
duties: of patriotism 108–19; and rights 32–8

Eagleton, Terry 81n1–81n2
Écrits politiques (Gouges) 124n74, 124n77–124n78, 159n59, 194n33
Ecritures du corps. De Descartes à Laclos (Deneys-Tunney) 156n9, 157n33, 159n60
Edelstein, Dan 36, 42, 46n26, 46n34, 46n42, 47n76, 49n97, 49n99–49n100, 153–4, 160n70, 188, 191, 194n37, 195n55, 196n81, 197n93, 206n5
Edgar, ou le Page supposé (Chénier) 72
"Editor's preface" (Laclos) 129
Egret, Jean 85n66, 122n51, 123n68
Encyclopédie méthodique. Economie politique et diplomatique (Demeunier) 120n11
Encyclopédie ou Dictionnaire raisonné des sciences, des arts et des métiers (Diderot and d'Alembert) 8–9, 17n29–17n32, 18n38, 33, 42–43, 138, 158n36, 179
Engels, Friedrich 18n44, 194n45
Enlightenment 5–8, 11, 13–14, 24, 38, 57, 60, 97–8, 101, 165, 171, 187–8
The Enlightenment: A Genealogy (Edelstein) 84n34
"Enlightenment Rights Talk" (Edelstein) 160n70, 194n37, 197n93, 206n5
enmity 38–49, 93; *see also* inhumanness
Entretiens avec Cathrine II (Diderot) 107
Entretiens sur le fils naturel (Diderot) 78, 88n120, 185, 196n65
Éphémérides du citoyen (Du Pont) 62, 84n39
equaliberty 12–13; *see also* Balibar, Étienne

Equaliberty: Political Essays (Balibar) 18n41, 18n43, 18n52–18n53, 19n46–19n49, 48n83, 124n45, 125n88, 194n42
esclavage des noirs, L' (Gouges) 194n36
"Essentially Contested Concepts" (Gallie) 17n24
Estates General 25–6, 67–8
Études de littérature préromantique (Estève) 194n24
Étude sur le théâtre de Marie-Joseph Chénier (Liéby) 88n124, 195n53
The Event of Literature (Eagleton) 81n1–81n2
evil, lack of see utopianism
Evil in Modern Thought: An Alternative History of Philosophy (Neiman) 197n85
Exclusion, political and social 10, 38–43, 104, 154, 167, 191

familial recognition 175–8
The Family on Trial in Revolutionary France (Desan) 131, 157n16–157n17, 157n30, 193n18, 194n26, 194n29
Fauré, Christine 22, 44n5, 47n59
Feher, Michael 132–3, 157n20, 157n23, 158n39, 159n49–159n50, 159n54, 159n58, 160n63
Feilla, Cecilia 75, 87n92, 87n97, 87n101, 87n107, 88n121, 166, 173, 193n13, 193n16–193n17, 194n24, 195n57, 196n75, 196n80
Félix, Joël 155n2, 160n74
Fénelon, François de 18n37, 97, 112, 120n23, 195n55
Fénelon ou les religieuses de Cambrai 9, 16, 71, 73–4, 76, 78–9, 164–201; background 164–7; convent life and paternal inflexibility 167–73; humanness, problems of 173–8; political agency 178–84; politics of happy ending 185–92; *Tableau vivant* 185–92; unhappiness/happiness 178–84
Festa, Lynn 87n108, 174, 178, 194n39, 206n5
fils naturel, Le and *Entretiens sur le fils naturel* (Diderot) 70–71, 78, 86n80, 88n120, 185
"Financial Origins of the French Revolution" (Bossenga) 45n18, 123n61, 124n70

fiscal system, future 96
Fléchier, Esprit 179
The Forbidden Best-Sellers of Pre-Revolutionary France (Darnton) 83n26, 119n1, 119n3–119n4, 120n6–120n7, 120n21, 121n35, 121n38, 124n49, 125n82
foreigners 39
forgiveness 190
"The Form of Government" (Mercier) 102–108
Forms: Whole, Rhythm, Hierarchy, Network (Levine) 136, 144, 157n31, 159n51–159n53
Forsström, Riikka 59, 83n24, 83n28, 83n31, 120n21, 120n25, 124n75
Forsyth, Murray 47n72, 48n85–48n86, 49n91, 124n78
Foucault, Michel 10, 18n42, 118, 125n88
Fowler, J. E. 151, 160n66
Framed Narratives: Diderot's Genealogy of the Beholder (Caplan) 196n75, 196n83
French Drama of the Revolutionary Years (Rodmell) 88n116
French Finances 1770–1795: From Business to Bureaucracy (Bosher) 123n69
The French Idea of Freedom: The Old Regime and the Declaration of Rights of 1789 (Van Kley) 17n15, 45n8, 45n12, 122n60
French Nationalism in 1789 according to the General Cahiers (Hyslop) 45n20, 123n64
The French Prerevolution 1787–1788 (Egret) 123n68, 124n51
The French Revolution and the Creation of Modern Political Culture (Furet et al.) 48n86, 88n128, 124n52
Friedland, Paul 57–8, 74, 83n17–83n20, 87n94, 193n20
From Deficit to Deluge: The Origins of the French Revolution (Kaiser and Van Kley) 45n17–45n18, 123n61, 124n70, 155n2
Furet, François 88n128, 206n1
future, dream of happy: background 93–6; duty of patriotism 108–19; *L'an 2440* form of government 102–8; taxation 108–19; temporality, utopian thought 96–102; see also utopianism

gabelle tax 111
Galilei, Galileo 133
Gallie, Walter B. 7, 17n24
Gauchet, Marcel 17n14, 22, 24, 30, 45n7, 45n10–45n11, 46n45
"general will" *(la volonté générale)* 35, 104
Geneva School 30, 157n32
Genlis, Madame de 67, 85n61–85n62
Geoffroy, Julien Louis 88n122, 180, 195n58
Gerber, Matthew 157n19, 171, 193n18, 194n30
God's name 28; *see also* religion and God
Golden Age image 42
Goodman, Dena 88n128
Gossec, François-Joseph 73
"'Gotta Serve Somebody': Service; Autonomy; Society" (Maslan) 206n3
Gouges, Olympe de 15, 59, 83n16, 112–16, 124n74–124n75, 124n77, 159n59, 164, 167, 172, 194n31, 194n33, 194n36, 195n49, 197n89
Grand Peur, la 27
Grégoire, M. l'abbé 28, 33, 47n57, 47n61, 47n65
Grievances, lists of *see* Cahiers des doléances
Grub Street authors and writers 6, 57, 59
Guillaume Tell (Lemierre) 75

Habermas, Jürgen 88n128
happiness 26, 44, 95, 119, 166; background 3–5; *bonheur* 7–8, 131, 156n14; "Bonheur" 17n29; *bonheur commun* 13; *bonheur de tous* 3, 13; *bonheur générale* 26; collective happiness 26; *Eudaimonia* 7–8; *felicitas* 7; human rights 130–1; interpretations 7–9; manipulation of 10; natural happiness 142; "political anthropology" 10–14; *vs* pleasure 8–10; politics of happy ending 185–92; politics of words 6–10; of women 104; *see also* Déclaration des droits de l'homme et du citoyen; *malheur* (unhappiness)
Happy Days (Beckett) 7
"Headscarf Affair" 39
hearing/seeing, sympathy 175–7, 183
Henriette d'Aquitaine (Chénier) 72

Henri VIII (Chénier) 73
Herbois, Collot de 83n16
hierarchies of social forms 144–52
The History of Human Rights: From Ancient Times to the Globalization Era (Ishay) 44n2
Hobbes, Thomas 158n41
Holm, Isak Winkel 121n34
Homo Sacer: Sovereign Power and Bare Life (Agamben) 195n45
Horace and Horatian concepts 69–71, 77, 79, 86n74, 86n80
Horkheimer, Max 120n20
hors-la-loi legislative category 42
hostis humani generis 49n100
Huet, Marie-Hélène 83n17
humanness, problem of 173–8
Human rights xiii, 11, 14, 16, 18n45, 22, 47n66, 48n86, 62–63, 109–110, 173–175, 191, 204–205; and happiness 10–19, 130–131; and literature 14–15, 62–64, 95–96, 117, 130–131, 153, 173, 191, 201; self-evidence of 24–5, 29–30, 95; *see also* humanness, problem of
Human Rights and Empire: The Political Philosophy of Cosmopolitanism (Douzinas) 44n4
Hunt, Lynn 15, 17n12–17n13, 18n60, 24, 45n13, 46n43, 48n82, 55, 62–3, 80, 84n42, 95, 118, 120n14–120n15, 122n50, 123n63, 125n91, 153–4, 159n61, 160n69, 173, 191, 193n6, 194n44, 197n92, 206n2, 206n4
hunter metaphor 146
Hyslop, Beatrice F. 45n20, 110, 123n64

ideal future 118; *see also* utopianism
"The Idea of a Declaration of Rights" (Baker) 17n15, 45n8, 45n12
"Idées sur la poésie" (Du Pont) 84n39–84n40
imagination 79–80
"impeached" agents 38–40
inclusion 38, 167, 191
indirect taxes 111
individual will 104
inequality 144
"The inequality of common utility: active/passive citizenship in French revolutionary human rights" (Kjærgård) 195n63

The Ingenu (Voltaire) 97, 120n22, 120n24
In God's Shadow: Politics in the Hebrew Bible (Walzer) 121n34
inhumanness 38–39, 80, 167, 190, 204–205; *see also* enmity
In Praise of Love (Badiou) 160n64
"In Praise of Richardson" (Diderot) 196n73
Intellectual History of Economic Normativities (Thorup) 47n66, 123n62
The Interior Distance (Poulet) 156n4, 157n26, 158n37–158n38
interpellation 118–19, 155, 192
Inventing Human Rights: A History (Hunt) 17n12–17n13, 18n59, 45n13, 48n82, 62, 84n42, 120n14–120n15, 123n63, 124n50, 125n91, 160n69, 193n6, 194n32, 194n44, 197n92, 206n4
Inventing the French Revolution (Baker) 17n24, 47n72, 82n13, 88n128, 89n129, 122n55, 124n53
Ishay, Micheline R. 44n2
Israel, Jonathan 17n18, 44n3, 46n26

Jacobins 4, 7, 16, 24, 42, 60, 66, 180, 187, 195n57
Jameson, Fredric 136
jealousy 151
Jean, Joan de 84n53, 157n25
Jean-Jacques Rousseau: La transparence et l'obstacle (Starobinski) 159n61
Jefferson, Thomas 27
Jessé, M. le baron de 32, 47n58
Jouhaud, Christian 14, 17n20, 54, 82n4
Journal de la Montagne 180, 195n57

Kaiser, Thomas 45n17, 123n61, 124n70, 155n2
Kelly, George Armstrong 66–8, 85n56–85n57, 85n59–85n60, 85n63, 85n65, 85n67
Kennedy, Emmet 87n106, 192n2–192n3
Kosseleck, Reinhart 17n24
Kwass, Michael 16n16, 45n18, 109, 111, 115, 122n54, 123n61, 123n68, 124n70–124n72, 125n81

Laclos, Choderlos de 6, 14–16, 54–55, 57, 63, 77, 79–80, 95, 119, 129–164, 178, 192, 202–3, 205–6; background and poetics 66–72. *See also Liaisons dangereuses, Les*
Laclos et la tradition: Essai sur les sources et la technique des Liaisons dangereuses (Versini) 158n44
Laclos et le libertinage (Pomeau) 156n4, 156n6, 156n8–156n9, 158n38, 160n65
Lafayette, Madame de 134–5, 157n28
Lafayette, Marquis de 27, 45n23–45n24
La Fère artillery school 66
La Harpe (critic) 85n71
Lally-Tollendal, M. de 36–7, 39, 42, 47n75
La Mettrie, Julien Offray de 8, 18n35
Laveaux, Jean-Charles 179, 183, 195n57
Leaves of Grass and Other Writings (Whitman) 22, 44n1
"'Le choc des opinions': Le débat des droits de l'homme, juillet-août 1789" (Baecque) 45n6, 45n16, 45n19
"Le citoyen/la citoyenne: Activity, Passivity and the Revolutionary Concept of Citizenship" (Sewell) 48n86, 48n89
Leibniz, Gottfried Wilhelm 97, 99, 121n32
Lettre à M. D'Alembert sur les spectacles (Rousseau) 77–78, 88n117, 121n44
Lettre au peuple, ou projet d'une caisse patriotique; Par une citoyenne (Gouges) 112, 124n74, 124n77
Lettre au roi, contenant un Projet pour liquider en peu d'années toutes les dettes de l'Etat, en soulageant, dès-à-présent, le Peuple du fardeau des Impositions (Mercier) 115–16, 125n83, 125n85
Levine, Caroline 136–137, 144, 157n31, 159n51–159n53
Liaisons dangereuses, Les (Laclos) 14–15, 66–72, 79, 129–164, 178, 192, 203–204; hierarchies of social norms 144–60; Laclos-Ricciboni debate on 66–72; politics of social forms 131–6; rhythm of social

Index 217

forms 136–44; *see also* Laclos, Choderlos de
libelles 6, 57, 67, 154
liberté (statistics) 7–8
libertinism 15, 66–71, 131–5, 137–52, 203–5; *see also Liaisons dangereuses, Les;* love
L'idée de bonheur (Mauzi) 17n26, 18n36
Liéby, Adolphe 78, 88n124, 195n53
Literary field 5–6, 14, 17n20, 54, 59, 70
The Literary Underground of the Old Regime (Darnton) 5–6, 17n21–17n23, 57, 83n15, 83n27, 160n74
Locke, John 12–13, 19n55, 38–39, 152
Lotman, Jurij 178, 195n51
Louis XVI 1–3, 16n4–16n6, 25–6, 29, 60, 67, 73, 78, 135, 171
love 132–5, 137–52, 173, 185; and enjoyment 137, 139–140; family love 177–178; for the state 110–111; forbidden love 164, 170, 190; *see also* libertinism; paternalism; patriotism
Lubersac, M. de 33, 47n61–47n62
Lukàcs, Georg 136

Mably, Gabriel Bonnot de 5
Machiavelli, Niccolò 112
malheur (unhappiness) 3, 16, 95–99, 119, 135, 138, 176, 178–185
Malouet, Pierre-Victor de 29–32, 42, 46n40, 46n46–6n47, 47n55
Man-citizen 10–11, 79–80, 117–119, 153, 180–181, 201
Marat, Jean-Paul 59, 83n17, 173, 180
Marie-Antoinette 154
marriage 66, 132, 135, 137–40, 146, 157n33, 170, 177–178, 185; arranged marriages (*mariages de convenance*) 132–5, 137–40, 143–4, 152, 204; marital happiness 132, 135, 138, 148–149
Marsaillaise, La 43, 49n102, 190
Marshall, David 87n109, 176, 187, 195n48
Marxism 10–11, 18n44, 109, 122n59, 136–137, 187, 194n45
Maslan, Susan xiv, 11–12, 30–32, 58, 64, 78–80, 87n95, 88n119, 117, 143–144, 153, 166, 181, 187, 193n20, 201
Maupeou coup 15, 106–8
Mauzi, Robert 17n26, 18n36
McMahon, Darrin M. 7–9, 66–67, 157n24
melodrama 75, 164–5, 190, 192n4
The Melodramatic Imagination: Balzac, Henry James, Melodrama, and the Mode of Excess (Brooks) 192n4, 193n7–193n8, 197n87
Mémoire de Madame de Valmont (Gouges) 194n36
Mercier, Louis-Sébastien 6, 9, 14–16, 54–57, 68–69, 77–80; background and poetics 59–66; form of government 102–108; *L'an 2440* 93–129; taxation and patriotism 108–125; temporality 96–102; *see also An 2440, rêve s'il en fût jamais, L;* enmity; utopianism
Mirabeau, Gabriel Honoré Riquetti comte de 82n11
Mirabeau, M. le comte de 28, 46n29, 56, 82n11
Mirabeau, M. le vicomte de 46n32
"mirror of prince" 112–14
Moderation, moderates 9, 29, 32, 60, 73, 179–180
monarchy 18n45, 67, 73–74, 76, 78, 135, 155n2, 171; *see also* royalism
Monastère Saint-Lazare 2
Monastery vows 135, 164, 168–9, 196n64
Monde, le 5–6, 57, 129, 152, 172, 202
Montesquieu, Charles-Louis de Secondat 15, 97, 103, 120n20, 121n42–121n43
Monvel, Jacques-Marie Boutet de 164, 167, 180–181, 189–90, 193n21, 195n59–195n61, 197n84, 197n86, 197n88
Morals 38, 93, 131–132, 134, 165; and law xiv, 22, 174–175; and literature 5–6, 62–69, 71–2, 76–81, 85n71, 96–97, 99, 105, 108, 112, 124n80, 142, 186; and politics 38–40, 191; *see also* nature
More, Thomas 96; *see also* utopianism
Moribus 1 120n17
Mothe-Fénelon, François de Salignac de la 179
Mounier, M. 27, 32, 45n21, 47n59

Mousset, Sophie 194n31
"mouvemens délicieux" 9
"moving vantage point" 94
Moyn, Samuel 10, 18n45

Naigeon, Jacques-André 86n77
Naissance de l'écrivain. Sociologie de la littérature à l'âge classique (Viala) 54, 81n3, 82n5–82n6
Nancy, J.-L. 16n4
national lottery 116
nature 9, 62, 70, 152, 165, 170, 181, 183–184, 187, 189; natural children 16, 70–1, 167, 170–4; natural jurisprudence xiv, 3, 12–3, 18n45, 26–8, 42–3, 55, 95, 98–9, 146, 152, 183, 190, 203–5; naturalist philosophy 132; and Physiocracy 55–6; and society 29–32, 141–4, 154–5, 202
Necker, Jacques 85n57, 110, 116–117, 123n65–123n68
negative liberty 67–8
Néologie, ou vocabulaire de mots nouveaux (Mercier) 96–7, 120n18–120n19
The Novel of Worldliness: Crébillon, Marivaux, Laclos, Stendhal (Brooks) 130, 132, 134, 156n13, 157n18, 157n27

Of the Social Contract (Rousseau) *see Du Contrat social*
Old Regime (ancien régime), the 1, 5, 16, 25, 33, 36, 38, 44, 74, 76, 79–80, 93, 107, 111, 130, 143–4, 154, 166–7, 169–70, 177, 187–8, 191
Old Testament 99–100, 118; *see also* religion and God
"On the Education of Women" (Laclos) 68, 160n63
"On the Silver Mark" (Robespierre) 41, 49n92, 49n94
"On Women and Their Education" (Laclos) 158n39, 158n42, 158n48, 159n49–159n50, 159n58
order, search for *see Liaisons dangereuses, Les*

paintings/painters 86n79, 186; as metaphor 64–65, 72, 101, 153, 168
Parlements, les 106–107, 122n54
paternalism 1–2, 114–115, 167–73
patriotism: 60, 65, 75, 80, 113, 179, duty of (in Mercier) 108–19; reawakening the virtue of (Mercier) 59–66
perfect future society 15; *see also* utopianism
Persian Letters (Montesquieu) 97, 120n22
personhood 12–4, 38, 58, 108, 118, 152–3, 191–2
Pestré, Jean 8–9, 17n29–17n32, 18n38, 138, 158n36
Philippe-Egalité 66
Physiocrats and Physiocracy 54–6, 61, 79, 82n8, 82n10–82n11, 84n37–84n38
Pigault-Lebrun, Charles 179, 195n56
pleasure *see* happiness
politics: agency 178–84; of happy ending 185–92; of social forms 131–6; of words and happiness 6–10; *see also specific issue*
populationism 135, 171, 173, 182, 196n64
pornography 93, 154
positive laws 11, 27, 42, 76–7, 104, 152, 202
Poulet, Georges 134, 140, 156n4, 157n26, 157n32, 158n37
Préliminaire de la constitution. Reconnaissance et exposition raisonnée des droits de l'homme et du citoyen (Sieyès) 48n85
Princesse de Clèves, La (*The Princess de Clèves*) (Lafayette) 134–5, 157n28
privileges, system of 13, 28, 37–8, 44, 74–6, 111, 166, 170
The Promise of Happiness (Ahmed) 9, 18n39–18n40
property *vs.* useful labor 39–40
Public opinion (*opinion publique*) 67, 80–81, 88n128
The Pursuit of Happiness: A History from the Greeks to the Present (McMahon) 17n28, 17n33–17n34, 157n24

querelle des anciens et des modernes, la (quarrel of the ancients and the moderns) 60, 63, 78–79, 84n34
Quesnay, François 54, 55, 82n8

Rabaut de Saint-Etienne, Jean Paul 25, 45n15, 56–7, 82n13, 166, 193n15

Rancière, Jacques 31, 47n54, 195n45
Ravel, Jeffrey S. 87n97, 88n118, 187, 196n74
Raynal, abbé 93
Reason and Revolution: The Political Thought of Abbé Sieyes (Sewell) 47n72, 48n85–48n86, 49n91, 124n78
"Réflexions sur les hommes nègres" (Gouges) 124n75
reincarnation 60
Religieuse, La (The Nun) (Diderot) 169, 193n22, 196n64
religion and God 28, 33, 99–100, 105, 118, 166, 169, 177–8, 182–3, 189–90
Révolution des droits de l'homme, La (Gauchet) 17n14, 45n7, 45n10–45n11, 46n45
Revolutionary Acts: Theater, Democracy, and the French Revolution (Maslan) 83n21, 86n89, 87n95, 87n100, 88n116, 88n119, 159n61, 193n14, 193n20, 196n74
rhythms 135, 136–44
Rials, Stéphane 28, 29, 32, 45n22, 46n31, 46n35, 46n39, 47n60, 48n84
Riccoboni, Madame de 68–72, 80, 86n73, 86n75–86n77, 86n85, 153, 196n68
Richardson, Samuel 69, 75, 186
rights *see* Human rights; *Déclaration des droits de l'homme et du citoyen*
Robespierre, Maximilien 9, 15, 41–3, 48n90, 49n92–49n98, 59–60, 75, 179, 190–1, 195n56, 204
Rousseau, Jean-Jacques 5, 9, 13, 15, 18n54, 30–2, 35–6, 38, 41, 46n49–6n50, 47n69–47n70, 49n93, 57, 59, 69, 77–8, 88n117, 93, 95, 103–5, 108, 119, 121n44, 122n46–122n47, 141–4, 148, 155, 158n40–158n41, 159n62, 165, 170, 179, 195n55
royalism 1–3, 8, 16n3, 67, 75, 107, 113–115; *see also* paternalism

Saint-Just, Louis Antoine Léon de 7, 18n27
"*sanguinocrate*" (bloodocrat)" 60
Sartre, Jean-Paul 81n1–81n2
satire 61, 64–5
Scott, Joan Wallach 194n31

seeing/hearing, sympathy 175–7, 183
Seneca 148, 160n63
sensory recognition 175–7
Sentimental Figures of Empire in Eighteenth-Century Britain and France (Festa) 87n108, 194n39, 206n5
sentimental literature 75, 85n70, 164–97
Sentimental Narrative and the Social Order in France (Denby) 87n110, 165, 193n10–193n12, 194n38, 195n46–195n47, 196n75, 196n78, 196n83
The Sentimental Theater of the French Revolution (Feilla) 87n92, 87n97, 87n101, 87n107, 88n121, 193n13, 193n17, 194n24, 195n57, 196n80
Seven Years' War 25, 66, 110
Sewell Jr., William H. 17n25, 37, 48n79, 48n86, 48n89, 82n11
Shklar, Judith N. 113, 124n76, 195n55
Sieyès, Emmanuel Joseph: 2, 15, 27, 36–7, 39–41, 43, 45n25, 47n72, 48n86, 49n91, 56–7, 65, 76–7, 79–80, 82n11, 114–6, 182, 191, 195n63
Sixth Bureau (le sixième bureau) 27–8, 35–6, 46n37
The Sketch (Condorcet) 82n11, 98, 120n27, 121n28–121n30, 124n44, 124n48
Skinner, Quentin 7, 17n24
Sliwinski, Sharon 174, 194n40–194n41
society, alternative visions of 32, 99; *see also* utopianism
Sonenscher, Michael 45n18, 47n72, 47n77, 48n86, 82n10, 82n12, 88n113, 109, 123n61, 124n79, 195n63
The Spirit of the Laws (Montesquieu) 121n42–121n43
Staël, Madame de 124n80, 170
Stalnaker, Joanna 83n23, 83n32, 101, 120n10, 121n37, 121n39, 196n
Starobinski, Jean 159n61
Stene-Johansen, Knut 85n55, 157n22, 158n44
Strength in Numbers: Population, Reproduction, and Power in Eighteenth-Century France (Blum) 157n29, 194n27–194n29

The Structural Transformation of the Public Sphere: An Inquiry into a Category of Bourgeois Society (Habermas) 88n128
The Structure of the Artistic Text (Lotman) 178, 195n51
Subjectivity 10, 14, 80, 108, 118–9, 129–130, 135, 191–2, 202, 206
suffering 175–7, 183
The Surprising Effects of Sympathy: Marivaux, Diderot, Rousseau, and Mary Shelley (Marshall) 87n109, 176, 195n48
synecdoche 188
Szondi, Peter 187, 196n76–196n77, 196n79

Tableau de Paris (Mercier) 59, 64–5, 83n23, 84n37, 84n48, 100–1, 116, 121n37, 125n84
Tableau historique de l'état et des progrès de la littérature française depuis 1789 (Chénier) 73, 98
tableau vivant 16, 60, 167, 178, 185–92
Tackett, Timothy 45n19, 46n28
taille tax 111
talents 35–9, 62, 69, 182, 191
Talleyrand-Périgord, M. de 36, 41, 47n71, 68
taxation 30, 94–5, 108–17
Taylor, Charles 81, 89n130, 122n60
temporality 15, 96–102, 137, 140
the Terror 42, 60, 175; *see also* Robespierre
The Terror of Natural Rights: Republicanism, the Cult of Nature, & the French Revolution (Edelstein) 49n97, 49n99–49n100, 195n55, 196n81
theater 5, 11–2, 16, 57–60, 62–3, 65, 69–78, 80, 87n95, 87n107, 88n119, 88n121, 93, 118, 164–197
Third Estate 4, 25–7, 29, 37, 47n77, 48n78–48n80, 76, 82n11, 88n113–88n114, 109, 111, 115, 124n79, 182, 195n63
Thouret 48n87, 49n91
Timoléon (Chénier) 74
Tocqueville, Alexis de 54–5, 79, 82n7, 82n9
Todorov, Tzvetan 156n5, 157n21, 160n72
Two Treatises of Government (Locke) 18n55

The Unfinished Enlightenment: Description in the Age of the Encyclopedia (Stalnaker) 83n23, 83n32, 120n10, 121n37, 121n39, 196n70
universalism/non-universalism 5, 11, 22, 30, 32, 104, 191; extensive/intensive universalism 11, 104, 191
useful labor *vs.* property 39–40
utopianism 15, 93–6, 120n21; anti-utopian utopia 98; and ideology 108–9, 116; in *L'an 2440* 93–125; and "mirror of princes" 113–4; social otherness 95–8; temporality of 96–102; uchronianism 15, 98, 119, 122
Utopian Lights: The Evolution of the Idea of Social Progress (Bazcko) 120n5, 120n11, 120n16–120n18, 120n21, 120n26, 121n31, 158n46

Vardi, Liana 62, 82n10, 84n38
veiled/unveiled perception of world 168–9, 175–6, 187–9
Vendée insurgents 42
Versini, Laurent 142, 155n1, 156n10, 158n38, 158n44
Viala, Alain 14, 54, 57–8, 81n3, 82n5–82n6
Victimes cloîtrées, Les (Monvel) 164, 180–181, 189–90, 193n21, 195n59–195n61, 197n84, 197n86, 197n88
Vidler, Anthony 102, 120n9, 121n41
Views of the Executive Means Available to the Representatives of France in 1789 (Sieyès) 56, 82n12; *see also* Sieyès
vingtième tax 111
The Virtues of Abandon: An Anti-Individualist History of the French Enlightenment (Coleman) 18n56–18n59, 122n56, 124n73, 125n89, 152, 160n68, 197n90–197n91, 197n94
visions of society, alternative 32, 99; *see also* utopianism
Voltaire, François de 5, 57, 75, 78, 93, 97, 120n22, 120n24, 143
voluntary tax offerings 110–12, 114
voting *see* active/passive citizenship

War of American Independence 110
Washington, George 27

Weber, Max 187
What Is the Third Estate? (Sieyès) 27, 37, 47n77, 48n78, 48n80, 76, 82n11, 88n113–88n114, 115, 124n79, 195n63; *see also* Third Estate; Sieyès, Emmanuel Joseph
Whitman, Walt 23, 44n1, 224n1
"Who Is the Subject of the Rights of Man?" (Rancière) 195n45
Wilkie, Jr., Everett C. 83n26, 119, 119n2

Winnett, Susan 130, 138, 145, 156n13, 158n35, 159n55
women 39–40, 104, 137, 141–2, 144–6, 155, 164–97
Wood, Ellen Meiksins 17n25

Zamore et Mirza; ou l'heureux naufrage (Gouges) 124n75, 194n36
Zuber, Valentine 24, 45n14, 45n22
"Zur Judenfrage" (Marx) 18n44, 194n4

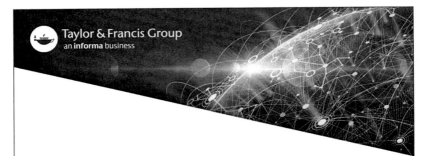

PGMO 06/29/2018